The Long Night
A True Story

Toby

Ernst Israel Bornstein

The LONG NIGHT

TRANSLATED BY

Noemie Lopian (née Bornstein)
David Arnold, MBE

The Toby Press

The Long Night
A True Story

First Maggid Edition, 2015

The Toby Press LLC
POB 8531, New Milford, CT 06776–8531, USA
& POB 2455, London WIA 5WY, England
www.tobypress.com

Original German edition © Ernst Israel Bornstein 1967
English translation © Noemie Lopian 2009

Cover design: Yehudit Cohen

ISBN 978-1-59264-440-7

Printed and bound in the United States

Author's Original Dedication

Dedicated to the sacred memory of my father
Usher Bornstein
Who always saw the best in others

my mother
Hella Bornstein

my sister
Noemi Bornstein

and my brother
Yehuda Bornstein

who in 1943 were all gassed in Auschwitz
by the Nazi barbarians

ೞ ೞ ೞ

This revised English translation is
dedicated to their memory
and
to the memory of the author
Dr Ernst Israel Bornstein
(26 November 1922 – 14 August 1978)

With gratitude to David Arnold MBE *who selflessly and graciously devoted his time over three years in assisting with the translation of this book.*

Tribute to the Author from His Children

Papa,

You will live with me always: In the short 11 years
I knew you, you taught me by example to love and give
to fellow man, to believe and give the best of myself.

Noemie Heli Lopian née Bornstein

ఠ ఠ ఠ

In memory of my father who taught me the essence of life.
He instilled in me the value of life, Right from Wrong
and to live life filled to the brim with love, joy, light and
no hate. I am forever indebted and grateful always.

Muriel Davis née Bornstein

ఠ ఠ ఠ

I look back at my father's all too brief life with awe and
admiration.

After suffering a harrowing physical and psychological
ordeal and losing nearly everyone he loved, he not only
rebuilt his life by qualifying as a dentist and medical
doctor, marrying and having a family, but he remained
true to his human and religious values. He strove both,
to help whomever was in need in any way he was able
and to keep the memory of his martyred brethren alive.

His enduring legacy was that he lived his life without
bitterness and hatred and, by his example (as well as our
mother's), ensured that we too live our lives in the
same way.

As a father, his love and warmth is fondly remembered
and very much missed. May his memory be a blessing.

Asher Alain Bornstein

1O DOWNING STREET
LONDON SW1A 2AA

5 November 2015

Dear Noemie,

Thank you for your email of 23 October and the accompanying translation of your father's book, 'The Long Night'.

I was touched by your family's story. It is truly commendable that your father wrote a book to document his experiences, despite how harrowing these must have been.

I absolutely agree on the central role of education in Britain today. I set up the Holocaust Commission to ensure that children in the future continue to learn from the horrific events of that time, and the experiences of those brave individuals who witnessed these first-hand are vital. Through the work of the United Kingdom Holocaust Memorial Foundation, established to take forward the Commission's recommendations, Britain will have a new National Memorial and world-class Learning Centre to commemorate the Holocaust. This will enable forthcoming generations to learn from well-preserved memories such as those of your father.

Please accept my best wishes for the success of 'The Long Night'. Thank you, once again, for taking the time to write to me.

Tom.

David

Ms Noemie Lopian

Contents

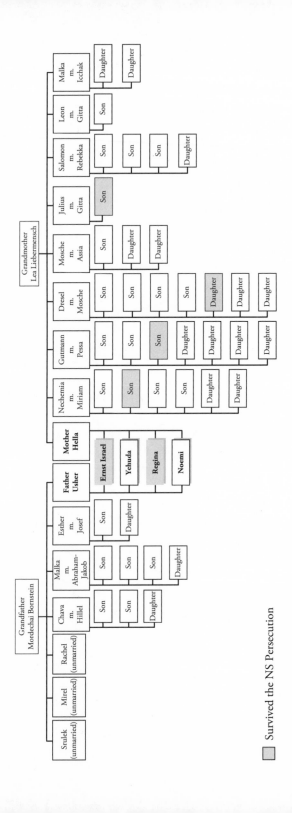

Survived the NS Persecution

Foreword

Astory that I was told about my grandfather when I was young always used to puzzle me. It was about his First World War medals.

When my grandmother and her three young daughters were arrested in Amsterdam and imprisoned in first Westerbork and then Belsen, they took with them Alfred Wiener's war medals.

My grandfather was by that point in London, setting up his famous Holocaust archive and contributing to the war effort, but unable to help his family. His wife thought that, perhaps, his medals might help in some way. They were proof – weren't they – that the family were loyal Germans. Maybe they would be of use.

Sadly, of course, they were of no use at all. My grandmother starved to death. She died just after arriving in Switzerland as part of a rare prisoner exchange, leaving her three daughters to fend for themselves in war torn Europe.

The girls managed to contact my grandfather, who was in New York collecting material, and they set off in a Red Cross ship to meet with him. And on the way, they discussed a problem. What should they do with the medals? Maybe when they arrived at Ellis Island and were quizzed, the insignia might make them seem like spies. They wrapped the medals in a handkerchief and dropped them out of a porthole.

And there they lie, in the waters by the Statue of Liberty.

Here's what confused me as a child. My grandfather was quite cross about his medals. And I couldn't understand it. Why would he want them? Why didn't he see immediately that disposing of them was the right thing to do?

As an adult, however, I think I understand. Or at least, that I understand better.

There were two things that were precious to my grandfather above all other values in his public life. The first was his belief that he was a German. A true and loyal citizen of a great country. The second is that he believed in the power of truth. That was his life's work, after all. Documenting the truth so that it could be used as a weapon in the fight for liberty.

And what happened with the medals offended against both these things.

I share these values. I too believe that Jews must be true and loyal citizens of their home country and must be recognised as such. And even more strongly, I believe in the power of truth. I believe that laying out, unsparingly, without bias, without embellishment, the truth, has a special force in argument and in the maintenance of social relations.

That is why I am so grateful, so moved, so taken with this extraordinary book. Because it is more than a book. It is a piece of armour. It is a declaration of intent. It is a cry for freedom and justice. It is a rock to cling to. It is a barricade that we can man. It is truth.

The Bornstein family bringing us this truth is a form of heroism. Not the heroism of fighters or mountain climbers or daredevil stuntmen. The heroism of people prepared to confront their emotions and expose themselves and their inner secrets, the secrets of their precious Ernst, so that others may live and others may learn.

This powerful testimony tells stories of those who stood firm under terrible pressure and those who crumbled. It affirms the humanity of all who suffered, whatever their response. It is brave enough even to deal with the way those who suffered sometimes imposed suffering on others, a beating, say, making them more difficult with other prisoners.

It copes with this terror just by calmly, clearly, with open eyes telling it how it was and letting the power of truth do its work. Its simplicity makes it luminous, its very lack of elaboration makes it complicated, its very straightforward narrative style makes it deep.

With every Holocaust story one learns something new. I never feel that I have read it before or that I know it already. Each one has the shock of new revelation, each one brings new questions. And that means that if you haven't read *The Long Night* you haven't read about the Holocaust.

At the party for my fiftieth birthday, I reflected to my friends how lucky I felt that I had reached that age living in the suburbs of a country at peace, in a nation that respects the rule of law.

By the time they were fifty, my grandparents had been turned out from their homes, deprived of their property, starved or murdered and the remainder left to start again in a foreign country, speaking a new language, trying to find an income, starting again as middle aged people.

There is much that is special about *The Long Night* but above all, I think Ernst Bornstein makes you feel that sense of dislocation and bewilderment as an ordinary family is torn from its roots and subjected to the horrors of the camps.

This publication derives to be seen as an important moment in holocaust literature. It makes available to a wide audience a particularly fine, particularly clear sighted account. It is impossible to read this book and fail to see the world a little differently.

In a way you finish *The Long Night* feeling less secure, because you realise that freedom and peace and even survival are contingent, that they may be fleeting, that terrors can come and you will be powerless to resist.

Yet I preferred to finish *The Long Night* feeling uplifted, that there are in life people like Ernst Bornstein and his family who share him with us. That even in the depths it is possible for someone to keep their wits about them, never to lose their humanity, not to miss a second of life or let something important go unnoticed.

At the end of the Long Night, we are awake, we are alive and we are free.

Daniel Finkelstein
House of Lords, 12 June 2015

Original Preface to *The Long Night*

Prof. Dr. Max Mikorey

I t is with great pleasure that I fulfil Dr. Bornstein's request to write a brief preamble for his personal account of his experiences during the time of national socialist persecution. Admittedly, a number of excellent publications have already dealt with this topic in various languages, among which "A Psychologist Experiences the Concentration Camp" by the Viennese psychiatrist Viktor E. Frankl deserves a special mention. Nonetheless, Dr. Bornstein's book fills a gap, given that the German invasion into Poland caused him, an A-Level-Student, to be torn from the security of patriarchal family life, forcing him to experience, step by step, every single phase of National Socialist persecution, culminating in the dreadful death marches towards the Tyrol where, on Himmler's orders, prisoners were to be exterminated in the Alpine ravines. Based on his astonishingly impartial observation of himself, his fellow sufferers and also his persecutors along the way, Dr. Bornstein's chronicle provides the foundation for a sociology of the catastrophic symbiosis between persecutors and their victims within the setting of a concentration camp. Dr. Bornstein's report is particularly harrowing for the very reason that the hellishness of concentration camp existence is related entirely without accusatory pathos, and facts are allowed to speak for themselves. It is reminiscent of the "Memoirs from the House of the Dead", published by Dostoevsky ten years after his release from the Katorga to portray "a world never previously described and entirely new to us… and the nation trapped and perished in it". I hope Dr. Bornstein's book will be as successful as Dostoevsky's celebrated "Memoirs from the House of the Dead", given that it constitutes a significant contribution towards the efforts of internally overcoming and externally providing the fairest compensation humanly possible for the injustice committed, and to render any recurrence of such injustice impossible for all time.

More than 100 years ago the great Austrian poet Franz Grillparzer presaged the tendency towards barbaric brutality in those twentieth century crowds, reduced to purely biological motives and gripped by a feverish frenzy of nationalism, when in March 1849 he wrote the prophetic epigram: "The path of present-day learning leads from humanity via nationality towards bestiality."

Without a shadow of a doubt, even after the elimination of the National Socialist regime, we are still facing the danger of an emerging moral ice age which, against the background of an extraordinary increase in living standards through technical progress, has already coined the phrase of 'megadeath' to conveniently cover the reporting of lives lost in future wars. I can think of no reading matter more suitable to unequalled since the time of Enlightenment.

However, the categories now being deployed in the medical assessment of concentration camp damages were outlined more than one hundred years ago by Anselm von Feuerbach, one of Germany's most eminent lawyers. In his book *Kaspar Hauser – The Crime against the Spiritual Life of a Human Being*, published in 1832, Feuerbach narrated an extremely dubious and problematic individual case and developed his theories. With great empathy Feuerbach thought himself into his protégé's situation, which in his day appeared to be a sensational novelty, but has turned out to be a mass phenomenon in our time. Even then, Feuerbach maintained that the hole which had been torn into Kaspar Hauser's life by the misdeed inflicted on him was beyond repair; the life not lived, his youth taken from him while his spirits were unconscious, could not be retrieved. Forever he would remain a man without childhood and youth, a monstrous creature who, against all laws of nature, started out in the middle of his lifespan. Thus, Feuerbach recognised that young people are disrupted in their development by such imprisonment.

Those who read Dr. Bornstein's book attentively will understand that a whole generation of Kaspar Hausers exists today, every one of them deprived of a different epoch of their lifetime through years of concentration camp detention. Feuerbach's conclusions apply to all the unfortunate victims of National Socialist persecution. For them, too "now and for all the future the various life stages will be shifted, separated and mixed up", the period of their persecution will "haunt them like a frightful ghost into their old age."

Feuerbach's words – phrased for the assessment of one individual phenomenon – apply, without a doubt, also to the mass phenomenon of the persecution of Jews and to its victims.

Indeed, more than a century ago Feuerbach's Kaspar Hauser book laid the theoretical foundations for the explanation of psychological after-effects of such mass crimes, which became a sad reality in our time.

I think we must be grateful to Dr. Bornstein for his book, written with many painful memories, a book so clearly striving for the truth and enabling outsiders to re-live this huge human catastrophe.

Prof. Dr. Max Mikorey was Dr. Bornstein's Psychiatry and Neurology professor at the University of Munich. Dr. Bornstein and Prof. Mikorey were to remain lifelong friends and met each other at least once a year with their wives. Prof. Mikorey died in November 1977 at the age of 78. In Dr. Bornstein's personal papers we found a copy of Prof. Dr. Mikorey's obituary.

Introduction

It was an unusually sunny December day in the year 1956 when I met my revered teacher, Professor Mikorey at the University of Munich. I had not chosen my PhD thesis from his suggested themes and I used the opportunity to approach him about it. As a dental student, I heard Professor Mikorey's evening lecture in the neurology clinic and, like my fellow-students, I was impressed with his knowledgeable personality and his humanitarian radiance. What I learned then also helped me with my other studies when I later studied medicine and again met Professor Mikorey at one of his lectures.

When I was striving for my doctorate we came to talk about the persecution of the Jews and he encouraged me to write down my experiences from that time. When I was nineteen years of age, I was locked away in the concentration camps and in four years and three months I had passed through twelve different camps. Professor Mikorey thought I was psychologically mature enough to relive those fateful times and to report as an eyewitness about the suffering of my people.

At that time I was still a member of the Jewish Scientific Institute in New York (YIVO[1]) and was occupied with collecting the experiences of young people who had years of imprisonment behind them. My job entailed reporting these events in the language of the eyewitnesses and keeping them free of literary embellishment. In the same manner, Professor Mikorey thought I should describe my experiences and the circumstances of the time in which man could lose his human characteristics to such an extent that his human nature was forfeited. In medicine, one knows by experiment about the impact of hormones on the human body. Under the Nazi terror, the psyche of man was completely changed or totally lost. Under Nazi terror, humankind descended step by step into inhumanity as the natural feelings of man were systematically destroyed. Thus a mother could give away her child to save herself and a hitherto decent person could become bestial under the impact of fear and hunger. Some were transformed into subservient slaves who served the master who later cold-bloodedly murdered them. In this report, I have tried to recall these experiences to let facts speak for themselves without commentary and without burdening the reader with personal emotions. Still, it will be difficult for my words to be always credible. After so many years, can one now relate events, thoughts and feelings as one saw, thought and felt them? Probably not. How does a person feel when he sees his companion being shot the moment he stops walking, and realises he can barely walk himself? Of course at first he carries on, he wants to live, he reaches for his companion's hand to support himself. But he (the companion) is at the end of his strength, he

---

1. In 1925 the YIVO Institute for Jewish Research was founded as the Yiddish Scientific Institute (Yidisher visnshaftlekher institut) in Vilna, Poland (now Vilnius, Lithuania), by key European intellectuals, including Albert Einstein and Sigmund Freud, to record the history and pioneer in the critical study of the language, literature and culture of the Jews of Eastern Europe. YIVO's founders worked tirelessly in collecting the documents and archival records of Jewish communities across Eastern Europe, years before anyone could have predicted the devastation that would befall them. In 1940, YIVO moved its permanent headquarters to New York City, becoming the only pre-Holocaust institution to transfer its mission to the United States from Europe.

pushes the hand away, he won't support the laggard. The weak one is left behind. But that one must have seen for oneself the lifeless face, the flickering eyes of a person about to confront his fate. The bullet strikes his neighbour and soon he will also be struck. Who can say what such a person experiences whilst walking the final steps of his life? Who can describe what he feels and suffers in these moments? And what did I myself experience on this day? As 'chosen' inmate I had to carry the bread sack for the Kapo and as the last one in the line I had to march next to him and the ss man. The ss man shot all who stopped and the Kapo had to record their concentration camp numbers. I looked into the barrel of the gun before the bullet struck the neck of the tottering person, looked at the thin stream of blood that ran slowly as life departed the body. I observed the ss man and saw how he ate with appetite his carefully prepared open sandwich whilst continuing to walk, despite his bloody deed. In the nearby fields there were farmers sowing, and at one of the houses by the roadside a woman was watering flowers. In this moment a bullet pierced the head of a straggler, a small stream of blood ran down the temple. And all that happened in the midst of built-up fields and lovingly tended flower gardens! Are we still living in this world or was all this a nasty, unending nightmare? How was it possible that people within fifty metres were quietly going to work whilst, in their midst, exhausted defenceless people were being shot?

At first I wanted to abandon my plan to record my memories because, once I had started, I was continuously tormented with nightmares of my experiences in the camps. One day a young patient visited me. Amongst other things she asked me if I was a Jew and if it were true that there had been concentration camps where Jews had been gassed. Were women and children really gassed? I told her of my fate and that of my parents and grandparents. Deeply moved, she said that she believed me. Until then she had been of the belief that reports of this nature were pure propaganda disseminated by the occupying army to damage the reputation of the Germans. So I understood that this was the opinion of democratically educated post-war youth. If this youth believed that the bloody era of the Nazis was only an invention of the propaganda, I will play my part in shattering these illusions. I owe my parents who were gassed in Auschwitz, the truth. I owe my little, funny, impulsive brother and my delicate little sister who were murdered in the gas chambers at Auschwitz, the truth.

Today, over twenty years later, young people often pose the question, "how was it possible that large masses of people who were numbered in their millions could be led to their extermination and that these masses went without a fight, like Iambs to the slaughter?" From today's perspective these events are hardly believable; but I hope, with the publication of this book, that this question will be answered, at least in part. It is not a collection of the worst experiences of the Jews; it is a portrayal of day-to-day Jewish life in the years 1939–1945. This account should enable the reader to feel the situation in which the Jews found themselves and to understand their responses. In none of the camps through which I passed were there gas chambers in which women and children were gassed. Even in our camp that was less than one hundred kilometres from the extermination camp Auschwitz, everything was so veiled that it took us more than a year before we understood that, not far away from us, masses of heaps of men, women, children and elderly were gassed and burnt daily. The secrecy of the extermination system was part of the devilish method through which humankind was enslaved step by step, and so every possibility of collective resistance was eliminated. Even so, in hundreds of cases, individuals and groups bitterly resisted either with weapons or with bare fists, but from the beginning this was futile and led only to death. I portray a chronicle of events that happened in a century in which animal protection was vigorously promoted and demonstrations against the use of rabbits for vivisection took place. In the same century, in the same society, a murder machine was operated, whose wheels were apparently silently grinding so that even sensitive ears were not disturbed.

My story has another purpose. It should help provide a connecting theme for those scientists who deal with Survivors of this catastrophe, that is, with people whose unique and unprecedented psychological and social profile form part of society. This is because on the whole these Survivors are broken in their psyche through a trauma that cannot lead to 'restitutio ad integrum'. Although many Survivors seem to be very much part of life and achieve successes, they have remained psychologically sick people. Their present life is burdened by their past and no success can compensate for their horrific experiences. Not infrequently, in intellectual circles of Survivors, the fateful words were heard, "Actually we already died in the years between 1940 and 1945. However, we have won our external life, but our inner self is dead." I heard this phrase often when I noted down the life stories of young Survivors for the Institute in New York. As dehumanised creatures we could never free ourselves from the burden carried by those condemned to be exterminated. The years of fear and oppression left behind damage to the psyche that is just as irreparable as damage to the grey matter of the brain. The ex-concentration camp inmate can laugh and be happy with others but within himself he bleeds and is in pain because the old wounds will not close. Although one has left the confinement of the concentration camp, the terrible atmosphere of the camps still embrace him, it is as if the camp is still inside him. All this must be taken into account by those who diagnose or concern themselves with the welfare of the psyche of camp inmates. How often do I myself hear, especially in the evening, when I am on my own, my parents and sister speak? I see their faces, which often appear calm and contented. However, when suddenly my little brother comes, a ghostly turmoil rises in my mind. I see myself again as someone drags me from our flat; I hear the screams of my relatives and I think that they also screamed like that in the gas chambers! I see only my father as a quiet, silent man with a serious appearance, as he says to Mother and the children, "One shall meet the murderers with calm. With pride one shall exit this world. The murderers will get their punishment". My surviving sister told me that those were my father's words on their arrival at Auschwitz.

I will continue to write because my little brother's voice is still ringing in my ears; because you were suffocated, you with your happy heart, with your serious child's eyes with which you watched over my shoulder as I was reading. For you dear brother, with your innocent eyes which were barbarically extinguished in Auschwitz. You look at me in the darkness when I lie awake, and your eyes warn me, "Don't forget it!" For you I will have sleepless nights, my little brother. For you I will tell the story of the long, bloody night.

We were a happy family before The Night began, which lasted five years and eight days. We four children (I was the eldest of two boys and two girls), were cared for by good parents and a large circle of relatives. My father, who was a respected and revered central focus of the family, advised on difficult questions and had the final word on difficult decisions, probably because he was the eldest of seven siblings. His attitude of putting the mental and moral above the material won him the respect and regard of his community. For many years he strove for the education of Jewish youth and was on the honorary parents committee in our town. His work in the Zionist movement took a large part of his free time; I well remember that his evenings were filled up with meetings and lectures for these movements. He saw his life's work as being active for them. He saw the realisation of the Jewish future in a Jewish State in the area of what was then Palestine. Our education was strongly influenced by his ideals. I can say that my parents complemented each other in their efforts to prepare us psychologically for our future. Their harmonious family life was only the outer frame of their constant endeavours but, with one blow, our strong family life was derailed.

In the autumn of 1939 the first repercussions of decades of constant black propaganda against the Jews manifested in decrees and restrictions succeeded one another. Yet we still would not come to terms with the first measures: as for example the wearing of a white armband with a yellow Star of David or the ban to visit certain streets and places. There then followed the ban not to use the train, the expulsion from the schools, and the order by punishment not to leave the flat. Life continued, even though shops and flats were dispossessed, even though huge sums of contribution monies were collected, and gold, jewellery and furs and radios had to be handed in. The Jews were gradually locked away for the time being in a large ghetto. Life carried on, despite the daily degradation to carry out demeaning jobs for the police and army from which one would often come home beaten and bleeding. It carried on until the abduction to forced labour camps. The final stage was then the 'Final Solution' of the

Jewish question, that is, the death in the gas chambers in Auschwitz. In August 1943 my parents, my brother and sister and my relatives were killed in the gas chambers and crematoria in Auschwitz. And with them the last Jews of the town were abducted. Now follows the family tree which depicts a family whose fate, under present circumstances, showed mercy because two young people were able to save themselves from the mass murder. Of many families no one survived, their traces were wiped out and destroyed, like the ashes of the crematoria in Auschwitz, Strutthoff and Treblinka.

Chapter One

Life in the Ghetto

On 1 September 1939 we were woken up early in the morning by bursts of thunder. We could not decide if it was exploding bombs or thunderous gunfire. At the same time, the radio ordered that the country be defended: by way of anti-aircraft defence, by way of service of the Red Cross and the digging of trenches. The war between national socialist Germany and Poland had undoubtedly begun. Planes were continuously cruising overhead, but we could not see if they were our planes or that of the enemy. Towards the afternoon, news had spread that the German army had crossed the border and had already advanced thirty kilometres into Poland. Strangely, this news did not scare me. At first, it did not occur to me to go to one of the air raid shelters. I was full of curiosity but unafraid as I watched the planes manoeuvring overhead and I felt that a new chapter in history had begun.

The hopeless situation of the Jewish youth, under the ultranationalist Polish regime of Colonel Beck, meant that I too yearned for change in our current circumstances. Admittedly, I only had vague ideas of how these changes should come about, they were just dreams and premonitions. By chance, at lunchtime during an air attack I was with the Chief of Police of our town. I observed how the hands of this much-feared man trembled so violently that he was unable to smoke his cigarette because of the shock of the exploding bombs. This man, whom the whole town feared and revered, stood hidden, cowering and trembling under the stone staircase. I was shocked by this image, and I was suddenly filled with foreboding as I realised that the situation was far more serious than I wanted to admit at that moment.

This was also the first Friday night when Shabbat[1] was not sanctified. It made me sad that this regular family celebration went silently by, unmarked. Many of our neighbours assembled in our flat and we listened together to the boastful speeches of the Polish military leaders who promised that the German invaders would soon be defeated and chased away.

News reports came thick and fast. Shocked Polish soldiers spoke of regiments of German assault infantry rolling towards us in trucks. The atmosphere became oppressive and my appetite for interesting experiences evaporated. Slowly it became clear to me that the planes were all of German origin and the Polish Army was unable to resist the German invasion. On Saturday morning we watched the municipality buildings being evacuated. Public life and traffic had come to a standstill. Rumours abounded that German tanks were already close to town, and that the German army's capability to perpetrate acts of violence should be feared.

With little hand luggage, my father, a few neighbours and I made our way to the next village to the east. My other relatives had fled the day before. The streets were packed with refugees, many pulling oxen, cows and goats behind them. Others pushed small carts filled with all their worldly goods, on top of which sat crying children.

---

1. Shabbat is the seventh day of the Jewish week and the Jewish day of rest. On Shabbat, Jews recall the Biblical Creation account in Genesis in which God created the Heavens and the Earth in six days and rested on the seventh. Shabbat commences at sundown on Friday evening and concludes at sunset on Saturday night.

Children who had been lost by their parents were screaming for them in this chaos. The whole exodus appeared eerie and unruly. Artillery shells whistled overhead and filled us with fear and dread. We were only able to progress slowly because the army blocked the road. I saw frightened faces everywhere. Everything seemed to be disintegrating. Rumour had it that hundreds of spies dressed up as Polish soldiers and officers among the fleeing masses were signalling to the German planes overhead. A Polish officer rode at our side. Next to him, tied to a horse, walked a soldier, apparently a German spy. The outraged masses shoved and beat him. On Sunday at dawn, we arrived at my grandmother's in Pilica where my mother, brother and sisters were waiting. In the afternoon, families were discussing whether to flee further or to stay put. The advance of the German troops put a stop to the discussions. Front line German soldiers had already forced their way into the village. When we awoke the next morning, the roads were swarming with German tanks and soldiers. Neighbours said it was not as bad as we had been led to believe. The soldiers seemed amiable, they were chatting to the men, gave out chocolate to the children, and did not harm anyone. Our youngest aunt went out into the street to check whether this was true. After a while she returned and confirmed that this was the case. Several hours passed without further trouble. Suddenly, wild shots were heard. We peered out of the window on to the street and we were just able to see how German soldiers threw themselves on to the ground and fired their weapons. A neighbour came with the news that next door to us, German soldiers were already taking away men from the flats. We ran down to the cellar and hid. Almost immediately, soldiers appeared in our flat and ordered, "All men out!" Heavy steps and wild screams rumbled above our heads, "Cursed bloody lot! Where are the men?" For a moment we held our breath, then flashlights were shone into our faces. With kicks, we were driven out onto the street at gunpoint where several men were already assembled. After we had been joined to a larger group, several soldiers marched us to the market square. Hundreds of men stood pushed together surrounded by soldiers with loaded machine guns. Some soldiers shot their guns into the air to increase the general panic. Then an order resounded, "Stand in rows of five! Get on with it! March! March! Quick! Line up!"

So we marched out of the village to an unknown destination until we stopped in front of a large factory hall into which we were herded with screams and beatings. Immediately the older men gathered together to choose a delegation which would find out why we were being held prisoner. After their return, the men told us that someone had shot at the German soldiers from a hiding place and that every tenth man amongst us would be shot if we did not identify the guilty one. Our delegates demanded in German, Polish and Yiddish, "Whoever possesses a gun should step forward!" But no one came forward. Finally they pleaded with us urgently that those who possessed weapons should come forward. The elders of the town assembled themselves around the rabbi and discussed how to avoid a massive bloodshed. Finally a few old men approached the elders of the town and informed them of their decision to sacrifice their lives for the remainder of the community. I pressed more closely against my father who stood calmly but sadly to one side. He was full of gloomy premonitions, "We ran away too late", he said to me, "we should have left Europe a year ago, that would have been the right thing to do". We were led under heavy guard by the soldiers, out of the factory hall into an open field and we were ordered to lie down. Everyone was trembling with fear, because he believed he could be that tenth one whose life would be forfeited. At this moment a few military cars stopped in front of us. A high-ranking officer stepped out and gathered the remaining officers around him. After a few minutes consultation we were ordered "Get up! You can go home again! You are free!"

Afterwards we found out that German soldiers really had been shot, whereupon the commander had ordered that all the Jews should be herded together and every tenth one shot. Meanwhile the local police tracked down the real culprits. They were a few highly motivated Polish soldiers who had resolved to fight back regardless of the odds. They had taken cover in a church tower and from there they had shot the German soldiers.

We were able to return to our grandparents' home. My mother's eyes lit up with joy upon our return. In our fullness of joy, we set aside our anxieties and put the best possible interpretation upon events. We concluded that the Germans had nothing nasty in mind and their precautions were intended only to strike those who were guilty; we would have nothing to fear if everyone behaved as they should. However, more threatening news reached us from other towns. We were told that hundreds of men had been shot and, in the chaos of the occupation, whole villages had been resettled. There were contrary rumours that, in some small towns, peace and order reigned. In those towns the German occupiers ordered business to continue as normal and the shops to reopen; with one word they ordered life back to normal, making no distinction between the treatment of Jews and non-Jews.

Here in the small town of Pilica the initial tensions also subsided. We could see how the soldiers chatted with people in a peaceful manner, nobody was harmed, and slowly our fears were eased. We did not want to give credence to rumours about prisoners being shot, along with other atrocities which were apparently happening in other cities. There was a deep-rooted belief among Jewish people that the Germans were highly cultured and known for their humanitarian and liberal ideals, a nation of poets and thinkers. The older Jewish generation recalled encounters with the pre-1918 Germany that had inspired trust and respect. Therefore most Jews were inclined to believe that the different atrocities they had heard about were the inevitable consequences of a few riotous front-line soldiers, and in the main they hoped to trust the humanitarian ethos of the German people once the front-line troops had been withdrawn.

After a two week stay, my family decided to return to our home town of Zawierce. On our way back we encountered endless units of the German Army marching eastwards. However, on the way we were neither impeded nor harassed. When we finally arrived home we saw large placards ordering all male Jews aged thirteen or over to assemble in the large textile factory. The order was already one week old so we ignored it. The Jews that were already interned in the large factory halls were held for a further ten days and finally released.

The German invasion of Poland was completed quickly. The German occupying army tried hard to restore daily life. However, some restrictions on Jews were imposed: we were banned from leaving our home at night, and prohibited from assembling for prayer or for any other reason. The synagogue was locked and Jewish pupils were excluded from all schools where normal lessons were taking place. Increasingly and ruthlessly, we were made to do all kinds of work. Men were forced, especially on Shabbat and on the Jewish festivals to work. One day, on Yom Kippur, our Day of Atonement, our holiest of days, I was taken with many others to work, unloading coal at the railway station. On this, our most sacred fast day, we were herded into the wagons that were guarded by two young soldiers. The coal dust burned our eyes and dried our mouths but they did not allow us to leave the wagons for a drink. We were unaccustomed to heavy manual labour, and, as our hands burned from the shovelling, one of the young soldiers who was good-natured allowed us to take a break. However, when his much stricter superior appeared he conformed to his more severe attitude. This bullying made our situation abundantly clear. Still we wanted to try and emigrate. We contacted different consulates and for a while nourished hopes which then tragically faded away. On the whole, we submitted to the deceptive judgement that the war could only last a few months. Once the war was concluded there would definitely be the possibility of emigration. So we exercised self-control, despite the tyranny and deprivation of our rights, and understood they would only last as long as the war. We really did believe that the work we were forced to undertake by the occupying forces would be the worst that could happen to us and when necessary must be patiently borne.

A few months after the end of the Polish campaign, our region, Polish Upper Silesia, was annexed to the German Reich. Our town, which was always known by the Polish name Zawiercie, was renamed "Warthenau". The Germans coerced all non-Jewish Poles to declare themselves "Volksdeutsche"[2]. The Germans pretended to them that they would rise to become the "Herrenvolk"[3]. Many groups resisted, especially members of the Polish socialist party, the PPS[4], many of

---

2. Ethnic German
3. Master Race
4. The Polish Socialist Party (Polska Partia Socjalistyczna, PPS) was one of the most important Polish left-wing political parties from its inception in 1892 until 1948. It was established again in 1987 and remains active.

whom were arrested to break the resistance of the Poles. Above all the first new "Volksdeutschen" were Polish businessmen who displayed pictures of Hitler and swastikas in their windows. At the same time, Jews were forced under threat of heavy penalties, to wear white armbands with yellow stars on which the word "Jude" was imprinted. So we became marked people, second-class citizens.

On the orders of the Gestapo, the "Judenrat"[5] was established in order to collect a substantial sum of money and to put several hundred men at the disposal of the German authorities each day for various jobs. I had to present myself for work every other day. We were busy washing the roads, cleaning the police stations, maintaining the stables for the horses, and also we had to undertake various transport tasks. Often there were insufficient numbers of people at the Judenrat's disposal. Therefore the German police seized young men by force from their homes.

Beginning in 1940, Jews were uprooted from the border area close to the towns of Teschen and Kattowitz and resettled in our midst. A few hundred families arrived in our town. These exiles left their homes with just one suitcase of clothes and were totally destitute because all their money had been confiscated. We were confronted with the hopeless misery of the exile for the first time. We had to make space in our home for a few of the exiled families, share with them the little we had and give them money so they could purchase ration cards to procure the most basic provisions. Ultimately, all those in need were assisted by Jewish welfare. They set up soup kitchens where the needy could eat for free and they distributed food without charge. Amongst the families who took refuge in our house was a family with many children from the Polish-German border town of Tarnowitz. The father of the family, Mr Hadda, was a proud German nationalist, and had been an army officer in the First World War. He had fought in Upper Silesia in the Battle of Annaberg and had received a high military decoration for his heroic deeds. He proudly recounted how, due to his initiative, Annaberg had been defended and retained in the German Reich. Every day he preached to us that

---

5. Literally "Jewish Council", in effect a puppet Jewish administration

the harassment and persecution to which the German Jews were subjected must surely be a mistake. He said, "It's only meant for Jews from the East". Often he even used the term "der Führer" with pride and respect. He thought the persecution of German Jews was only a precaution made necessary by war, and as soon as the war was over their rights would be restored. Even the military decorations, awarded to this enthusiastic German patriot for his brave fight in defence of the German Fatherland, were of little help to him. In 1943 he and his family together with other Jewish residents of Zawiercie were taken to Auschwitz and gassed and burnt.

Spring of 1940 revealed its first bloody traces. In one night, twelve people, mostly young men, were arrested, immediately disappeared and were never heard from again. It was rumoured that for the sake of security the German officials wanted old communists in their safe keeping. There were only a few old communists among those who were arrested. Our neighbour, Yehuda Grünkraut, was woken that same night by the Gestapo. He had to dress hurriedly and go with them. Grünkraut was an active member of the Zionist movement "Bejtar", a right-wing nationalist party. Grünkraut's arrest could be traced back to a denunciation. In general, denunciations became more common and Poles were the main perpetrators. The Poles announced themselves to the Gestapo as "Volksdeutsche" and presented themselves as eager helpers. They willingly volunteered lists of names to prove their commitment. People in whom the Gestapo had no interest were frequently arrested merely because their name appeared on these lists. After a few weeks Grünkraut's parents received a parcel of clothes and the news that their son had died from heart failure. During this time I once fell victim to confusion over names. As already mentioned, the "Judenrat", on behalf of the Jewish community, had to contribute a very substantial sum to the German municipal authorities. As the sum could not be collected in time, the Gestapo arrested thirty Jews who were all elderly and affluent citizens. The name Bornstein was also on the list. So it was that one day, when I happened to be at home alone, I was arrested by two Gestapo officials. Together with a few other suffering companions I was taken on a lorry to Sosnowitz where the ss had a training camp. There young members of the ss were taught how to deal "correctly" with subordinates and prisoners. For the first time in my life, I spent day and night in close proximity to the ss. It turned out that we were to be guinea pigs for the ss. We spent the nights fully dressed in draughty sheds lying on hard wooden boards. Early each morning we were woken by a piercing whistle. We received a cup of black coffee and a piece of bread, and then were driven out onto the exercise yard. Then began endless punishing exercises to which most of us were unaccustomed. Those who collapsed were helped to their feet with beatings. Thus a few days passed in constant hounding. Later, they sent us home without explanation.

We found terrible changes in our hometown. Suddenly we encountered such unaccustomed restrictions and limitations that the humiliations we had so recently endured paled into insignificance. Jewish families who lived near public offices and officials had been forcibly resettled in other streets and parts of the town. These measures grew in scale until their true purpose could not be concealed from even the most well-meaning person. It emerged that the plan was for us to live in a ghetto in which we would soon be confined. As Jewish people continuously streamed in from outlying areas, pressure on living space constantly increased, not to mention the financial and social crisis. Educated and clerical workers in particular were forced out of their jobs and had no opportunity to build up a new existence or to establish a new livelihood.

We viewed the future with trepidation and prepared ourselves as best we could. There were persistent rumours that labour camps were being built from which there would be no escape for Jews, so during the summer we strove to get hold of heavy winter shoes and clothes. However, a few Poles still found ways and means to come into our ghetto and provide extra groceries and other things that were no longer available to us. Textiles were particularly valuable for bartering. Slowly our worldly goods were depleted by bartering.

The constant strain and danger and our efforts to eke out our daily existence distracted us for the time being from all our future plans. This nightmare existence must eventually end. We long since lost the possibility to control our destiny. We all knew that escape from this imprisonment was doomed to fail.

Soon the abusive treatment to which we were subjected was intensified. A new decree compelled Jews to hand over their businesses to trustees. Jewish businesses were then transferred to several hundred Germans newly settled in the area. A few hundred Jewish families had to vacate their homes to make room for "Volksdeutsche". As the ghetto became forever smaller, the little space that remained became overcrowded with those who had been made homeless yet again as they were forced to find shelter with other Jewish families. In the late summer of 1940 the "Judenrat" received an order to make several hundred men available for work. They were to be used for the building of the motorway. When I discovered my name was on the dispatch list I fled and hid for two weeks in the neighbouring town. Only when the transport left for these forced labour camps did I return. In the meantime a few of my friends had been abducted. The grief of their relatives was so overwhelming that, understandably, I did not dare to meet them as, once again, I had escaped the abduction.

We had hardly recovered from this shock before the next one followed. Acute poverty and slave labour became the order of the day. We became fair game for the German police and occupying authorities, as each one of them had the power to confiscate Jewish possessions and to round up and abduct Jewish people. We were surrounded by harsh German guards. Our oppressors were eagerly supported by those malicious Poles who had become "Volksdeutsche". There were also some Poles who had a good relationship with us Jews. Mostly, they were simple labourers or small farmers, religious and upright Catholics, who seized every opportunity to help us. Admittedly their efforts were not without danger because those willing to help us had to fear the power of those influential Poles who were ill-disposed towards us Jews. Therefore we could not expect vital aid. Our escape was blocked by an impenetrable wall. We were blockaded by a large section of the Polish population and the occupying forces isolated us from the outside world. Systematic anti-Jewish propaganda, both written and pictorial, filled so many heads with prejudice that when meeting a Pole one never knew if they were well or ill disposed towards Jews. Occasionally, thanks to a fortuitous sequence of events, an individual was able to escape, but never whole families. Which responsible family head, be it father or son, could abandon their families in such desperate times? We had no alternative but to face up to the growing horror with which we were confronted with each passing day.

Chapter Two

Grünheide

From the beginning of 1941 there was talk that the Jewish youths from neighbouring towns were to be conscripted as a continuous source of new labour. Since insufficient young people volunteered for work, the Gestapo and the Jewish police under their command raided the Jewish community, seizing people by force from their beds at night and deporting them to the labour camps. We were convinced that sooner or later we would be subjected to these raids as well.

One Friday during these days filled with dread we sanctified Shabbat for the last time. The ceremony was conducted in great haste. With two small candles which flickered restlessly and our room barely lit, my father sanctified Shabbat by silently reciting the prayers which were normally so happily said but were now filled with fear. We four children, trembling and with fearful faces, sat at prayer. I could not get out of my mind the following thought "Who knows if this is the last Shabbat during which I will hear my father's prayers at our table?"

After this short service my mother quickly gave me a parcel containing my supper and, with a tear-stained face, accompanied me from our home. I had to conceal myself in my hiding place to avoid being picked up by the Gestapo during the night.

Some nights I hid with Christian friends who lived outside the town. Then I would return to my parent's home. On the night of Tuesday 25 March, somebody said that a raid was planned for the following night. People were terrified by shootings and murder during the last raid in a neighbouring town. Jewish inhabitants were greatly agitated by various versions of these reports. Could it be true that people who were discovered in hiding were shot on the spot; that whole families were seized as hostages when some sought-after family member could not be found? This news made our blood run cold and we were convinced that soon we would have to bid one another farewell. Some families ran hither and thither to conceal themselves in hiding places outside the town.

These fear-filled nights seemed endless. At night I wandered from one hiding place to another. Once I lived in an attic, then in a cellar, always in the hope of escaping my persecutors. On that particular Tuesday evening, as many of my friends ran to their hiding places again, I decided to stay at home. My mother begged me to hide myself, but to no avail. I was suddenly reluctant to play these nightly hiding games, my doubts evaporated, and I felt compelled, against my better judgment, to spend the night at home. I decided not to submit to the atmosphere of wild panic and went quietly to bed. At four o'clock in the morning the lady next door knocked on our door. We were wide-awake in no time. It was pitch black but the sound of tumult drifted up from the street. Our worst fears were instantly roused by the thumping noise of soldiers' boots striking the pavement. With one leap I was at the window and carefully pulled the curtain aside. I thought I was looking into an eerie abyss. The houses opposite were already under guard by the ss. In one hand they held an upturned rifle and in the other a torch whose beam scanned the front of the houses. Men and women were clubbed as they were pushed out of a door into the street. The ss quickly made sure that they were not men disguised as women. Then they were pushed and beaten back into the house. My mother and siblings observed this scene from the window and began to cry loudly. Their plaintive cry and the paralysing fear of what was to come suddenly made my hands and feet tremble. My teeth began to chatter and I struggled to remain erect. I was totally helpless, what should I do with myself now? Where could I run to hide myself? Nothing made sense anymore, it was now too late to escape. I embraced my mother and tried hard to stop her tears, "I will run away quickly and try to hide somewhere", I promised her. "I think I can shelter at the neighbours". I ran quickly downstairs to the first floor to our neighbours. In great haste we decided to put a large wardrobe in front of the door behind which we would hide. However, the wardrobe was not large enough to conceal the entire door. Without further ado, the neighbour's wife shoved us into the cupboard and hid us with the clothes hanging inside. Before we had a chance to settle into our hiding place we heard the deafening shouts of the Gestapo and the police, "Men out, damned Jews out!" Heavy steps approached us and before we had time to think, the ss were already in our neighbour's home and ripped open the cupboard door. They cheered as they rummaged through the cupboard. They forced us out under a hail of blows from the butts of their rifles. We were kicked and pushed and we ran to the staircase. With one shove we were forced down the flight of steps. At the bottom of the stairs, I was pushed towards our neighbours who were already assembled there. My mother stood on the second floor and watched this scene with tears in her eyes. I looked up at her, yearning to give her a final farewell hug. With poundings and beatings with batons we were driven further and further away from our home towards a large crowd of fellow sufferers. On the street, a large group of men, their heads bloody and bowed from beatings, stood huddled together. At that moment we were surrounded by gendarmerie and the police, their weapons at the ready. Finally, when we had all been gathered together the order was given, "Forward, march!" Eventually we reached a factory where a large group of other prisoners was already waiting.

The gendarmerie, police and Gestapo, equipped with rifles, truncheons and cudgels, formed a cordon, striking us right and left, and forced us through an opening. Bloodied and groaning, we reached the hall of the factory. The entrance to the hall was drenched in blood and wounded people lay everywhere. Old men had their beards ripped out and their bloody faces were stamped on with boots.

In all this misery I found my father again. Silently he laid his hand on my shoulder. Our shared grief stifled the words in our mouths. We both must have thought the same, about our families that were left behind without help or protection.

My father, with a few acquaintances, had hidden in a neighbouring house, but they were finally also discovered. The Gestapo and police had searched the attic and cellars with sniffer dogs and drove them out. There, a few of his friends who were wounded from beatings lay together and succumbed to their injuries; others were shot where they hid.

Towards midday the factory was overcrowded, over a thousand men of all ages were assembled. Finally Gestapo Chief Knoll, the head of the Arbeitseinsatzes (labour camp organisation of Upper Silesia) appeared, accompanied by Gestapo Chief Lindner, several officers and some members of the Judenrat[1].

---

1. As already mentioned, the Gestapo established the Judenrat to provide Jewish self-government who were entrusted with the distribution of food ration cards, pest and infection control, burying of the dead, recruitment of (forced) labour, and the (enforced) collection of money. Some members of the Judenrat who at first did their duty only because they were compelled to do so soon became willing Gestapo henchmen. Only a few recognised that their situation was hopeless and kept their human dignity. However, next to the many ignominious denunciations which emerged from the ranks of the Judenrat, one must not forget the many high-minded life-saving deeds with which a few seriously endangered themselves.

Cooperation with the Gestapo produced temporary advantages for the members of the Judenrat. They were exempt from forced labour, they could save members of their family from deportation, they received a bigger food ration. However, the obvious advantage of harmony with the Gestapo proved to be a delusion. The Gestapo abused their control over the Judenrat to discover the exact number of people in the Jewish ghettos and to inform themselves about the internal circumstances in the ghetto, for example: about possible resistance groups. They were also compelled to confiscate and hand over gold, silver, jewellery and furs. As there was a well-organised Jewish militia that was an integral part of the Judenrat, it was possible for the Gestapo, working together with this support, to keep hundreds of ghettos in check, even though they were widely scattered. The preferential treatment of the Judenrat lasted only as long as the help of their henchmen was needed. After three years the town of Warthenau

The men from the Judenrat selected a few from the crowd to be supervisors, and finally they produced two doctors who quickly bandaged the wounded and isolated them from the healthy. With help from the supervisors, the doctors had to choose five hundred of the strongest men from the ranks. We had to undress and march past the doctor who was flanked by the Gestapo. The doctor determined our fitness and assembled the healthy. Suddenly we heard the command "Silence!" Gestapo Leader Knoll climbed onto a table and made a drastic speech which left nothing to the imagination. "Your time is up anyway," he said, "whoever comes forward of their own volition will go away to work, will be treated well there, and after a while will be able to return to their families. They will be treated the same as the non-Jewish workers." Horrified at the sight of the wounded and shot I said to my father that I wanted to volunteer to work; but he should strive for his own release so he could remain with the family. In total, one hundred and fifty young men willingly stepped forward. We were then led out of the hall and bundled off into buses. Only then did we see the large crowd of women and children outside the factory gates. They stared anxiously into the buses searching frantically for their husbands, sons or fathers. On the lookout for my family, I finally caught sight of my little sister Noemi, then a thirteen year-old girl. In desperation she ran from bus to bus, searching to discover one of us. Finally she spotted me, but we were forbidden to wind the windows down. No one was allowed onto the bus. Silently we stared at one another through the window; we both had the feeling that a terrible fate awaited us. My final memory of my little sister is of these lingering glances.

After driving for a few hours through the night we reached a clearing behind a forest on which stood half-ready barracks, our accommodation for the coming weeks. A few of us were immediately

---

was rendered Judenrein (cleansed of Jews) by the liquidation of the final remnant in the ghetto. The Judenrat and the Jewish militia still helped the Gestapo to load the remaining ghetto inhabitants into goods wagons which were destined for Auschwitz. Suddenly and without warning or explanation the families of the Judenrat were taken aside and led behind a house. There they were shot and cut down by the Gestapo.

ordered to collect straw. When they returned we were informed that the entire clearing was under observation by armed guards in SA[2] uniforms.

When we entered the barracks, empty walls stared back at us. There was no lighting. The straw was spread out on the floor and we were ordered to lie down and to remain calm. We laid awake for a long time, struggling to come to terms with the events of the last twenty-four hours. Like a bad dream these cruel images kept passing before our mind's eye. We still had not fully grasped that we had been finally torn away from our families and homes, that for us there would be no return. We could not and did not want to understand that all we had read and heard about had finally happened to us. The screams with which the ordeal started were ringing in our ears: "Jews out! All men out!" Innocent and unsuspecting men were beaten with rifle butts, old men were trampled on, their faces bleeding, the skin of their faces shredded where their beards had been ripped out. These pictures were imprinted forever in my memory, images which always returned to torture and torment us during our imprisonment.

Despite all these events, we did not want to abandon our hope of life. Hadn't the Gestapo promised us that as voluntary workers we would be well treated?

With uncertainty of what had happened to my father, with the thought of my sorrowful mother, with the worry about my remaining siblings, I finally fell into a restless sleep. The next morning we were shocked and startled awake by whistles and screams, "Get up! Out onto the Appellplatz[3]!"

So called group leaders showed us how we had to stand, while opposite us a hundred youths arranged themselves in formation. They were counting in a military fashion and marched out to the camp flanked by SA guards with cocked rifles. Jewish underlings approached us and instructed us how to line up, be counted and how to march off. The camp had been partially built by prisoners who had been

---

2. The *Sturmabteilung* (SA) was the Storm Detachment or Assault Division which functioned as the original paramilitary wing of the Nazi Party.
3. Literally "the place where prisoners or troops lined up for roll call".

there for several months and they were now partially responsible for its administration. The SA had appointed a Jewish Elder in overall charge and he had chosen his block and group leaders. For better or worse, the prisoners were at the beck and call of these leaders. Prisoners were allocated easy or heavy, pleasant or dirty jobs depending on the liking or antipathy they evoked. These group leaders introduced the newcomers (our group comprised several hundred people) to the discipline of Grünheide Forced Labour Camp.

After being instructed as to how we should march, stand to attention and be counted, we were allocated to our barracks and quarters. Suddenly a prisoner from my home town approached me and said, "Your father is standing at the back over there." Quickly I tried to get into the column further back in order to get closer to my father. Finally I stood before him. Father told me that after our deportation the men who remained were inspected and declared fit by a Jewish doctor working under the supervision of the SS. They were then loaded onto lorries and brought here during the night. Consequently the volunteers and forced labourers were gathered together in the forced labour camp.

Then we were given shovels, spades and hoes, divided into groups and set to work in the vicinity of the camp. Others had to work, building the barracks into which we were later to be housed.

Although it was the end of March the weather was bitterly cold. We were inappropriately dressed as we were still in the same clothes we had been wearing when we were surprised and deported from our homes. At dawn we had to dig a ditch around the camp. We were not properly equipped for the work we had to do. Some could barely conceal their clumsiness. Albeit unwittingly, they made a grotesque image; dressed in dark suits, their socks pulled up over their rolled-up trouser legs, awkwardly holding their spades. The SA were unstinting in their mockery, and abused us, calling us lazy. One SA man shouted at us, "You lazybones, you Jew-pigs! You don't even know how to hold a spade!" Most of us had not done such work in our lives because we mostly worked in administrative or professional occupations. It was all too easy to reduce us to caricatures, to brand us as inferior, useless people.

The day stretched endlessly before us until we were allowed to return to the barracks in the evening and to rest from this unaccustomed outdoor work. Then everyone received a spoon and was given a meal as we walked past the kitchen. This we consumed in the so-called dining hall. Many men put their plates down and returned to their barracks where they huddled together in small groups speaking about the families they had left behind and their bleak future. In the evening I was very hungry and ate all my food. My father stood next to me, having hardly touched his food, pushing his plate towards me. At first, I refused to accept his portion but he forced me to eat. He encouraged me with his kind, fatherly countenance not to be downcast because the first goal of the Nazis was to destroy our souls. He pulled me towards him and passionately admonished me to fight for my life. The seemingly inescapable present would eventually give way to a future that would disclose other prospects. "You have your whole life in front of you" he said, "every morning your future can be renewed." He spoke calmly and I felt that he wanted me, the inexperienced pupil who had always been protected, to be reconciled to our situation. Never before had my father spoken to me with such urgency, his words weighed heavily and left their mark forever.

When we were later ordered to go to sleep I found it difficult to be separated from my father. We spoke about our mother at home and speculated what my three siblings would be doing without their father.

During the morning Appell[4] we were allocated to different workgroups. Then we were mixed with the more experienced prisoners forming new work groups. Under the watchful eye of the SA we marched out to the motorway where they handed us over to the building contractors who were working on the motorway. I was directed to the "Kaltwasser Hoch-Tiefbau" firm and joined a group loading clay into tippers. It was impossible to work continuously outside because of the changeable spring weather. March brought a lot of snow and overnight the clay ground was often frozen solid. Early every morning we were punctually marched outside, but it was

---

4. Appell, literally "roll-call".

frequently impossible to carry out the work. Finally they allocated us to various transport jobs or we were made to break up cement with wooden boards or planks. As we wore neither gloves nor winter clothes the work was agony. Many had frostbitten hands and others could not withstand the work, unable to overcome the freezing cold with constant movement. Sometimes, when the foremen and civilian workers were unable to direct the work because of the constant slush or rain, we were sent from the building site back into the camp. Anton, the guard, begrudged us this enforced break. He chased us for hours around the Appellplatz in order to force us to do pointless work. Despite this we could pass a few hours in our quarters. Then we cooked and fried potatoes and dried our clothes. Nearly all of us wore ordinary clothing that soon became damp and stiff with clay from shovelling.

April brought sunshine and rain, and still changeable working conditions. With rain came the order to cease work; that only happened when we were completely soaked. The German master craftsmen and foremen and the SA guards wore raincoats with hoods, but we were soaked to the skin. April brought one of our great festivals – Pesach[5], which usually coincides with Easter. During those spring days we remember great biblical events that brought freedom to our people. This is when Jews traditionally celebrate their liberation from slavery in Egypt. It is the custom to organise great family celebrations in the company of guests on the first two evenings of the festival. This patriarchal ritual starts with the head of the family telling the story of how the Jews were enslaved in Egypt and were liberated, and ends with a celebratory meal. Children await this festival with great impatience. We could mark this Pesach only in our minds. We felt the separation from our families even more deeply. Our hearts were heavy with homesickness and our minds were seared by burning questions about our future. Was our bitter destiny to be torn away from our families and end our lives as deportees behind barbed wire? Would we ever escape our imprisonment? Nobody knew the answer. A few believers decided to observe the ritual even under the present

5. Pesach, also known as Passover.

circumstances, resolving not to eat leavened bread[6]. My father was a member of this group. In secret they managed to obtain flour and to bake the matzah, which only consisted of flour and water, in the oven at night. In the evening when the festival began, the religious sat huddled together, recited the prayers, ate the matzahs and recounted from the holy books the story of the Exodus from Egypt.

For some weeks, I worked building up the earthworks for a bridge. This arduous work with a shovel soon reduced my hands to a very poor condition. I could lift it only with the greatest difficulty. Enviously, I watched those few who were already accustomed to this heavy labour and managed to cope with their difficult situation.

Schachtmeister[7] Greguletz, a Silesian, drove the strong ones among us to load the trucks even more quickly; those who could not keep up were beaten sadistically and prodded with a spade handle. I used all my strength to fill my truck as quickly as the others but I managed only poorly. The shovel waved in every direction when I lifted it up to the truck and sometimes I could not stop it overturning. Greguletz was watching me. Occasionally he even picked up a spade to help me because he saw that even with the best will in the world I could not completely fill the truck.

We were correctly treated by a Silesian called Heiduck who was responsible for greasing the truck. He gave us words of encouragement and often brought us a sandwich. He thought the Nazi regime must soon end and the Jews would resume their former lives and homes. One morning, Heiduck did not come to work. The trucks began to squeak as the bearings ran hot. Suddenly Greguletz called me, "You little squirt, come here! I will show you how to grease the wagons. If you do well you will remain our wagon-greaser, if not you will be beaten and sent back to loading trucks." I was delighted to be allocated this new job. Finally there was a chance for my hands to heal.

---

6. During the eight days of the festivals we are permitted to eat only unleavened bread, known as matzah. The eating of bread or other leavened products is strictly prohibited.
7. Literally "Pit Master".

I worked to the best of my ability. After a while, Heiduck returned but I remained his assistant greaser. Old Heiduck smoked and coughed continuously while I did his work. For this he gave me all his food at lunchtime and sometimes he also added something for others. Despite the rationing there was sufficient food in Silesia. Greguletz never once gave any of us even a piece of bread. What remained from his portion he threw to the passing cows, and many hungry eyes followed his hands as he offered the bread to the animals.

Now, I could walk around the building site without any guard and talk with the ordinary workers. Some of them obtained certain articles for me that one could still then buy from the canteen of the Kaltwasser Railway Station, for example pocket mirrors, combs and other things that could be bartered. I was also often able to send my mother a letter. As a matter of fact, at that time, we were only allowed to write a card, which was censored, once a fortnight. My father and I prepared detailed reports which the good Heiduck took to the post office in Kaltwasser. We wrote to calm my mother, stressing above all that we were getting on well and not to worry on our account. However, the reality was very different. My father was not at all well. Although he tried to conceal his poor health from me, by chance I discovered he had numerous ulcers on his body. I also noticed that on the march he had difficulty keeping up with the group. Quietly, he tried to make little of his condition. But as I observed him at his work I was filled with anxiety and worry for him.

As already mentioned, Greguletz regulated the tempo of the work according to the strongest and fastest. At the first truck stood the tall Mydlarz. He was a labourer by trade and he filled his truck as quickly as possible in order to please Greguletz. As most of the others found it extremely difficult to lift a full shovel we often whispered to the strong Mydlarz to work more slowly because the others could not match his speed. His only response was to smile proudly and stupidly at us. He maintained his work rate for barely a year before he died, weakened by his endeavours. Many other strong men shared his fate.

When I saw how my father struggled to fill the sand trucks to the brim and kept falling behind the others, I was frightened that Greguletz would soon appear with his stick, so I went to his truck to help him fill it quickly. Suddenly I felt a severe beating on my back. When I turned around I saw the pit master Greguletz in front of me, his raging rat's face wrought with anger, "You damned arse! What are you doing here? Just get back to your work!" I tried to explain to him that I had a few free minutes. The group elders approached us to pacify him but Greguletz chased me away, and with a heavy heart I had to abandon my father and leave him to his work. How could I now help him? After the evening Appell in the camp, I went to the medical orderly, Kristall, who originated from our neighbouring town. I begged him urgently to write my father a sick note. At first he did not want to listen to me. However, he admitted that he knew my father and that lately he had been coming frequently for dressings. However, his illness did not conform to the regulations that would otherwise have allowed him to be excused from work. Incidentally I mentioned to him that I had good contacts on the building site and that I was able to obtain useful things, including some medicines. Suddenly he mentioned to me that he had to send a letter and asked if I could pass it on. As medical orderly in charge of the Ältester[8] his authority exceeded that of the Jewish Elder and he was able to receive uncensored post. However, he himself could not send letters off since he rarely left the camp and he had no contacts outside the camp to post any letters for him. I shared everything in the camp with my friend Kanatzky. His parents manufactured confectionery and occasionally he received parcels from them that he would share with me. To secure the medical orderly's goodwill I gave him a bag of sweets. Every few weeks an ss doctor came to the camp and reviewed the medical reports. He also decided whether those who were too sick to work should remain or be sent home. When the doctor next came, the medical orderly wanted to do his best for my father and

---

8. Ältester, literally "oldest", the term used by the Germans to identify the Jew who answered to them for all his peers.

have him declared unfit. He warned me, however, that the Ältester would have to be present and give his consent as well.

Our Judenältester Sorski from Kattowitz was not exactly malicious but he really imagined that the ss had chosen him to be the Judenältester because was superior over the others. He acted with supreme self confidence in his "role". Since I was occasionally able to send letters secretly, I also came into contact with him and he sent some letters through me. He checked me thoroughly and when he recognised my reliability he began gradually to trust me. One Sunday, when I knew he was in a good mood, I went to his room and made my request. I sought for Sorski's understanding for my father's current circumstances since he could hardly work because he was in such pain. I impressed upon him that as a son I could not remain indifferent to my father's suffering. Sorski, still in a good mood, replied, "If he is ill I have nothing against it, provided that the medical orderly puts him on the sick list." I thanked him and left the room very happily. Now, I had to obtain the medical orderly's agreement. I knew only too well that many similar requests had been submitted. There were still people in camp who still had concealed diamonds and jewellery with which they wanted to purchase their freedom to at least return to the ghetto.

In a subsequent conversation, the medical orderly enquired about my financial circumstances at home. I told him truthfully that we could not bring any money with us because we were overtaken by events when we were seized and taken away. I reassured him that my mother still had some trinkets. After that he suggested that I write to my mother and tell her to give a few hundred marks to his father. His father would confirm in a coded letter that he had received the money, and once this had been accomplished he would try to put my father on the sick list. He also promised to speak up for my father and make it clear to the ss doctor, whose decision was absolute and final, that my father was unfit for work and to approve his release. In a constant turmoil, I worried about what else I could do and kept sending my mother fresh instructions. She had to take certain other measures to ensure that no further difficulties would be encountered upon my father's return. The sick were not necessarily returned directly to their home towns. Instead they were brought first to the transit camp in Sosnowitz called Dulag, which served as headquarters for the administration of Jews in East Upper Silesia. Dulag served as a transit camp both for those who were to be dispatched to labour camps and the sick who were returned from them. As in all camps, corruption was rife here. The Gestapo and the ss, who were in overall control, with the help of the judischer Hilfspolizisten[9], obtained diamond rings, gold teeth and large sums of money. The camp leaders "bought" freedom for their favourites and therefore sent others back to the labour camps in their place. So we could never be certain that the sick who reached Dulag would really be sent home. Without money and without connections one was completely at the mercy of the camp leaders. To forestall any risk, my mother sought the help of a certain Windmann, a senior member of the Judenrat of our town. I can still remember early in 1940 that Dr. Frick, who was then Lord Mayor of our town, threatened all those who failed to pay ransom with the death penalty. (After the war, Dr. Frick was living in Munich and worked as senior counsellor for the government.) The Judenrat strongly urged all influential members of the community to help with the collection of money. My father was also enlisted to help with these collections, but at home he told us that on many other matters his views differed from those of Windmann. Windmann's position as leader of the Judenrat had gone to his head. Even though he and my father were longstanding friends and for years had worked together leading a party, during 1940 their friendship cooled more and more. Now, however, my mother was forced to seek this man's power and protection to secure safe passage home from Dulag for my father.

After a few days, the ss doctor appeared in the camp to make a routine visit. The medical orderly kept his word and put my father on the sick list. Everything went well until then because the ss doctor included my father with a few others who were also unfit for work. When I returned to camp from work that evening, the medical orderly

---

9. Judischer Hilfspolizisten, Jewish Auxiliary Police.

whispered the good news to me on the Appellplatz. I quickly wrote to my mother that our efforts had been successful and my father would be sent home in a few days. She should do her utmost to ensure that our plans came to fruition for my father to reach home from Dulag. I reconciled myself to camp life with renewed courage. Prior to deportation I had always totally relied on my parents' guidance, but the basis of my behaviour changed completely as I was forced to depend upon my own judgement. Now my father's return home should become reality. However, this was insufficient to make us happy. An improvement had arisen in other respects, in the last few weeks. I had put on weight and my appearance had improved and I was in roughly the same physical condition as when I had first arrived in the camp. This by itself was sufficient to fill my father with hope and happiness for the future

On Saturday afternoon when I returned from work we were counted on the Appellplatz. The sick who were to be transported back to their hometown were called out. They had to tie up their bundles in an hour. I went to my father in his quarters and helped him to pack his belongings, in any case these were very few. He gave me some of his laundry, some he gave to others. His locker was cleared in a moment. We were to be separated in an hour and for both of us his quarters suddenly seemed too small. We went behind the barracks and for a while walked silently together backwards and forwards. I tried to dispel the oppressive mood and break the unbearable silence. So I told my father that I too would enlist the help of the medical orderly and try to get home. If I were to succeed then together we would seize a final chance to escape or emigrate. My father replied briefly, "We have missed that, we failed to recognise the danger in time. Now it is very difficult to get away, only great events can change our fate." Then we relapsed into silence. The Judenältester blew his whistle and ordered, "March to the railway station! The three pairs who are now to march away must go up by the gate where they will be accompanied by the SA guards to Sosnowitz." Only a few minutes remained before our final farewell. Tears stuck in my throat as I tried to control my emotions and appear cheerful. I still said, "Mama does not need to worry about me. I am well, and with my connections I can even help others." My father hugged me and tenderly he stroked my hair and said, "Who knows when we will see each other again, perhaps you will experience and endure a great deal. Don't forget who you are. Stay strong and full of hope." When the SA man approached the other side of the camp gates my father added, "Promise me one more thing." With it his words stuck in his throat, "Remain a good Jew." He was also no longer able to control his emotion and his eyes filled with tears. I could only nod in agreement as I silently cried and swallowed my tears.

The camp gate opened and my father stepped out with his companions. I remained behind the wire fence and hastily wiped away my tears as I wanted to appear cheerful in that final moment. I pressed tightly against the wire fence as I waved to my father. With each step he became more distant. I could no longer control my emotions as I saw how my father's progress pained him. The final picture still etched in my memory is of an unclear silhouette of a sad group trudging in the footsteps of an SA guard with a rifle over his shoulder. The more distant my father became, the stronger were my tears. "When would we see each other again?" I asked myself. My father was already far away. The menacing rifle now seemed to overshadow his vague silhouette. So I saw him for the last time – for the very last time. After a week I received news that my father had arrived home.

I now had the good fortune to work often as a locomotive stoker and when necessary to stand in for a German worker. Apart from that I was not required to do other work in the camp. I began to gradually ascend the camp hierarchy, which consisted in the main of camp tailors, cooks and other staff.

Other work in the camp had to be undertaken during the evenings, Saturday afternoons and Sundays. These included cleaning the barracks, sweeping the camp grounds, taking away rubble and rubbish, cleaning the washroom and latrines and other tasks, all of which we sought to avoid. Camp personnel decided who should do these jobs. If someone was kindly disposed towards a prisoner because he did errands for him he would be spared from these tasks. This was also true in my case. The engine driver brought me the "Breslauer Zeitung" (Breslau Newspaper) which I could pass on to the prisoners who wielded influence in the camp. In contrast to me, my friend Kanatzky, to whom I was particularly attached following my father's return home, had an unenviable lot. Even in the camp itself he had no special privileges and was forced to work on the tip, in a group closely guarded by a craftsman called Kuptschik. Kanatzky knew from me the route by which my father had returned home and begged me to make contact with the medical orderly so that he too could be put on the sick list. Naturally I would have preferred to get myself onto the list and finally return home.

However, my friend thought it might be unwise to repeat the arrangements by which my father had returned to our home. He also thought that in comparison to him I was not doing too badly, so I could afford to delay my return, and I had to agree with him.

Once again I made contact with the medical orderly and the Camp Elder and everything went smoothly. After a few weeks my friend was allowed, as a sick person, to go home. I accompanied him to the barbed wire fence. We had a final embrace and wished for a speedy reunion. But that is not how things worked out. He joined the Jewish Ghetto Police and worked for the Judenrat. In the first few weeks he sent me some parcels, but then I did not hear anything further from him. With the benefit of hindsight, I now think I did him no favour by arranging for him to go home. Had he remained in the camp, he would have had a small chance to be among those who survived. As I later found out, he strove to conscientiously fulfil the instructions of the Jewish Ghetto Police and often had to inflict injustice on others. As part of the campaign to clear the country of Jews (Judenrein) he too was sent to Auschwitz where he was gassed with all the others.

The first Whitsun (Pentecost or Shavuot[10]) we spent behind barbed wire. We got up for work as usual. Our thoughts dwelt on our families. Although we knew that our relations at home were subject to persecution, they were at least allowed to stay together and could move freely within the area in which they were confined. Filled with

---

10. Shavuot, Jewish festival which falls seven weeks after Passover (hence Festival of Weeks) which celebrates the giving of the Torah.

nostalgia, we recalled how our families assembled on the Holy Days to honour the elders and learned. Our yearning for our parents was so strong that even during work all we talked about was our families at home and how we celebrated the festivals. We expressed our hope to spend Shavuot with our families again, but none of us could quite believe it. Rumours circulated that after the completion of the motorway we would be released. We could not substantiate these beautiful fantasies. We willingly succumbed to the hope that our forced labour was only a temporary measure of the national socialist regime. We did not feel guilty of anything and hence could not imagine why we should be held in a forced labour camp for any length of time.

I was not a member of the work gang that was guarded by a watchman and supervisor, so as truck greaser I had considerable freedom to move about. One could walk alongside the railway lines towards the tip and would be unguarded and left to my own devices. Each day I had to walk to the engine shed, which was located in the village called Kaltwasser, and collect lubricating oil. At the same time I ran errands for the supervisor and collected bits and pieces from the forge and engine shed. I often used a track across the fields where I frequently saw a girl sitting on a large stone eagerly reading a book. She had to guard the cows grazing in an adjacent field. She also noticed me and gave me a friendly glance but I did not dare to start a conversation because we were forbidden under threat of heavy punishment, to speak to civilians. However, one day she jumped up and with a stick in her hand she stood in my way and began speaking to me. I remained still, looked first to the right, then to the left, but there was no one in sight. With some embarrassment I stood uncertainly in front of her. As I looked up I recognised blue eyes and a pretty cheerful face smiling at me. Then she asked, "What kind of work do you do?" I replied, "I work on the motorway." She pointed to our place of work, "Only Jews work there." "I am also a Jew," I answered, and pointed to the oil and soot-stained yellow star on my chest. "But you don't look like a Jew" she said. "The people that work over there are probably criminals, they are never unguarded." Briefly I explained to her that these people were all Jews and not criminals, we had been seized from our homes at night and brought here for forced labour. Her smile evaporated and she looked downcast as she walked towards the field to herd the cows together. The following day I waited impatiently to collect the oil in the hope of seeing the girl again. I was not sure whether she would show me her smiling countenance once more or if she would treat me with contempt because I was a Jew. But she waved to me from afar and with a gesture invited me to approach her. I made sure I was not being observed and then walked into the field. She handed me a parcel of sliced bread and told me to enjoy it. From the beginning, she did not think of me as a motorway worker. She was not a herdsmen, it was just her compulsory military service. Finally she consoled me that time would pass quickly and we would definitely be allowed to return home to our families. I was deeply moved by her modest gift, friendly face, kind eyes and the consolation she tendered. I thanked her and set off on my way in a daydream. This meeting gave me renewed strength. So my life was not yet completely lost. Perhaps I would succeed and reach the Jewish autonomous region[11] that the Germans apparently intended to establish. Even before I reached the camp I had heard of this plan that all Jews should be taken from the ghetto into a reservation in the region of Lublin and, under Jewish control, set up labour battalions. I could only hope that all my experiences in the labour camp would not be for nothing, but would help my family and me if this plan would come to fruition. It did not even enter our minds that

---

11. "Der Endlosung" (literally, The Final Solution), G. Reitlinger, published by Colloquium Print, page 77, "The decree of 26 October 1939 ordered that all male Jews had to serve two years public service. Later, the qualifying age for this duty was extended to 16 – 60 years of age, and the Judenrat was responsible for allocation of the contingents. In this way, almost 500,000 Jews were obligated to do hard labour." The Jews in these work camps were hired out by the security police, the civil authorities or the town council to private businesses. Embezzlement was widespread. In the beginning, the senior ss and police leaders were not part of the ss administration. Odilo Globocnik, later leader of the extermination programme, founded cooperative workshops in the province of Lublin, and transformed them into labour camps for his own profit. In July 1941, Himmler visited Globocnik, and his friend's profits worried him so much that he established his first plan for a centrally managed concentration camp in Lublin that would take over all these workshops.

our total extermination was being planned. Was it not enough that we had been robbed of our civil rights, used as slave labour without any medical care in unhygienic conditions?

22 June 1941 marked not only the day on which the Germans marched eastward and invaded Russia, but also heralded the introduction of new and even more stringent measures. The guards were reinforced. The watchmen in the Appellplatz loudly cocked their guns in our faces to intimidate and terrify us. This was accompanied by an order to sew a yellow star on our shoulder and trousers, which until this time we had worn only on our chest, to make it more difficult for us to escape. One summer's day, when we returned from work, we were assembled for counting as usual on the Appellplatz. We noticed the concern and anxiety on the faces of the camp personnel and the Judenältester. During the count we noticed that the sick were not present and were not included in the count. The medical orderly who normally loudly announced how many were bedridden and how many were unable to work was silent. We did not know what these strange changes and the unprecedented tension signified. Only when we left the Appellplatz to line up for our soup did we hear quiet murmurings that there had been an "important visit" to the camp that day by Major Lindner, Chief of ss and Police of Upper Silesia. He had inspected the barracks and counted the sick. They were ordered to step into a waiting vehicle and were taken away. This caused tremendous speculation, where had the sick been taken? One of the camp personnel let it be known that Lindner did not want useless mouths in the camp, and they had probably been sent to Auschwitz to be exterminated.

Until this time the name Auschwitz was unknown to us and we heard it for the first time. The term "extermination" was unthinkable because until now the sick had been sent to the transit camp in Sosnowitz. The official explanation of the Judenältester was that the sick had been sent to a camp to recuperate. He probably was acting on instructions from a higher authority. We were inclined to believe him. Others knew better. According to them, the reports of extermination camps were deliberately circulated to increase the inmates' will to work, and to prevent unnecessary use of the sick barracks.

After the visit of Obersturmbannführer Lindner, the sick were no longer transported home. The fantasy to leave the camp because one was sick was now a thing of the past. I had no time to mourn this loss because new restrictions made daily life increasingly difficult.

Until now, things seemed to be predictable. Everyone had their fixed task in a working group. This routine was interrupted by a tragic accident. A few of the strongest and most capable young men were working in a pit clearing muck and dirt with an excavator. However, one day there was a collapse and a bloody body emerged from the pit. Anxiously they searched for the medical orderly to care for the injured man but there was only one medical orderly available for all the working groups. When the guards discovered that a man had been injured, they ordered two young men to carry the injured man to the cement hut. I as the wagon-greaser also had access to this hut and recognised the injured man, Salomon Dunkelblum. He was a tall, slim, strong man with a ready smile for his friends and very well-liked by all of us. Since he was a capable worker he enjoyed a certain respect from the pit boss. Now he presented as a pitiful sight. He lay there covered in blood and quietly groaning. Blood flowed from a large wound at the back of his head, staining his work clothes and a collar of blood accumulated around his neck. The medical orderly tried to stem the bleeding and bind his wound, but the blood soaked through the bandages. The medical orderly realised his powerlessness and turned to the guard and begged to send the injured man to a doctor or a hospital, so that the dangerous bleeding could be stopped. The guard's response to this plea was to send everyone back to work and he ordered the medical orderly away. The groaning of our bleeding friend was like a knife in our hearts, and we were filled with bitterness and resentment. A little while later, I sought an opportunity to approach the cement hut. The groaning had ceased and everyone approaching the hut was driven away. Finally, it became clear to us what this signified. Instead of sending for help they had let our friend bleed to death.

When the working day came to an end, our group assembled for the march back to camp. A guard accompanied by two strong young men entered the barracks where Dunkelblum lay. His rigid corpse was shrouded in cement sacks and carried out on a long board. Dunkelblum showed no sign of life. With clenched fists we carried our first dead back to camp. We were greatly troubled by the death, what we felt was pity and sorrow. At the same time we felt oppressed by gloom as we bore our friend's corpse and any remaining hope to the grave. Until then, we had believed we were living in a labour camp with the expectation of being treated like ordinary workers. Dunkelblum's death demonstrated clearly to us that we were merely cheap labour without any claim for help and without rights.

In the evening during Appell, the guards announced, "So and so many Jews back from work, one dead because of a work-related accident. Dismiss. March. March!"

We experienced summer as prisoners behind barbed wire. At the same time as our being completely at the mercy of our tormentors, trees and bushes came into bloom. We felt the warm rays of the sun and hungrily inhaled the fragrance of summer. All around us cornfields billowed and the blue and cloudless sky spanned the warm summer earth. Our circumstances had shockingly changed and we felt a similar transformation of our inner lives. However, nature remained unchanged and reminded us of home. This image faded with each passing day, so that only sometimes we could see it in our dreams. The fragrant earth and growing com evoked memories of home.

Just as before, the sun shone down on us as if there was nothing to separate us from those free, happy people of years gone by; as if our present could not be separated from our past. Even now, its warmth sparked our hope in life and freedom. Soon we began to harvest the cornfields. The stubble-covered fields reminded us of the shaven heads of the inmates and once again we were grieving and melancholy in our hearts. Whenever we marched past a field of stubble it was as if a vast crowd of shaven heads passed us by, as if nature was reflecting the ridiculous image of our humiliation. The coming of autumn coincided with the major Jewish festivals. On the morning of the New Year Festival[12] we marched as usual to the motorway.

12. Rosh Hashanah, literally "the head of the year", the Jewish New Year. According to tradition the world was created on Rosh Hashanah. Each year, every one seeks

Some moved their lips in silent prayer as we marched; others wanted to try to secretly recite the traditional prayers during a break from work. I, myself, marched in silent protest against the doctrine that we should quietly accept our fate. Again and again I asked myself the question, "Are we really a chosen people, and if chosen, for what, chosen only for suffering?" I reflected on fragments of Jewish history: reports of the Spanish Inquisition and pogroms perpetrated by God fearing Christians streaming from church after Holy Mass. "And now" I thought "that those of us who were marching were also writing another chapter in the history of this chosen people, another chapter of suffering, humiliation and extermination." All my thoughts and feelings rebelled against the notion that our people were destined to suffer in order to fulfil a certain mission, a mission that I could not understand. I refused to accept that my faith obliged me to endure suffering, conspiracies and torments as a gift from God. I could not and did not pray. The days after New Year were filled with work and the daily monotony of camp life.

The Day of Atonement[13] fell eight days after the New Year. When we returned from work that evening, many men secreted themselves in corners and between bunks and prayed. A few of us sat on our beds and stared blankly into the night. The future loomed before us like a dark abyss that threatened to consume us. Slowly my heart turned to stone. I was seized with a single thought: "How can one still pray in such a situation? To whom could one pray, for what could one give thanks?" This moment was suddenly broken by three

---

to renew their soul by repentance, in the hope of a merciful judgement. It is also sanctified as a day of remembrance, "Yom Hazikaron". Its primary significance is for one to reflect upon oneself and upon God.

13. Yom Kippur, the Day of Atonement, is a fast day that begins in the early evening and lasts about 25 hours, and during which religious Jews completely abstain from both eating and drinking. On this day one tries to come clean with oneself and the world. We must reconcile ourselves with our fellowman before we can seek God's forgiveness. On this day all work and earthly matters are set aside. The house of prayer glows with (candle) light. Religious Jews assemble in the synagogue, dressed in white shroud-like garments, and are uplifted by holy thoughts and prayers. It is a day of repentance, reflection and self-examination before God.

sharp blasts of a whistle. This was our cue to assemble instantly for
Appell. Immediately after, we heard the screams of the Blockältester
who called us to attention. We assembled quickly in the darkness.
Then we were counted by the guards and the Judenältester announced
to the guard in charge, "Everyone is present and ready for Appell".
One of the guards called Anton, who was from Kattowitz in Upper
Silesia, stood in front of us legs apart and striking a Hitler-like pose
to give a speech. In appearance and speech he tried to model himself on Hitler. "Listen, you damn Jews," he said, "It is not only your
businesses and way of life that have been terminated, it is also your
customs and service to God. If I catch one of you who has not eaten
his bread he will get fifty strokes on his naked arse. I couldn't give
two hoots about your God."

We stood there petrified. The darkness and silence that enveloped the camp seemed to transform Anton into a demon spouting
mean and devilish words. We had to hear his blasphemy in silence.
Why did this blasphemy go unchallenged, why did the heavens not
open and give a visible sign of help? But no man and no God stood
by us. We felt we were enveloped in a hostile silence.

Soon we discovered the reason for this night time Appell. The
camp command had heard that many of us had not eaten in order to
fulfil the ritual of the Day of Atonement. The demeanour of those
friends who fasted was so much more remarkable because despite their
poor general condition, they resolved to hunger. The Nazis wanted to
rob those who remained true to their faith of their inner strength.

Anton was a casual labourer from Kattowitz. His parents were
caretakers in a Jewish house. So as a child he already had the opportunity of contact with Jewish people and grew up in close proximity
to them. Inevitably, he also learned their customs and traditions. He
knew the Jewish festivals very well and knew that the Day of Atonement was the holiest day for Jews. This holy day was even observed
by Jewish free-thinkers and assimilated Jews, just as in Christian surroundings, atheists celebrated Christmas. Anton, who was a primitive
anti-Semite, was intent on violating our Jewish beliefs and for that
he had chosen our holiest night. "Lights out! Silence in camp!" came
the command of the Blockältester. Tears streamed down our faces

in the silence of the night as we swore to ourselves to take revenge for this blasphemy.

Until then we had received parcels and packages from home, but this suddenly stopped by order of the police leadership of Upper Silesia under whose jurisdiction we fell. Then we discovered from friends who occasionally received illegal post from home that the situation of our relatives had worsened considerably. The persecution became more oppressive, the borders of the ghetto were ever more restricted, and the hunger in the ghetto became unbearable because with the closing of the ghetto it became more and more difficult to obtain grocery. The ration of grocery available for distribution by the Judenrat was wholly insufficient. As long as the ghetto was not closely guarded, the inmates found ways and means to barter with Christians for food: but the closure of the ghetto made such transactions almost impossible. Hunger and disease spread through overcrowded flats in which not only the local Jewish population was herded together, but also other Jews resettled from elsewhere. There was a growing number of victims of neglect. They could not bathe themselves nor could they launder their clothes, and many of the weakened ones finally succumbed to infectious diseases.

At the onset of winter, the construction firms building the motorway stopped work. Many of the strongest young men from a number of motorway construction projects were assembled and dispatched to an unknown destination. It was implied that they would be allocated to important war work and they would enjoy the same status as German workers. Many in our camp willingly volunteered to join this group. I held back and left the selection to fate. When we were scrutinised on the Appellplatz, I was considered unfit for this work as I was not strong enough, so I remained in the camp.

After a few weeks we learned that the young men on this transport were dressed in OT clothes and placed at the disposal of regular OT troops in order to build roads and railway lines behind the Eastern front. The harsh winter on the Russian front imposed many massive difficulties on the German reinforcements and our friends had to labour with all their strength to accomplish these difficult tasks. In spite of that they were not treated as free workers, as they had been originally promised. They were forced to live in the same freight wagons in which they had been transported. The most elementary hygienic requisites were completely absent. The resultant increasing dirt and neglect soon made its presence felt. After just a few weeks there was a severe outbreak of typhoid among the Jewish workers. A Jewish doctor called Dr. Leitner was responsible for the medical care of his fellow inmates. With the authority of the armed forces responsible for this transport, Dr. Leitner intervened after the outbreak of the epidemic. He suggested that all Jewish workers, including the sick, should be returned to the region from which they had come. The ss administration did not want to hear of this suggestion. Those afflicted with typhoid were to be isolated. The possibility of returning to the old camp remained open only to those who were fully fit. However, contrary to expectations, there were a few people among the OT troops and authorities who took up Leitner's suggestion and ordered the entire transport, including the sick, back to its mother camp. So at the end of winter, a group of young men returned from the East to Grünheide, and were immediately placed in isolation. We wanted to ensure that typhoid did not spread throughout the camp. However, because guarding and fencing around these isolation barracks was entirely our responsibility, with the permission of the Blockältester it was possible to smuggle oneself into barracks in order to look out for relatives and friends. I heard a few young men from our hometown were in the sick barracks. I did not want to be excluded from those who went to the barracks and I too managed to gain entry. A large majority of the inmates lay in fevered delirium babbling incomprehensibly. My school friend Lieber was delirious and unconscious. Some of the sick had survived the fever only to be afflicted with acute pangs of hunger, which usually follow typhoid. They wolfed down a large plate of soup as soon as it was placed in front of them. They also gobbled an enormous amount of potatoes that had been boiled in buckets. The atmosphere and mood in the sick barracks was rather jolly and optimistic, and not at all depressing. Paradoxically, the delirium of those who were seriously sick was accompanied by a euphoric mood. One example was a delirious man who smeared his jam ration on his chest before licking it off as he sang. Another sang prayers sitting on his bunk, and I could not distinguish whether he knew what he was singing or if it was a symptom of his fever.

However, not everyone could withstand the burning fever, and many perished before the typhoid epidemic eventually abated. Moreover, there was a complete lack of medical support. The camp medical orderly had no medical training, but he tried to help the sick with medication. The dead from the epidemic were buried in the forest behind our camp, where our first victim, the unforgettable Dunkelblum, was already buried. My friend Jakob Adlerflugel also died of typhoid. He was a man who was well respected and held in high esteem. My grandfather had business dealings with him and was extremely happy to welcome him to his home. He left behind a young wife and children. He was ordered into action in the East soon after his deportation to the concentration camp because he was so powerfully built. He was so weakened by this military service that he lacked the strength to resist the burning fever of typhoid.

In deadly silence we carried Adlerflugel into the forest. We wanted to extend to him all the formal respect and rites prescribed by the Jewish religion. However, there was no opportunity to wash the body of the deceased and wrap it in a linen shroud. So we buried our friend dressed in his work clothes and wrapped in his prayer shawl (tallit). As we covered him with earth, I quietly recited the memorial prayer for the dead, which is normally only ever recited by a close relative of the deceased.

When we returned to the camp, we left behind nothing more than a small freshly dug mound of earth – no fence, no sign, be it of wood or stone, marked the grave of our brothers. Only a small mound marked the place where a person, a father, rested in foreign soil. Later, no one would be able to determine who lay there.

Work on the motorway progressed more slowly. Instead we started building barracks at a feverish pace on a large site surrounded by a fence we had already erected. We could only speculate for whom these barracks were intended. Would others from the ghettos with whom we had originally been resettled be brought, or other foreign workers?

One day we went to the building site to find it was already guarded and crammed full with Russian prisoners of war. We were no longer permitted to enter the camp. Instead we worked in the barracks intended for the guards. Moreover, our own guard was reinforced and we were strictly forbidden from approaching the camp fence that separated us from the prisoners of war. The prisoners of war called to us and tried to make contact with us in every way imaginable. When no other guards were present, one of the guards with whom we got on well gave us permission to talk to the Russian prisoners and swap news.

On Whitsun 1942, the order was given to clear Grünheide camp. We had a day off work to prepare for the march. The following day after Appell we marched to the camp gate. It was a beautiful, warm spring day. We were ordered to keep pace with the guards who marched alongside us, and sing songs as we did so.

Singing marching songs, we made our way through Upper Silesian country lanes. The road was shaded by a green canopy formed by the tops of trees that had grown together. We were so intoxicated by the feeling of awakening Mother Nature that we marched not like prisoners but like high-spirited youths on a spring outing. It took several hours for us to complete the twenty kilometres to the Annaberg Camp.

This camp was organised on the same lines as Grünheide. It was a forced labour camp for the construction of the autobahn (motorway). In Annaberg, I met up with old acquaintances from my home town. Some of them had returned from the Eastern Front and had recovered with time from their torturous ordeal. But soon we realised that life had been easier in Grünheide. There we could still obtain our rations of bread and potatoes from outside, whereas in Annaberg it was not possible to get hold of extra groceries.

One day I met my acquaintance, Natek Schapiro, who was working as a medical orderly. He reunited me with other of my acquaintances from our home town, one of whom was called Feder and worked as a cook. He immediately provided me with extra food rations. Also Kuba Rosenzweig was there, who, as group elder, stormed through the streets with a rubber truncheon beating the "innocent" and the "guilty" without distinction. He ranted again and again his old saying, "God curse me again." Kuba no longer made a normal impression. Probably the after-effects of a stint with the army in the east where he had contracted typhoid had transformed him psychologically into an uninhibited camp-beater. (He hanged himself after the end of the war.)

On arrival in Annaberg Camp that first night, all those in our transport from Grünheide were housed together in empty barracks, not in separate rooms. The following morning we were given one day's ration of food and with the majority of the inmates of Annaberg we continued our march further. Our feet still ached from the previous day so we did not find it so easy, but we withstood the stress and were still reasonably fit when we reached Sakrau labour camp. Sakrau was part of the network of labour camps committed to motorway building.

As brief as our stay in Sakrau was, it was still very oppressive. Where in previous camps we were numbered in the hundreds, here we were numbered in the thousands. Where previously we had sufficient potatoes, here we suffered with increasing hunger. When after two days stay the order was given to continue the march, we were somewhat relieved. Our transport grew even larger with the addition of some former inmates of Sakrau camp. We marched a short way to the next train station where passenger wagons were waiting for us. We were crammed into the compartments and locked in from the outside. Beyond the train window, life and trains continued as usual as if there was deepest peace and perfect harmony between mankind.

Chapter Three

Markstadt

We still found life interesting, and here we saw a world that was completely different from the one in which we were forced to live. Quickly other landscapes, other villages, other houses passed by. We passed non-stop through new stations, saw people walking up and down and waiting, saw families with their children getting on and off trains. After several hours we stopped at a quiet peaceful village served by a small station. The notice board announced the name of Markstadt, a place that until then meant nothing to us. Reluctantly, we stepped off the train. Although the railcars were locked and armed ss guards stood on the steps outside, after one year's imprisonment this journey was for us an event. Until now we had been surrounded by sand from Grünheide autobahn, the monotonous fields around our barracks, by civil workers, fellow-inmates and the personnel who guarded us. This train journey made a welcome break from the tedious everyday routine.

At the station we were put into rows of five, we were counted and checked and finally we were signalled to march into the new camp. First we passed through the peaceful village, but then before our eyes another picture emerged. Before us lay a town of barracks that was partly surrounded by barbed wire. With astonishment in their eyes, people stared at us and called to us in foreign languages: Czech, Polish, French and Russian sounds assaulted our ears. Thousands of foreign workers lived in this camp, those who were there of their own free will lived in the "free" barracks, in marked contrast to the forced labourers, such as the Poles who had a little "P" sewn on their chests, and the Ukrainians whose clothes were inscribed "Ost". Some Poles and Ukrainians greeted us with shouts of abuse so our shared slavery had not healed these people of their anti-Semitism. That was a bitter realisation.

Kapos and a group of supervisors ordered us to march in step because the head of our column had already turned into the camp. The camp leadership, supervisors and Jewish Elders met us at the gates of the camp. We were seized with anxiety, impatience and curiosity as we contemplated life in this new camp. What would our new workplace be like, what should we expect from the hierarchy of this new camp? Instinctively, we sped up the tempo of our march and made a conscious effort to assume a military gait. Finally we stopped in the Appellplatz, the huge camp square. At the front of the square there was a growing crowd of Kapos and Jewish Elders all screaming. The Kapos, who were officially known as "Group Leaders", wore plain military boots and white armbands and swung rubber and wire truncheons in their hands. The Jewish Elder was clad in a leather coat, leather trousers and highly polished leather boots; he wildly screamed a staccato torrent of orders at us; but at first we were unaccustomed to such treatment and simply could not understand him. With truncheons and sticks our supervisors abruptly taught us how to stand upright and erect and in ranks and files.

The Jewish Elder, who we knew came from a refined Jewish family from a small town in Upper Silesia, gave a short speech which he concluded with an inelegant warning, "You sons of bitches! Whoever deviates from camp discipline will get fifty on their naked arse!" To amplify his meaning he gestured towards two well-built, sturdy men, Herschel Moch and Bossack, who stood slightly apart, idly toying with their truncheons.

The Jewish Elder, Baruch Meister, issued his orders in a military manner to the Block Elder, and as we waited with our hearts in our mouths, we were led away in groups of three hundred men to our various blocks. Quickly we plunged into the barracks; everybody wanted to be the first to get the "best bed", that meant a bed that stood in a corner and ideally, close to the wall, so that it was at least partly concealed from the supervisor. From experience we knew that those unfortunate enough to occupy beds close to the door were in full view of the supervisor, and after a day's work they were often taken to do extra labour, such as off-loading of cars, etc. Also, the occupants of beds at the front were more frequently inspected. It was much more obvious when their beds were not properly made or a single strand of straw lay underneath. Each of these petty offences would be rewarded with a beating.

The weaker ones fought for a lower bed, so they were spared the painstaking effort of climbing to the higher level. Soon after, the Block Elder came, accompanied by a thug, and cautioned us concerning the absolute requirement for perfect neatness; then he selected the strongest of us as Barrack Elder (Stubenältester). From that moment the Barrack Elder was responsible for neatness of the entire hut. If any mess was found, whoever was responsible would receive a severe beating. "Straw on the floor is totally prohibited! Not a single speck of dust must be found anywhere!" Then the Block Elder wiped the window sill with his finger and ostentatiously shoved it under the Barrack Elder's nose; of course it was dusty. "In future it is prohibited to find any dust here", he said in a menacing tone.

Then the eating cards were given out; but we still had to wait a long time for our lunch. Only after we had queued for hours did we receive our warm soup. The kitchen personnel and equipment were wholly inadequate to meet the needs of the four thousand prisoners who descended upon them.

Here we discovered for the first time the difference between thin and thick soup. With sore, burning feet we often had to queue for an hour or more because the soup kettle was frequently emptied before we all received our portion; we had no choice but to wait until another cauldron of soup was ready. Often the kitchen personnel just poured water into the soup to make it go further, so it would suffice for all those still waiting in the long queue. As soon as we received our soup, we were urged to finish our ration quickly and return our bowl. Of course we would have preferred to slowly savour our soup together with any bread or potatoes boiled in their jackets which we were occasionally able to obtain with an exchange or swap. However, we were pressed from all sides to gobble our food as quickly as possible. "Empty plates, plates to the kitchen!" echoed endlessly.

We were continuously harried as we hastened to complete our roster of routine daily duties. We received the order, "Lights out!" at ten o'clock each night with a great sigh of relief. We were woken at four o'clock each morning. Exhausted, we emerged from our straw sacks and set about making our beds in the shape of matchboxes that were perfectly smooth. The Barrack Elder bellowed at everyone to sweep the floor and not to leave even a speck of dust. Hurriedly we swallowed our crust of black bread and our sludge-like coffee, then we were shoved out of the barracks so that every speck of dust could be removed.

After a few days we heard loud screams from next door where the Barrack Elder was beaten because his charges were late. We also heard a scream – Achtung! Although we were as if paralysed from lack of sleep, we immediately stood to attention as the Jewish Elder, the Block Elder and the thug appeared; they commenced a detailed inspection of our beds and the room, checking that everything was as it should be. One of them wiped his finger on the frame of a bed and when he found a trace of dust the Jewish Elder immediately ordered that the Barrack Elder should receive at least twenty five lashes. Without delay a stool was brought and the Barrack Elder was held down by the Block Elder and the Camp Dentist (actually only an ex-dental technician) who was responsible for "camp hygiene". The thug Bossack, who had a pockmarked face and was a repugnant tyrant from Sosnowitz, then administered twenty-five lashes on the Barrack Elder's naked bottom. Then many of the beds and the straw on them were deliberately messed up. "I will return in fifteen minutes", said the Block Elder, "and the barracks better be spick and span!" The beating only made the Barrack Elder even more ruthless and truculent. No one could understand exactly what he wanted them to do, so chaos ensued. Without thinking, he kept ordering his comrades about from one corner to the other, but everyone was completely bewildered by the screaming and raging confusion. It seemed as if everyone had lost their mind and was working to a plan that made no sense; the inevitable result was total chaos. To understand our situation you have to appreciate that while this treatment was "the normal daily life", we were not yet accustomed to it. Although we were prisoners, we were usually halfway reasonably treated as long as nothing untoward happened. So we were relieved when at six o'clock in the evening we heard the whistle that commanded us to go to roll call. The count of the prisoners and the parade of the workers' colony followed with rigourous strictness and the Block and Group Elders used their batons and whips liberally to impose strict discipline. We had experienced less harsh treatment at the camp in Grünheide; there it was only prisoners who had committed serious offences such as theft who were subjected to severe corporal punishment. In Markstadt, however, severe corporal punishment was such a daily routine occurrence it did not even merit comment. The dentist Jakubowitz, whose job it was to remove inmates' teeth without anaesthetic, was prominent among the rows of guards who applied themselves energetically to the task of beating prisoners.

In our minds Grünheide now seemed like a peaceful village. There, they did not count out the potatoes in a pedantic fashion! They just heaped them on to our plates. The bread was tastier and at lunchtime we were allowed into the dining room where we sat at large wooden tables and ate in peace. In Grünheide we resented the fact that on Sunday mornings we had to polish the tables and benches with sandpaper until they gleamed. In retrospect, how small these problems seemed compared with the oppressed, hounded life we were now leading. Here, we were no longer among just a few hundred inmates who one felt one knew and among whom one felt like a human being.

In Markstadt, I felt completely lost among the anonymous masses. More than five thousand forced labourers were assembled in the one place; people from different countries, different professions and ages.

The new arrivals were allocated to various working commandos. They immediately sought out and urgently enquired of the old camp inmates about their chances and prospects in their respective working groups. In some working groups we had sufficient freedom of movement to "organise" something for ourselves. Unfortunately I was not able to speak to any of the experienced prisoners because they were all instantly surrounded by seven or eight new arrivals gathered around them. So I stood, lost among the crowds of inmates. One question dominated my mind, "What was going to happen to me? What was my destiny to be, a good or evil fate?"

A large commission composed of civilians, high-ranking uniformed ss officers and other ranks approached the Appellplatz, abruptly interrupting my thoughts. The Jewish Elder, Baruch Meister, assumed a military pose and bellowed out his orders: "Achtung! Hats Off! Eyes Right!" He specifically repeated the command "Hats Off!" several times, until everyone simultaneously removed their hat and slapped it against the seam of their trousers; there were so many assembled in this vast square it produced a dull drumming sound.

Then, on instructions from one of the ss commanders, the Jewish Elder called out, "Workers with professional skills should step forward. Only highly skilled, experienced workers who really know their trade are required. Workers with insufficient experience who think they can secure easier work by pretending they are skilled will be put into a punishment commando." He called for locksmiths, joiners, plumbers and electricians to step forward in turn. Before I was taken away to the camps I went on a training course organised by the Judenrat. During the few weeks of the course I received basic training as an electrician. I could only carry out electrical installations in flats. My knowledge and experience as an electrician was quite modest. When skilled electricians were called for, at first I wavered, wondering if I should step forward as a skilled worker. Finally, I took the plunge and joined the skilled group. Locksmiths stood facing us.

It then became apparent that more skilled workers had volunteered than were required. Each group was then carefully scrutinised. The Commission began examining the locksmiths facing us. They required detailed information about the practical skills of individuals and posed devious questions about how these had been acquired. Apparently, the Commission picked out a few amateur locksmiths who had no work experience or knowledge. They had to leave their groups and were encouraged by blows from batons to rejoin huge crowd of other inmates.

To his disgrace, Baruch Meister started a brutal practice of beating inmates on their heads with a rubber truncheon or club; his example was energetically taken up not only by group and column leaders, but also by professional beaters such as Moch, Bossack and Machtinger.

These beatings were not initiated because of any order from the camp leadership or because of any instructions from the guards. The guards in Markstadt were made up of the Green Police, the leaders of the police and ss and ss-Obergruppenführer Lindner from Upper Silesia, all of whom were specially trained to guard and manage forced labour camps throughout Silesia. These police were very humane when compared to the sa in Grünheide, and later on, the ss guards in Fünfteichen; this was due in no small part to the fact that these people had received proper military training and did not feel the need to resort to force.

When I saw how the unskilled workers were beaten back into the masses I was panic-stricken. With hardly a moment's thought I slipped back and rejoined the masses that had remained standing in five rows. I was overwhelmed by an uncertain instinct that I had escaped danger. I always tried my best to avoid attracting any attention to myself. Later, it emerged that it was more important to avoid beatings than to find ways and means of escaping or organising extra rations. In order to survive in this inferno I had to be totally inconspicuous, to extinguish my identity and lose myself amongst the protection of the faceless masses.

When the various skilled groups were finalised the remaining thousands of inmates were allocated to different companies. The group in which I stood was allocated to a company called Schallhorn. The group was mainly composed of prisoners who had come here from the concentration camp of Grünheide. While the work groups were assembled it began to rain and soon our clothes stuck to our bodies. Despite that, we were detained for hours on the Appellplatz. Originally the site had been a large grass meadow, so it lacked tarmac and gravel; and the rainwater accumulated in large puddles that took days to disperse. We were drenched with water from above and our shoes became sodden, so for the remainder of the day our feet were damp and cold.

Finally the work commando was assembled. We received a resounding command, "Schallhorn, line up", and had to promptly assemble at the Appellplatz. Whoever imagined that they need not be punctual was beaten.

Among the group leaders who supervised the Schallhorn[1] Group were some who had served as group leaders in Grünheide, including Bromberger from Hamburg and Sorski from Katowice. I had the misfortune to be included in Bromberger's group. It consisted of about forty men working under the direction of Meister Berger, a pure bred German, to construct railway tracks. Our task was to construct narrow tracks to connect different parts of the construction site. Whilst one group was preparing the groundwork for the track the other group in which I worked had to unload and connect the rails. Since I did not have any gloves, I was compelled to carry the steel rails in my bare hands. Bromberger resented me because without his protection in Grünheide I had nevertheless secured "light" work as a wagon greaser, so he did everything he could to embitter my life. Bromberger made me take up a position where I had to bear the main weight of the rail. Like everywhere, there were some inmates among us who only pretended to take up their share of the load. Although they gripped the pieces of iron they bore little or none of the weight.

It was not very long before I injured my hands on the sharps edges of the rails, so that each time I gripped the rail it really hurt. With it came the hunger. In Grünheide we were able to cook potatoes that we had been able to "organise". There was sufficient for everyone. However, here in Markstadt this was not at all possible because we were cut off from the outside world. Occasionally in Grünheide we

---

1. Schallhorn was the name of the group, it may also have been the name of a contractor.

had received small packages, parcels and letters, here we waited in vain. Parcels and packages were collected in the store where the camp commanders and the Jewish Elders were free to choose whatever took their fancy. The remainder ended up in the soup kettle. What happened to the letters, nobody knew. In any case, we did not receive any post, nor did we have the chance to write ourselves. Gradually, we lost our last hope. None of us seriously believed we would be able to return to our family.

A difficult time began. Each one of us groaned under the increasing physical and psychological burden. The physical burdens were beyond my power and slowly my mental strength was also eroded. However, the Group Elder took no notice of my condition; he chose not to notice my sore and badly swollen hands. Whenever I did not move quickly enough he would prod me and shout, "You rested enough in Grünheide. Here you are in Markstadt. Get on with it, wagon greaser!" I stumbled from side to side from sheer exhaustion. I expended my final reserves of energy lifting and carrying the tracks. In the evenings, after I had eaten my soup and bread ration I sank like a lead weight onto my bed, but despite overwhelming tiredness, I could not sleep.

Gradually I became afraid. I saw clearly that the work was more than beyond my strength. I knew I could not cope with the strain for very much longer. I felt completely alone and abandoned because it was so long since I had received news from my parents and siblings, who at this time were still all at home as a family unit, working in the ghetto. My loneliness and helplessness weighed heavily on my mind. I feared that I could not bear the physical and mental pressure for much longer, but my will to live was greater than my weakness.

My Uncle Leon, my mother's brother, came to me from Camp Otmund. He was taken away in June 1942 in the first big raid. This raid had been the first action in which not only men, but also women and children had been transported as "emigrants" to Auschwitz and hounded into the gas chambers. Uncle Leon's wife and child had been taken in this transport. He had been separated from his family and came to Markstadt where he was allocated to the firm "Grün und Bilfinger" which was contracted by Krupp to build huge factory sheds. Uncle's Leon's situation was doubly difficult. He was not accustomed to regular hard physical labour; he had to work mixing cement. As a newcomer to the camp, he was confronted with a situation with which he was completely unfamiliar. The severe camp regime in Markstadt depressed him. When we were thrown together by chance we looked into each others' eyes and exchanged helpless glances. We all knew our situation was hopeless, we knew we could do nothing to help one another.

When the rations became even more meagre some of the inmates began stealing whatever they could lay their hands on. The mammoth building site provided ample opportunities. In addition to five thousand Jews there were thirty thousand foreign workers and a few thousand Reichsdeutsche (Germans). They all worked in a Krupp munitions factory where anti-tank cannons were manufactured.

Many firms were engaged in this construction; the Jewish workers were allocated to the following firms: Grün & Bilfinger, Beton & Monier-Bau, Wayss & Frietag, Lenz & Co. and, among others, Schallhorn. Each of these firms provided a canteen for the workers they employed. They were all provided with a hot lunch, with the sole exception of us Jews. Often the smell of cooking wafted towards us so that we salivated and our empty stomachs went into painful cramps. Although we did the same work as others we were excluded. Some German and foreign workers occasionally gave us their plate of food when they had no appetite.

Often those who were starving cast caution to the winds and stole potatoes, carrots, in short, anything they could get their hands on, from the canteen storerooms. Of course sometimes they were caught; if they were in luck they were reported and released, if a report was submitted the thieves were held back on the Appellplatz and received twenty five or fifty lashes on their bare bottom, according to the scale of the theft. Often the whole group would receive collective punishment. When the Appell was dismissed we had to remain standing for hours and submit to a humiliating search of our bodies. Often we were stripped naked because some would attach potatoes to their bodies under their clothes. These body searches lasted for hours and when they concluded we swayed and tottered exhausted into our barracks.

I lay in Block Three. My room was next to the Jewish Elder. He did the office work. Every evening after work the "sinners" who had been caught "organising" food were paraded in front of him. Others due to be punished were also sent to his room had to submit to his judgement. Usually the verdict was either twenty five or fifty lashes. The two beaters, Bossack and Moch, were joined by a third one, Moischel Machtinger, who supervised the cobblers who made boots for the camp VIPs. He was without doubt the cruellest of the three beaters and had a particularly sadistic way of toying with his victims. He pulled his victim towards him by the neck, then smashed him in the face with his elbow. The victim went black before our eyes. Then he asked in an ironic tone, "How old are you?" If the beaten one answered truthfully, "Twenty-five years", he replied, "You have lived long enough". This typical reply rapidly circulated around the camp and inspired fear and terror in us all. (Machtinger was later arrested in Poland and imprisoned for twenty-five years for torturing his comrades.)

I was very unhappy to be in the room next to the Jewish Elder because every evening I could not avoid hearing the screams of those who were being beaten. I witnessed at close quarters the impact of these punishments upon the victims who were broken both physically and mentally. These daily sentences frightened me so much that I took particular care not to "organise" or steal anything. The other inmates appeared to show little pity and gave no support to the victims. As a result of the injuries inflicted, some had to attend the sick bay from which they often did not return. In the best cases, the damage was confined to a period during which their physical movement was restricted, and this impaired their work.

During this period of time an incident took place which affected an inmate from my home town. This young man was called Lubling. He could no longer bear the arduous work and the appalling psychological pressure. He was incensed by these creatures, the camp functionaries, who were once fellow-prisoners. His will to live was probably suffocated by his psychological desperation, because one day he committed suicide.

Suicide was an infrequent occurrence. It was peculiar. As our lives became more difficult and helpless, so our hopes for freedom were diminished, and yet our determination to cling to life was strengthened. Even the doomed, the so-called "Muselmänner[2]" clung desperately to life. There were only a few odd inmates who voluntarily chose death from amongst the thousands of sick, weak and desperate ones.

Again and again my instinct for survival asserted itself. I observed that some prisoners often managed to avoid heavy work. Not everyone appeared to be starving. There were still hundreds of inmates who could last because their work was lighter. They had opportunities to contact foreign workers, and so were able to find ways and means of making semi-legal arrangements to "organise". I was constantly preoccupied with one question. How could I change my situation? I did not want to remain at the rail track under the supervision of Berger and Bromberger. I did not want to be killed by hunger and weakness. I lay sleepless for many hours on my bunk and longed for a way out.

Then a coincidence helped me. As usual, I carried my rails and did not attempt to avoid heavy labour, although each morning I was already worn down and exhausted. My endurance won me recognition by Meister Berger. When two inmates stumbled, their slipping rail crushed my foot, and it was Berger who bothered to send me to the barracks. The medical orderly applied a makeshift bandage and

---

2. In a report by an expert witness in the trial of the camp leadership at Auschwitz, Professor J Olbricht gave the following description of a *Muselmann*: atrophy of the fat tissue and muscles, the face took on a mask-like expression, the eyes were wide open and the pupils unnaturally enlarged, apathy, indifference, somnolence, weakness of all living processes, especially the psychological, his hearing and vision was poor, various reactions and associations and response to pain were all impaired. The ss and camp officials often wrongly interpreted all the forgoing as passive resistance and subjected them to repeated torture and beatings. Their interest in their surroundings and their ability to take care of themselves gradually disappeared until, without being aware of it, they were inevitably overtaken by death.

notified the Group Elder Bromberger that I must take care of my injured foot, and that I should remain on my bunk until the march back from work that day. Two fellow-inmates supported me as I limped back to the camp. That evening the camp doctor bandaged me and the following day I had to return to work. Meister Berger removed me from the group and appointed me as track leader. I was equipped with a tool bag and given the task of controlling the tracks.

I had escaped from Bromberger's clutches and new possibilities opened up before me; above all I could get hold of additional food. As well as that, I could move freely, without guard, without Meister, without Kapo. Slowly my hands healed and my tortured back straightened. Now I thought more often of my family in the ghetto, because horrible rumours circulated about the fate of those who were left behind. We heard reports that Jews were ejected from towns in the occupied territories, forced to dig large pits and then pushed to the bottom where they were shot. As my circumstances improved, so anxieties about my family doubled. The Polish, Czech, Ukrainian and French foreign workers brought sad news about the emigration of Jews from the ghettos, and the mass shootings. For a while we did not know if we should give this credence because all these gruesome stories sounded like a fantasy; we could not imagine that women and children, old and young, were all murdered only because they belonged to a certain people. It appeared to us that it was still possible that they were taken away for forced labour. Some of the foreign workers were hostile towards us and so we thought they wanted to frighten us with rumours, and to take away and destroy our last hope, our families. Unfortunately, it later became clear that all their reports were based on truth.

Since I had freedom to move about as track leader, I met free workers and also Germans with whom I came into conversation in different ways, and sometimes I was able to barter with them. Once, a farmer drove by. When he saw my track key lying there, he suggested to me that I swap it for a small parcel of tobacco. I did not think for long. I just looked around in all directions and when I saw I was unobserved I exchanged my track key for his tobacco. I was lucky because the keys in the workshop were never counted, so I was able to slip another into my pocket. I did not smoke the tobacco myself but instead, I divided it into small portions which I was able to swap for bread and soap. Due to this, I was able to stem my hunger and my interest in the world around me returned. I observed how the track supervisors of Beton und Monier-Bau harassed my comrades as they worked. They carried heavy sacks of cement to the mixers. Their faces were so caked with cement dust that only the slits of their eyes and the opening of their mouths could be recognised. Emaciated figures shrouded in the grey dust moved like ghosts.

I clearly remember one incident of prisoner abuse that outraged us all. Two young lads, both under the age of twenty, had been caught stealing from the food stores for which the Jewish Elder was responsible. They were both publicly beaten on the Appellplatz until they collapsed unconscious. The buckets of cold water were thrown over the motionless figures and they were unceremoniously rolled to one side. To add insult to injury, as one of the boys recovered Moischel Machtinger stepped up and urinated into his mouth. These horrific incidents inflamed our hatred of the Jewish Elder, Baruch Meister, and although later on he revealed a helpful side to his nature, he could never atone for all the evil for which he was responsible. (After the war, Meister roamed the world under a pseudonym until he apparently died in South America.)

My position as trackside courier gave me advantages. I was able to swap and "organise" things, and thus I joined the ranks of the well-fed of the camps. As I could often obtain tobacco and had bread and soap, I could again recruit friends among those in charge. I had to consolidate my situation. I collected tobacco and soap and swapped them for a watch. It was my intention to bribe Meister Berger with the watch, no easy task, because he had a reputation for being both strict and incorruptible. After much hesitation I took this crucial step.

I used a work break when Meister Berger was sat quietly in his hut after a meal. I entered the hut and put the watch in front of him. I said that I did not know what to do with it. He took it and examined it from all sides. Then he asked me if I had stolen it. "No", I reassured him, "the watch belongs to me." Then he pocketed it. I hoped and felt sure that Berger would let me stay in my present post.

Since I had a small and continuous supply of bread, I was never short of friends, mostly other inmates who also had light work. So I joined the circle of those who worked in the "forge" run by the firm Schallhorn. The "forge" was the collective name given to an enormous factory complex to which the camp was attached. This served the building sites. There were metal workers, plumbers, electricians, locomotive carriage and truck repair workshops, as well as surveyors, foremen, kitchen and other skilled workers. Many of these workers were ethnic Germans employed by Schallhorn. This worked in favour of the few foreign workers and Jews because the Group Elder Vogel, a simple but very good man, refused to oppress or beat those in his charge. He took care that the stipulated work was carried out and he protected the comrades from the supervisors when they were resting or cooking. There was a relaxed atmosphere at the "forge", not only amongst the forced labourers, but also among the ethnic Germans, craftsmen and foremen. The supervisor of the construction work was called Schallhorn. He always wore the Nazi party emblem. He did not treat the Jews like slaves, but instead just like all the other workers, that meant fairly and decently. Machine Foreman Kuka won our affection and respect because he showed such an understanding of our needs and was very sympathetic towards us. The attitude of the senior management towards the craftsmen had a favourable effect. Nearly all of them treated us as a working population rather than inferior slaves. Nearly all of them gave away bread and part of their daily lunch, which was cooked only for the non-Jewish crew. This benefitted the Jewish workers.

One day, my friend told me that a craftsman electrician was looking for an apprentice to work in the "forge". He suggested I should try my luck; I could hardly be worse off because the electrician already had a reputation for giving away bread and speaking out clearly against the Hitler regime.

So I decided to take the small risk and apply to be his apprentice. However, fulfilling my plan was not straightforward, because it needed the approval of a few Group Elders. Before I could count on their help, I first had to secure the approval of a prominent camp official.

At this point I want to go into more detail about the overall circumstances in Markstadt Camp, and especially the relationships between the prominent camp officials and the inmates. It was already my second year in the camp and I had acquired a good understanding of how the camp hierarchy functioned. About a hundred people worked as camp officials, some of whom were numbered among the "Prominenz" (prominent camp officials) who worked for the Jewish Elders as well as the camp leaders and supervisors. The camp personnel consisted of kitchen workers who prepared food for the supervisors in a special kitchen, kitchen porters who were in charge of the transport of groceries, shoemakers, toilet attendants, carpenters, etc. These "Prominenz" who worked within the confines of the camp were in every way favoured. They only started work at seven o'clock in the morning. The working columns marched the long way to their worksite in storms, rain and snow, and were already often browbeaten and exhausted from the march. When they arrived at their destination, the camp officials were still sitting and enjoying their breakfast, where they did not even lack for jam and sugar – things which for most us were unknown for so long. For lunch, the "Prominenz" often received double portions and even scooped out the nourishing residue from the soup kettles. They often finished their work during the afternoon. Then they were free to bathe or attend to their clothes and laundry. They wore highly polished leather boots to signify their position.

How different were the lives of the masses of inmates! Although the workers on the building site undertook an unfair and very heavy burden of work, they were fed only a thin soup and they hungered for bread. Despite the debilitating twelve hour work shifts they received nothing more. Every evening, when they were utterly exhausted by their labours, they still had to "march" back to the camp, and even then they sometimes had to queue for hours for their portion of "soup". Often wagons loaded with goods for the construction firms had to be immediately unloaded. Even though they were exhausted to the point of collapse, they would often be rudely awakened from their slumbers, driven out of their huts, and forced to work through the night. They also had to work unloading wagons, even on Sundays. In marked contrast, the "Prominenz", who were fit and well-fed, were never compelled to do additional work. The masses had to be available for work at all times, they were not allowed any respite, even on Sundays.

A similar number of "Prominenz" were to be found at the construction site. They included the Group Elders, foremen, medical orderly, the managers of the building project and a few people who worked for them.

The "Prominenz" who worked on the building site had contacts with foreign workers and Germans with whom they conducted a flourishing barter trade. Occasionally they even received alcohol and chocolates from English and French prisoners. Cigarettes and tobacco were always available. The easier work, the good food and the opportunity to keep oneself clean enabled the privileged to look fit and in good health. At all times there was a friendship and fellowship that embraced all the satiated and prosperous "Prominenz" on the building site. They were extremely anxious to distinguish themselves from the dispossessed masses at all times.

Gradually my eyes were opened: we had been misled by assurances that everyone in the camp would be treated the same, and that those who worked harder would receive more and better food. In fact, the opposite was the case. The hard labourers were woken at the crack of dawn each day and had to make their arduous way to the work place. Not only did they have to undertake heavy labour under crude supervision, they were scornfully abused as they were forced to unload wagons, they were given only the thinnest soup. They were robbed of the possibility to receive "presents" and the opportunity to "organise" or barter for essential foodstuffs. Those who got up and went to work later did not have to rush and work so hard. They received good food to excess, they had access to such things as tobacco, and were able to keep themselves clean. They were spared extra work and were even able to befriend girls who smuggled food for them which they obtained from the German staff's kitchens. There were about a hundred women who lived in their own barracks, separated from the rest of the camp by barbed wire. They worked mainly in the kitchens and laundry for the camp personnel and supervisors. Ordinary inmates were threatened with punishment if they even approached the women. The "Prominenz" found many ways and means to help each other. Many had girlfriends who they were able to meet in secret.

There were some who were neither "Prominenz" nor the dispossessed. They were something between the two; they undertook less arduous work and did not go hungry. However, they did not enjoy the authority of the "Prominenz" and so were dependent on their patronage. Prisoners in this category obtained bread and luxury items such as soap, alcohol, tobacco and chocolate to bribe the camp "Prominenz". I was a member of this intermediate category. I had connections with the "Prominenz" because I could obtain such things, so I had opportunities to seek their favours. When my friends advised me to change my workplace, they also put in a good word with the Group Elders. Thanks to their hard work and "protection" I was assigned to the master electrician in the "forge" as his assistant.

On the first day, master electrician Hermann pressed a bag of electrical tools and roll of cable into my hands. Together we went about our work on the building site. My master put on climbing boots and climbed up the electricity pylon. In accordance with the customary working practice of electricians, he called down to me to throw him the cable and necessary tools. I had never done anything like it before. I tried to follow his instructions, but the cable and tools went everywhere except in Hermann's hands. Angrily he cursed me, "Do you want to be an electrician? You are a shit! Go to hell! Don't stop me working!" Angrily he climbed down, collected the necessary tools, and continued working by himself. Dejected, I stood alone at the bottom. I thought fearfully that my efforts to get better work and to work for nicer people was all for nothing. Maybe I would have been better off if I had remained a track runner.

I contemplated my future with dread. I had a vision of endless masses of emaciated workers all coated with cement dust like motionless robots serving the pounding machines.

When Meister[3] Hermann had completed his work and descended the pylon he was still very angry. He took the tools from

---

3. *Meister* means "master" in German, as in master craftsman or as an honorific title such as Meister Hermann.

me and there was no work for me to do. I still followed him so that I could at least carry his bag, but he took it himself and he strode away. I knew that a decisive moment had arrived – the moment when he would decide whether I could remain with him or be sent away to work with my old track commando or at the cement machines.

I was determined not to give up without a fight. I walked up to Meister Hermann and apologised for my failings. I explained that I was not an electrician, only an apprentice, and that I had completed only a few weeks working on domestic electrical installations. I begged him to have patience with me and promised that I would try very hard with his help to learn the necessary skills so that I could make myself useful to him.

Hermann did not take his eyes off me as I pleaded with him. He still looked very critical and his expression seemed to suggest that I was merely seeking a comfortable position for myself. However, he gave me back the bag of tools and together we walked to his workshop. There he asked me about my home, my origins, my family circumstances and how I had come to be a forced labourer in this camp. I told him about home and the unfortunate night when we had been taken away. Hermann listened to my account with growing fury, took hold of the hammer and banged on the table with it. He called out in horror and anger, "One people, one Reich, one Führer, one mass grave, one lost civilisation!" He told me that his brother-in-law had been appointed as leader of the Gendarmerie in our home town. The reports about how the people of the town had been driven out and their homes plundered were true, because his brother-in-law went home every second weekend, laden with luggage full of goods stolen from the homes of people who had been deported. Meister Hermann took a piece of bread covered with fat from his locker and invited me to share his snack with him. Then he pointed to a particular compartment in the locker and remarked, "What lies in there is yours." From then on he always put into the compartment a ration for me like his own.

A new era of my camp life had begun. My Meister let me see newspapers and we had daily discussions about issues such as religion, politics or social problems. For me, the way to work was not only a welcome change but I also very much looked forward to it. It relieved me, at least for a few hours, from my world which consisted only of degradation and humiliation. Meister Hermann made me feel like a human being again, as opposed to a mere work slave; with him it was a given that I was treated as an equal and with respect.

Until that time, at intervals, we got post from home. More recently this connection with our families had been disrupted because we were no longer permitted to exchange letters. In this way, the Nazis kept secret from us how our homes in the ghetto had been searched. With increasing frequency we were threatened that if we escaped they would take revenge on our families.

When Hermann found out that I no longer got any news at all from my parents and siblings, he suggested to me that I should write a letter with his address on it, and that they should in turn address their post to him. I did as he suggested, and for a while I actually did receive letters from home. My parents sent me ration cards for grocery which Meister Hermann exchanged for bread for me. He also had a radio on which he could listen to English broadcasts. So I had access to a source of news which I was able to share with my comrades in the camp, who were naturally attentive when I gave them reports based on the English station. I also smuggled the daily newspaper that Hermann gave me each day into the camp. This was greatly valued by the camp "Prominenz", so my reputation and prestige was enhanced.

While my own position improved in every way, the number of Muselmanner steadily increased until there were a few hundred of them. Full of anxiety, I observed my Uncle Leon, who worked for Grün und Bilfinger. Alarmingly, he had lost weight from his face. When I met him one evening I was able to "organise" some food for him, and I observed that his body was already very emaciated. His face was covered in cement dust, his eyes were rimmed with red and lips were dry and cracked. Uncle Leon was one of the unfortunate souls who had to do hard labour working on the cement mixers.

He shared his doomed fate with hundreds of others. The sick bay was filled to overflowing, and one could readily see that those who continued to work belonged to the sick bay and were not fit for the workplace. About this time a Commission entered the camp and after a selection procedure removed all the sick people from the sick bay. At this so called selection, all the camp inmates had to undress and stand naked. Then they were inspected by the ss doctors. All the weak, the sick and those with boils, ulcers and running sores were singled out to be transported away. Some of the emaciated inmates who could still work were also taken away with them. They lied to us that they were to be taken to a camp to recuperate. We were inclined to believe this because we could not imagine anything worse than the hellhole that was Markstadt Camp. Only later did we discover that we had been deceived; from the beginning it was always intended that all those on this transport would be exterminated.

A transport of Jews who had been abducted from Belgium and Holland arrived in the camp. They were housed in two barracks separated from ours by a barbed wire fence. They were formerly well-off, mainly educated academic men whom the Nazis wanted to keep strictly isolated from us. They were not allowed any contact with us. They were taken to do heavy labour in separate commandos and were treated so inhumanely that after a few weeks many of them were laid out with exhaustion. After our transfer from Grünheide to Markstadt we had some time to accustom ourselves to our new circumstances. However, these newcomers were immediately compelled to perform the heaviest of labours, and quite naturally they could not withstand these unaccustomed and excessive burdens. After a few months both barracks were empty, and all that remained were a few sick men that were transferred to the sick bay. The harsh winter of 1942 – 43 made life for the inmates even more difficult because they had to continue working without a break, regardless of the weather. Inevitably the number of victims increased every day. I reported to Meister Hermann about our circumstances in the camp and we often spoke of the future. He had built a good radio receiver with a variety of switches. He could switch it off at anytime from anywhere in the hut the moment anyone suspicious approached our workshop. I was often present when Hermann tuned in to English broadcasts. I listened with him to the reports about atrocities perpetrated against Jews in the East and accurately named those responsible for the extermination of Jews. Sometimes, Meister Hermann sent me to Machinenmeister Kuka and another Meister so that they could listen to the broadcasts as well. Naturally I made myself scarce.

Hermann was the most intelligent of the ethnic German Meisters. He was a social democrat. Against his will he had been elected as "Obmann" of the Deutschen Arbeitsfront (DAF)[4]. He also wore the symbol of the DAF, complete with swastika. Occasionally he would point to it and call it "the death-wheel". He was friendly with Machinenmeister Kuka who shared his political views. Although it was strictly forbidden, he kept some Polish literature hidden in our hut. Sometimes I had to deliver one of these to his confidants, particularly Kuka. Hermann was also very well-regarded by those who managed the building work. Only a few of the inmates who worked in the forge could speak German fluently. I was one of the few who could make himself well-understood in German and also read German literature. On one occasion when I took a book from Hermann to Kuka I was invited to enter the room and he carefully locked the door behind me. He asked me to sit down and tell him about my background and my parents. He was very interested in my home life. Finally he asked me how I had come to the camp. I recounted to him all the details of our deportation. Kuka jumped up. He strode back and forth and banged himself on the head with his fist. He shouted, "And that should be our New Order! And we want to be a cultured People!" A large map hung on the wall. It was covered with coloured pins that marked out the current battlefronts. Kuka led me to this map and asked me to point to my home town. I indicated the place and at the same time followed the line of the battlefront. This was completely different to the official German Army reports. Kuka enquired of me in great detail about the conditions in Grünheide and Markstadt camps. I described the camp organisation and life to him. He called out in anger, "This will have terrible consequences for us!" I felt an inner satisfaction as I left the room after

---

4. *Obmann* – Shop Steward. The *Deutschen Arbeitsfront*, DAF (German Labour Front) was the National Socialist trade union organization which replaced the various trade unions of the Weimar Republic after Adolf Hitler's rise to power.

this conversation. I was strengthened by this human contact, sharing of trust, treatment and attention as a human being.

However, one thought continually asserted itself until it dominated all my thinking: how could I save myself from the certainty of the extermination that confronted all of us Jews? As I carried out electrical installations at different building sites I saw my comrades doing heavy labour at the cement machines. Those who were caught up on this treadmill could think of neither freedom nor escape. These inmates were harassed, enslaved, starving, caked in cement dust and so exhausted and worn down by the constant frenzy that body and spirit always teetered on the brink.

I became more and more depressed by my Uncle Leon's situation. Already, he had visibly lost his strength and had not managed to change his work. During this difficult period we were drawn closer together, and when on Sunday we had a few free hours we spent them together and reminisced about our relatives at home. Sometimes this yearning was overwhelming, and he was gradually and almost completely consumed by the memory of his young child. "Now he would be three years old." He told me in detail how clever and sensibly the child already spoke, "What has become of my child?" He sighed with a heavy heart, "he was two years old when he was deported to an unknown destination with his mother." I found it difficult to console him, any hope I could offer was an illusion. We heard reports from our hometown of the so-called "resettlement" – actually extermination – of the Jewish People. The small town of Pilica, where my uncle's mother and sister (i.e. my maternal grandmother and aunt) lived also succumbed to the same fate. The Jewish People from the town were transported to the extermination camps and the town became Judenrein – empty of Jews. How could I support, comfort and reassure my uncle that his beloved child was still alive? I almost choked as I did my best to suppress my tears when he talked of the young child that would by then have developed into a big, strong and clever boy. At these moments, I speculated whether I could flee to my home with my uncle. However, I knew that people in the ghettos were deported, some for forced labour, some for extermination. Finally I discussed this situation with Hermann. He agreed that I should give his home address as my own, so that I could receive a parcel of decent clothes, laundry and a few hundred Marks. Unbelievably, a parcel arrived and Hermann hid it for me in his workshop. My friend Meier Rosenthal was working as Kalfaktor (boiler man) directly under Senior Meister Homuth. He undertook to obtain work passes with Czechoslovakian names. However, there was one issue upon which Hermann himself could not advise us. He did not know of any secure town or place where we could stay if we escaped. He tried during his free weekends in Breslau to make contact with people who might be able to help us but all he could find were Mischling (people who were partly Jewish) and because their own future was so precarious they could not offer any kind of refuge. Quite apart from this, Hermann's home was close to the border with Switzerland so he was unfamiliar with Silesia. Our work site was a massive munitions factory, so our only hope of escape was that the Allies would bomb it one day. With luck, we might be able to flee with our Czech identities in the resulting chaos.

The heroic fight in the Warsaw Ghetto in April 1943 encouraged and stimulated us to think about resistance but it also convinced us that we Jews were condemned to death and that nothing in the world would stop the Nazis from completing their criminal plans. A single thought gnawed constantly at all our minds, "Everyone would have their turn, some sooner, some later. Should we remain passive and wait until they took us to our extermination?"

During the final few weeks we spent in Markstadt, the camp discipline became a little more relaxed. The Jewish Elder Baruch Meister appeared to try hard to improve our situation, but even he could not persuade those who regularly beat us to stop doing so. However, he tried to create more order and ensure we could rest properly after work. We no longer had to queue for ages for our food. There was also an easing of the harassment and cruelty to which we had been routinely subjected upon completion of our working day which made our camp life after work so bitter. Baruch Meister was on the lookout to ensure that privileged camp workers could no longer steal food allocated to ordinary inmates, and everyone got the ration to which they were entitled. Obviously, he wanted to improve the general health of the inmates. Occasionally, he conducted body searches of men and women inmates to check if they had stolen any food intended for us. When he caught inmates with stolen food he authorised their punishment: twenty-five lashes on their naked bottom for stealing from their comrades. He even arranged some entertainment on Sundays; thus some inmates performed and sang songs. We were frequently utterly exhausted and, given the choice, would have preferred to rest on our boards. But the Block and Room Elders followed the instructions of the Jewish Elder and drove us out on to the Appellplatz where these performances took place.

Camp life became somewhat more bearable. Maybe this was in response to the latest terrible news we received about many of the ghettos in the occupied territories; they had been liquidated in a most bestial manner. We thought it might also be because the Jewish Elder knew we only had a very limited life expectancy in the camp and he did not want us to have to suffer unnecessarily.

There was a steady flow of transports from the ghettos in Upper Silesia to Auschwitz, but one day one of these transports arrived in our camp. It contained former Jewish ghetto police and orderlies. Most of them were obsequious dogsbodies who had ingratiated themselves with the ss and Gestapo, and we abhorred them for it. The Jewish Elder locked them up in another barrack to keep them apart from us. They had to strip naked and give up everything they had with them, some of which were valuables they had definitely stolen. Then the Jewish Elder closely questioned them to discover who amongst them had behaved contemptibly or ruthlessly. These inmates were singled out and beaten so severely that finally they lay in a terrible state motionless on the ground.

As time passed by we received more terrible news about the "Aussiedlung" – the resettlement of the Jewish population from many towns and areas, many of which were declared "Judenrein" (cleansed of Jews). One morning, Meister Hermann brought me a letter. I opened it and read the few words. "We are standing in front of our wagons because our town is now Judenrein. Like other transports before us, we are probably going to the extermination at Auschwitz. Stay strong and make sure that you stay alive. And do not forget all this." Now my family had also met its inescapable fate;

its extermination. Sobbing, I sat in the workshop, my parents' final lines in my hand as Meister Hermann entered. I told him what was in the letter. He thought it right to lock me in the workshop and went to work by himself. So I sat alone in the dark room, alone with my pain. I grieved for my parents, brother and sisters who were at that moment en route to the gas chambers at Auschwitz, where like millions of other Jews, they had to succumb to their pitiless fate. The picture of my parents, my sisters and my little brother was etched in my mind. I do not know how long I cried, but I swore to myself never to forget the murder of my innocent family.

At lunchtime, the Meister returned and persuaded me to eat something but I had no appetite. I could not eat a thing. Was there any reason for me to carry on living, working and fighting for this wretched existence? At this moment I was overwhelmed with the futility of my existence. The news of the Aussiedlung, the "resettlement", actually my parents' death sentence, had for the time being plunged me into a deep despair from which I recovered only very slowly. Nevertheless, after some time I felt the will to live reawaken in me. I spent hours in solitude, agonising over my memories of parents, home and a happy childhood. In my mind I could clearly hear my father silently urging me to carry on. I knew I had to sustain my parents' legacy, for the sake of the love and care which they had given to me. I recalled countless small experiences, and I almost felt their presence physically. It was as if my parents' deepest desire was that I should remain alive and survive my ordeal.

Strangely, I always emerged strengthened from these sorrowful dialogues with the dead. While we had been compelled by gruesome experience to come to terms with our fate, nevertheless, perhaps even absurdly, I still did not lose the will to live. The mass extermination which surrounded us had reached its fullest extent. It was apparent that there was very little chance that we would escape with our lives. It was clear to each and every one of us that before long it would be our turn. Even so we lived as if our imminent death had no meaning for us. The rules of logic no longer played any part in our thoughts and feelings. The wish to survive did not arise from logic, but instead from a yearning for life and freedom.

My belief in God and faith in people and their moral code had long ago been broken. If ever I could breathe in freedom again I believed I could no longer respect any law, nor recognise any God or religion. From the moment my parents had started on the road to Auschwitz, love, compassion, goodness and justice were words that no longer held any meaning or significance for me.

Many of my comrades had similar thoughts. Some of them became Kapos and were so contemptuous of others that they did not even save their former friends and acquaintances. Some of these Kapos were seized by a barbaric and destructive instinct that I could not comprehend; sometimes, in an insane rage, they would persecute the innocent fellow inmates. Perhaps this was a futile protest against their own tormented existence.

However, not all Kapos were like that. Many helped their comrades, even though it may have endangered their position. Many had reason to fear that they too would be severely punished. Vogel, the Kapo of the Forge Group, was very helpful. Not only did he allow inmates to obtain food, when they cooked potatoes he would keep a careful watch to ensure the ss guards did not catch them.

When after a few days I was at last able to speak with a few of my comrades about the final letter I had received from my parents, news spread like wildfire throughout the camp. Friends came to me and wanted to know the exact content of the letter. I could only stammer a few sentences. We muttered to each other, "While we are compelled to do slave labour, our parents and families have already been exterminated." How long would it be before they could dispense with our slave labour and we too would become surplus to requirements? Some of my friends believed that the time for us to hatch plans for our escape had arrived. However, the hopelessness of such an enterprise was also very clear. Until that time, only a few had escaped from the camp. Where could we run to? Who would offer us a hiding place and protection when they might be the next victim? We heard rumours about nearby partisan groups but we had no connection to them and did not know how to contact them. Despite this, a few friends and I took the decision to prepare an escape plan. We had to obtain the necessary papers in a roundabout way. We intended to obtain, and if necessary to steal, food and other goods that we could barter in exchange for identity papers and money. Once we had escaped we planned to merge with other "foreign workers". We made contact with Czech people who obtained papers for us. After some time we were in possession of work papers that should enable us to escape from the factory. Every worker, whether German or foreign, had to show papers to the guards on leaving the factory premises. The entire perimeter of the factory was populated by a dense net of guards, so it was impossible to evade this control.

As my friends and I worked in the forge and did not belong to a closed group, we hoped that when we escaped our absence would not be noticed for a few hours. We wanted to steal bicycles to get a head start and defeat our pursuers. We hoped to be some distance from the camp when our absence would first be noticed at the evening Appell. If the first phase of our escape succeeded, we intended to head for a railway station and take a train to Czechoslovakia where we planned to make contact with the partisans. The increasingly frequent bombing raids by the Soviet Union and the West also created other opportunities for escape. What we really longed for was that our factory should be bombed. If we survived, we hoped to flee with the papers of those who were killed in the bombing and disappear. It may seem absurd, but we were very disappointed that despite the many alarms, we were never bombed.

By this time I had become a competent electrician and undertook various dangerous jobs by myself. When I climbed the mast I could hang on with just one hand, not having to use both as I did when I began. Sometimes, when the job was done, I would remain on the mast and observe the huge building site, which in my fantasy became an inferno that consumed the bodies of my friends.

In order not to interrupt production, I often had to connect cables without switching off the electricity supply. One day, in a careless moment, I received a violent electric shock. I fell unconscious to the bottom of the mast and that evening I was carried back into the camp. I ran a high temperature. I could not eat anything, and the next morning I could not get up for Appell. When in the early morning everyone left for work, only my friends Berek Fuchs and

Samuel Gelbart from Poremba, with whom I shared a wooden bunk in the corner, remained. I asked them for some water. I felt as if my life was drifting away. When I regained consciousness the following day, I found myself lying in the sick bay. I was told I had lost consciousness and my friends had covered me with a blanket and carried me to the sick bay. I was extremely stiff but still able to breathe. In the evening, my friends enquired after me and wanted to visit me but the medical orderly said, "You won't recognise him, and he won't recognise you". My uncle and friend from the forge urged the doctor and medical orderly to do everything they could to save me, but their options were very limited. Anyway, they put me in a small single room that was reserved for the dying, and when I came to they brought me to a "ward" managed by the medical orderly who was called Renja Schwarzfütter from Olkusch. My nourishment consisted of a few spoons of liquid and tablets which were probably Prontosil and Aspirin. After a few days, my uncle obtained some semolina and prepared a soup with it which he carefully fed me as he supported my head. Even though every movement of my head hurt, at least I was alive and making slow recovery. My uncle and friends from the forge, and in particular the good Jacob Bloch, obtained fruit and white bread for me. I could not swallow camp food, so Uncle Leon cooked soups for me.

Uncle Leon no longer had any illusions about the fate of his wife and child who had been deported to Auschwitz. Above all, he looked after me and even obtained for me a special light diet. After a few weeks, the supervising ss doctor came to the camp, and he visited me in the sick bay. The camp doctor reported at length about my illness because he was proud that he had managed to cure me just with the help of tablets. The ss doctor showed interest and ordered that my case should be written up as a recommended treatment for soldiers in a similar condition at the front. I was feeling better and better, and I no longer needed to fear that I would be transported together with the hopeless cases and "Muselmännern".

In general, there were very few remedies for the sick. The main job of the camp doctors, who came from our ranks, was to isolate cases of infection and to avoid the transmission of contagious diseases.

This was because we were in contact with thousands of foreign and German workers on the building site. Inmates at the end of their strength or whose internal organs were in a state of collapse were beyond help.

Finally, I was released from the sick bay. As I limped to work, I was supported on either side by friends. Even so, my left side was paralysed, and I dragged my left foot.

Meister Hermann was pleased when I reappeared. He immediately made room for me to lie down in his hut. The German storeroom foreman who I met shortly after also congratulated me on my recuperation and gave me a small glass of syrup to "strengthen me a bit", as he said.

I was still unsteady on my feet so, for the time being, the group elder Vogel put me in charge of changing points on the railway because this was a task I could do sitting down. I continued to get better and after a few weeks I was delighted that I was well enough to work once more with Meister Hermann.

During 1941 and 1942, while most of our relatives were still at home we thought of them constantly. We missed them dreadfully. We felt this most painfully during the Jewish festivals because for us these were always family occasions. This was despite the fact that during the last few years our relatives had not been able to celebrate our festivals for reasons beyond their control. By this time they were oppressed people whose humanity had been diminished; they lived in ghettos, herded together in cramped spaces where deportations and shootings were daily events. They too had to do forced labour. It was impossible to observe or celebrate our holy days and festivals. Only the very orthodox remembered these days. Only when they had completed their days' forced labour could they assemble in a room where they prayed devoutly.

In marked contrast, those of us who were in the camps were far from home and family but in our minds' eye the memories of past holy days shone in bright colours as we imagined ourselves reunited with our families. We were prisoners isolated from the rest of the world. We recalled the previous years as an ideal life, with our family as the central focus of our trust, togetherness and love. Especially during the festivals, in our fantasies the past took on wonderful colours which certainly did not always correspond with reality. So we remembered with pangs of longing and nostalgia, feelings of freedom, family and home. Our hearts were so full that we had to speak about our feelings. In detailed stories, which were often exaggerated, we talked about synagogue services and delicious dishes prepared for the different festivals. Only a few assembled in the barracks after work to pray on holy days.

In the Summer of 1943 we, from East Upper Silesia, received news that a total liquidation had taken place in that region. Now we knew that those sent for forced labour and "resettlement" had in fact been exterminated. This news depressed us all the more as the Holy Days approached. These days were always marked with great reverence. As September neared we were increasingly conscious of just how painfully our loneliness lay upon us. Disappointed by God and humanity, very few bothered with prayers and the Holy Days. Exhausted by our day's labours, everyone stretched out on their plank. Very few summoned up sufficient inner strength after the order, "Lights out!" to get up once more in the silence to whisper their prayers.

Thanks to the kindness of the good Group Elder Vogel in our barrack, a few very religious men formed their own group. Vogel gave them lighter duties and showed consideration for those who were weak.

The Day of Atonement approached, when the observant pray all day and fast for twenty-six hours without eating or drinking anything. Not even water is allowed to be consumed on that day. Again, it was Vogel who excused the religious men from work that day and arranged for them to remain in a hut on the building site. These people were prepared to work without food or drink. With their last strength, on empty stomachs, they were willing to undertake their workload. Vogel told Machinemeister Kuka about these men and the way they conducted themselves. Silently, Kuka also acquiesced to this arrangement, so the very religious men were allowed to remain in the hut during this fast day. They stood together and prayed, full of fear that they might be discovered and punished. Some had the tattered remnants of a prayer book from which one of them quietly lamented as he read out the prayers.

Late in the afternoon it suddenly became very dark. A heavy storm arose, driving torrents of rain before it, forcing everyone to stop work. With a few friends I also took shelter in the hut and saw the group of religious people swaying backwards and forwards, deep in prayer. The room was dark because the hut, which was made from wooden boards, had no windows. Like ghosts in rags and shrouded in the shadows, they swayed back and forth as the "Cantor" intoned the prayers. Very little light penetrated the gaps between the boards. Now the prayers reached the concluding climax (Neilah); these required a quorum of ten men to be present. With silent glances they turned towards us, inviting us to join them. We could see how fervently these men prayed, but we were also overwhelmed by feelings of disappointment and bitterness about God and religion. We were torn by this paradox. Our hearts were full of bitterness and uncried tears. We discovered it was impossible for us to recite the psalms and prayers. There was nothing we could do except mourn the terrible destiny and tragic misfortune that had befallen our people and destroyed our parents and families.

The rain drummed on the roof like a thousand tiny hammers. We huddled closer together in the room. Tearfully and with a quivering voice, we imperceptibly joined in the prayers of the faithful. "God, open the gates of heaven for our prayers. May the gates of The Merciful One not be closed." We became a large dark trembling mass shattered by the impact of our fervent prayers. Our hunger and tiredness evaporated, our protests and resistance were forgotten. The heartrending sounds of our prayers and sobs merged with the loud drumming of the rain and the howling noise of the storm. Once again the "Cantor" lifted up his voice and prayed, "God, the day is ending, we are drawing near to your gates. Oh God, forgive us, pardon us, excuse us, have pity on us, have mercy on us." Outside it grew darker and gradually the storm abated. We had to lower our voices. Wet from the rain and wet from our tears we concluded our prayers. Soon after, our Group Elder Vogel opened the door for us to march back to the camp together. With lifted hearts we lined up, leaving all our accumulated tears and prayers behind in the hut.

In Autumn 1943, our camp was due to be disbanded and we were to be assigned to other camps. The factory halls that we had built were now ready for use. In three of them, machines from Krupp had already been installed and tank and cannon production was already under way. Rumours about our dispersal from the camp had a certain ring of truth because we did not have the required skills to operate these machines. It was rumoured that those responsible for munitions production were reluctant to run a camp filled with so many Jews so close to their works. They feared that the factory would be bombed and destroyed. They also feared that the factory might be sabotaged by the inmates. Some of us thought that all the surviving Jews would be taken to Auschwitz, Buchenwald and other camps, since all ghettoes in Germany and the occupied territories had already been liquidated.

Comrades who were working outside the camps told us that they had met a group of men in striped cotton overalls, round prisoner hats and clogs. At this time we wore civilian clothes with a yellow star on our back, chest and trousers.

Even though the guards forbade us from speaking to the people dressed as prisoners some of them tried to attract our attention by calling quietly to us. That is how we found out that they were Jewish inmates from Auschwitz who were building a camp in our vicinity. We soon had a reasonable understanding of what was happening around us. A large concentration camp was to be set up at the adjacent village of Fünfteichen. This belonged to the main Grossrosen concentration camp. This camp was surrounded with a double wired electric fence which was surrounded by watchtowers. A transport of a few hundred inmates from the concentration camp at Auschwitz had already arrived, but many barracks with room for many more thousands remained available.

We thought our circumstances were about to change. The inmates in the striped concentration camp clothing now joined us on the building site. They worked only in the three production halls, but were not allowed to work outside. They had already made the first few barrels for cannons. They were closely guarded by the ss with Wolfhound dogs as they marched to work each morning. When most of the Jewish inmates were taken for the production of gun barrels we were no longer of the opinion that we would be removed because of the fear of sabotage. From camp friends who worked with the concentration camp inmates, I found out that many of them came from my home town. So I asked Meister Hermann to smuggle me into the hall where these inmates were working so that I could look out for relatives and friends. We were able to gain access to the hall under the pretext of connecting electrical power points. Hermann was in agreement. We draped electric cables around us and walked into the hall. Soon we met the first set of inmates who could not be distinguished from one another in their striped uniforms. Their faces were like pale masks. It was difficult to distinguish their facial features. It was also almost impossible to judge their ages. They differed only in their height. While they bent over machinery as they worked ss people and Kapos, armed with clubs, marched up and down amongst them.

When I discovered my Uncle Meisel in the masses I discreetly notified Hermann and we deposited our material close to my uncle. The first thing my uncle asked for was tobacco so that he could swap it for bread and soup. I hid a small packet of tobacco under a machine for him to secretly recover later. Then I urgently enquired about my parents and brother and sisters and asked what had happened to them. His eyes filled with tears and when he finally answered he tried to do so in a soothing tone, "Don't ask Srulutsch, don't ask! My wife and my two dear children are no longer alive. They have been gassed and burned at Auschwitz. Therefore don't ask any more! Make sure you stay alive and that you keep your strength! Tomorrow bring me more tobacco if you can, because Uncle Zimmermann is also here. His wife, Aunt Eva, and the three children are also no longer alive." As I noticed that the ss guards and Kapos were watching us I moved away from the area of the machines where I had spread out the electric cables. As I passed other inmates some quickly tried to whisper things to me which obviously had to do with their own fate or perhaps they knew me…but I could no longer recognise their faces. I could not comprehend anything of what they wanted to say to me because I was so shocked by my meeting with my uncle. Shortly after we left the hall, Meister Hermann, who had also been touched by the sight of these inmates, marched next to me with clenched teeth. Full of rage he exploded, "One people, one Reich, one Führer, one mass grave!" I told him of my conversation with my Uncle Meisel. After we arrived back in the hut, without hesitation he placed a packet of tobacco in my tool bag. Then he went to Machinemeister Kuka and reported to him about his first encounter with the inmates who had arrived from the concentration camp. People living in the neighbourhood had looked upon them as criminal prisoners. Prompted by their curiosity they asked the ss, "Who are the men in striped clothing?" but they were fobbed off and given misleading information. Their lies were readily believed when the inmates' every move was accompanied by guards with loaded guns at the ready. Only serious criminals could be treated like that. Now Hermann knew the truth and could explain to his friends that three months ago these prisoners had been peaceful family fathers, and were also craftsmen, business people, technicians, and academics. Overnight they had become unsuspecting victims who had been deported to Auschwitz where their families had been exterminated. The men had been found fit for work so they had been transported to our camp.

I waited a few days before I tried again, with Meister Hermann, to reach the factory hall and resume contact with my uncle. As we had done previously, we equipped ourselves with electric flex, other materials and a pass, authorising necessary repairs, to provide an apparently legitimate excuse for our presence. Again, I was able to speak to my uncle. He had bloody welts on his face. When I asked, he told me that after our last conversation a Kapo had searched him and found his tobacco. The tobacco was confiscated and he had been beaten. Then I told him I would again put tobacco in a hiding place. I pleaded with him not to take the small parcel as soon as I left, but to wait a while before retrieving it. As I was about to leave the factory hall, I was profoundly moved when I happened to meet one of my father's friends. I was stunned by what he had to tell me. "I know your father's testament." I stood still to hear more. I could see he was unable to find the words to express what he knew. I could not make sense of his confused stammering and I moved closer to understand him better. I begged him to tell me more about my father. At that instant I was called back by my Meister's voice. When I turned around an ss man and his Kapo beat me with their clubs and interrogated me. "Do you know it is forbidden to talk to prisoners? Are you involved in any secret activity?" Hermann rushed to my side and tried to protect me. The ss man insisted on searching my body. He wished to reassure himself that I did not have any letters or secret messages which I could pass on to other prisoners. At the same time he told me that if I wanted to avoid being severely punished I must hand over everything I had concealed about my person. I was able to be searched with a clear conscience because I had already hidden the tobacco for my uncle. After the search was completed without anything being found, the ss man kicked me and shouted, "Make sure you disappear, you dirty Jew!" Then he asked Meister Hermann to supervise me more closely. I was bitterly disappointed as I left the hall. I was filled with indignation because of the despicable behaviour of the ss man. However, what caused me even greater heartache was the conversation with my father's friend. It was so incoherent that I could not understand his account of my father's alleged testament. "Maybe I would have understood if I had been more careful and conducted myself more skilfully…" This thought occupied and tormented me for a long time. After a few days I tried again to meet my father's friend but I came too late. He was nowhere to be found. "He was already finished, he was no longer alive." What his companions meant was that when he approached me he was no longer of sound mind.

On my rounds through the halls I met Supervising Clerk Otto Sch. (Sch. lives today[5] in Regensburg.) He was in charge of a list of names of all the prisoners and was responsible for allocating them to their work groups. His father Max Sch. had a responsible position in the camp and in the stores. He was the only Jew who succeeded in having such a position. Otto told me that preparations had been made in Fünfteichen Concentration Camp to take in the inmates

---

5. Today = when this book was originally published in 1967 in German.

from Markstadt Camp. He also told me that when the camp would
be taken over we would be made to strip naked, give up our civilian
clothing and valuables, and we would be dressed in prison uniforms.
If I knew anyone who had jewellery or money I should warn them
not carry their worldly goods with them. It would be better to give
these valuables in secret to him. He would make sure that, with the
help of his father, any such person would get a good position in the
concentration camp, for example, in the kitchen or as Block or Room
Elder, and would be provided with bread and soup.

I reported this encounter to my Uncle Leon and my friends
Bloch, Scheyer and Rosenthal. My uncle asked me to put in a good
word for him so that he could have bearable work in the kitchen or
elsewhere. When I explained my uncle's request to Otto, he told me
that a few hundred marks per head were needed to barter for a better
working place. In fact, my friends managed to find the money. They
had lived in the camp since 1940, that is one year longer than me
and were specialists in "organising". Also, thanks to Hermann, I was
able to put aside a little money. Now everything went according to
plan. Otto bribed the Kapo of the factory hall so I got free access to
him and other prisoners working there. I begged Otto to help both
my uncles, Meisel and Zimmermann, first. Both no longer appeared
for work and the help came too late. Otto reported back to me that
Uncle Zimmermann had been heavily beaten up and Meisel was lying
in the sick bay where he died after some time. When we all no longer doubted that in the very near future Fünfteichen Concentration
Camp would be taken over, my friends Bloch, Scheyer and Rosenthal
entrusted their money to me. I hid the money in some crockery and
gave it to Otto. I added a few notes myself and pleaded with him not
to forget my uncle or me. Within a few days Otto came over to me
beaming. He told me I could choose my own position. I could work
in the kitchen or even be a Kapo or Block Elder. Many new kitchen
staff and supervisors were needed because a few thousand inmates
moved from Markstadt to Fünfteichen. Then Otto thanked me for
the tobacco I had "organised" for him and reassured me once again
that he would not forget me. Then I begged him that when he was
allocating work he should consider my uncle above all others. As far

as I was concerned, I wanted to continue working as long as possible as an electrician with Meister Hermann, and I was assured of this.

In the long Winter of 1943–44 we received news that gave us fresh hope. Stalingrad had fallen, German troops were retreating, and the German Western Front had been ripped open. In Italy, General Badoglio led a military coup which brought about the downfall of Mussolini. In the Mediterranean region, the English had moved over onto the offensive everywhere and in Yugoslavia the partisans managed to conquer strongholds. We knew all this, even if we did not know all the details. All those whose will to live had not been completely exhausted by hunger and suffocated by cement dust now began to hope again.

And yet, was our current situation not still hopeless? What would become of us if the war took a disastrous turn in favour of the Germans? Would they let us live? First, it was certain that the camp at Markstadt was to be abandoned and that we would be transferred to Fünfteichen Concentration Camp.

One evening at the end of December 1943 when we returned from work, our friends among the camp personnel told us that shortly we would have to leave Markstadt for Fünfteichen, but that the Jewish Elder would not be coming with us. Together with a one hundred other inmates he would be put in a camp in the Reichenbach region in Lower Silesia where he would once again be the Jewish Elder.

It was with this in mind that many tried to hide in the group of those chosen to accompany him, but in vain.

We were filled with great anxiety and consumed with the need to talk about our fears, hopes, and what might become of us. Inevitably, each and every one of us was gripped and overwhelmed by the fearful implications of the changes that now confronted us. We were paralysed by uncertainty, as always, whenever we found ourselves in this situation, in dread of whatever uncertain fate was in store for us. Some sought reassurance that the healthy ones would remain, and only those who were too sick to work would be transported to Auschwitz for extermination. However, others suggested that Krupp would take over the entire factory and only those who had the necessary "craft skills" would remain. The factory went over to a twoshift system, each shift lasting twelve hours. Skilled craftsmen were needed to fill all these vacancies. After lights-out in the camp, our small group sat in the dark for a long time together – Bloch, Scheyer and a few others. We talked about our parents, our families and our dear departed ones. We devised ambitious plans for our future, how we would organise our lives and which professions we wanted to pursue. And yet, what was the point of all this talk? What would await us tomorrow? Would we remain alive, and if so for how long? We were still deep in discussion when we were interrupted by the dawn wake-up call. Our friendship had deepened in the course of the night and awakened a shared wish that we should not be parted from each other. In the morning we promised each other to stay together and stick together come what may.

On Friday after the customary Appell we did not march to work. Instead we returned to our barracks. We discussed among ourselves the rumours that circulated between the latrines and the barracks. Suddenly we heard three shrill blasts of a whistle, the signal that called the Block Elders to the office of the Jewish Elder. There, orders and decrees were issued. Our curiosity and suspense mounted more and more. "What new information would our Block Elder impart to us?" we asked ourselves. Silently, and with serious faces they returned to the barracks and shouted out, "This block is now sealed! No one is allowed to leave the block, not even to go to the latrine!" So we waited impatiently, standing between the bunks, our minds racing. Suddenly, somebody outside loudly whistled and shouted, "Block three, line up!" Immediately the Block Elder drove us out of the barracks. We were made to line up in five rows outside and carefully counted to make sure no one was missing. We were marched as a single unit to the wash barracks. When we arrived, we were all made to stand in single file and undress. Once we were naked we were ordered into a room in front of a seated panel that consisted of several men in officers' uniform. We were continuously chased as we were forced to march past these men. As we did so, we recognised the death's head symbol on a few hats but we had little time to linger and look more carefully. Then we were chased back, forced to dress ourselves quickly, line up and then march back to the barracks. Nearly all of us returned. Since we all worked for the firm Schallhorn we believed that in future we would be able to stay together as a group. This was the only explanation we could come up with for the time being. The block remained sealed until the evening. Later we heard that this whole episode had been a selection in which a few hundred weak and starved men had been singled out. These men were taken out of the barracks and were closely guarded in a sickbay. We were relieved that very few were missing from our barracks. Since we worked for Schallhorn we had the opportunity to get extra food. Naturally, I wanted to know what had happened to my uncle. I was very relieved when I heard that he too had remained with his block. We were far too concerned about ourselves to be bothered about those who had been selected. Above all, we asked ourselves what would happen to us after Markstadt. Again, we heard rumours that those who had been selected because they were weak and sick would either be taken to a camp to recuperate or be assigned to lighter duties but deep down we were convinced that they were sent to be exterminated. We did not dare to voice our true thoughts. We all chose to push them to the back of our minds. We could not bear to confront such a grim fate, for this was the threat that hung over us all. Who could tell which of us would be reduced to feeble and emaciated Muselmännern in a few months? What kind of "recuperation" would await us? Our instinct for self-preservation drove us instinctively to ignore these thoughts. We were only concerned with our own destiny and whatever the next day had in store for us.

Night fell, and with it the distribution of food, this time in larger portions. It was the final one, the farewell provision from Markstadt. Our mood improved and eased our departure from the camp. Despite all the hardships we had experienced during the one and a half years we had spent in this place we were still reluctant to leave because of the uncertainty and danger that awaited us. We knew we had nothing good to look forward to.

Chapter Four

Fünfteichen

One early morning in December 1943 while it was still almost dark we left Markstadt forced labour camp. We were to be accommodated in a new camp in which we would have to submit ourselves to a new regime, the so-called concentration camp system.

Our route led us from the large factory area out to fallow land that stretched out for many kilometres ahead of us. Full of curiosity and fear we scanned the horizon for any buildings that might be our new accommodation and where our future destiny might lie. After a long march we stopped in front of an area that had been fenced off with barbed wire and was dominated by watchtowers, complete with searchlights and machine guns. In front of us lay a maze of barracks which altogether constituted the Concentration Camp Fünfteichen, a branch camp of Grossrosen Concentration Camp. The camp was very close to the railway. A passenger train made a deafening noise as it passed by us. The passengers were looking at us curiously. We turned towards the train which appeared to us to be part of another world. This picture of normality was in stark contrast to our own lives, which had been dragged down and fundamentally destroyed by daily torment. With whom could we share our misery, who really wanted to see it? The whole world was witness to our tragedy but remained silent, for us pitilessly silent.

We became more and more anxious about our future as the boundaries of the camp became clearer. We waited, full of gloomy premonitions, for confirmation of rumours of crematoria and gas chambers. In front of us lay the camp. On the other side, the unfenced railway line, our route to freedom, just a short step away and yet an abyss we could not hope to cross. We seethed with rage and indignation at our powerlessness. As we so often did in our despair, we asked ourselves, why don't the trains just blow up, why aren't the wells poisoned, why has the world not been demolished by plague and hunger? God had deserted and abandoned us. He had made a pact with the Devil who had sworn to exterminate us.

Our rebellious thoughts were interrupted by the bellowing, "March in step! Left, two, three four…" Together we marched through the gates. A group of Kapos and Block Elders came and stood on both sides of the column and yelled "Line up! Heads up! March in step!" When someone was not standing in line, they were kicked into place to give us a sample of our new regime. ss men appeared and counted us again. Rapport Führer Schrammel, who we later came to know as a bloodhound of an ss man, arrived while we were still standing in formation and commanded us, "Hats off! Hats on! Hats off! Hats on!…" Since we did not respond instantly and in unison we were ordered "Lie down! Roll on the ground! Get up!" We were driven forward by the Kapos and Block Elders. We had to wallow in the dirt. Those who failed to complete this "exercise" to total satisfaction were beaten. The ss compelled the Kapos to treat us as strictly as possible. Finally, we had to get up and once more the order resounded, "Hats off! Hats on!" We were threatened that this exercise might last for hours until every single one of us carried it out correctly.

There were some who were so frail they could barely stand up. They found this hours-long "exercise" very difficult and when the strain became too great they began to stagger and sway. This was the moment when the ss stormed at them and trampled some of them to death. Their bodies were pushed aside but remained in full view so that when we were counted nobody was missing.

Then the prisoners were ordered to give up their utensils and everything of value. Anyone failing to complete this demand would be shot on the spot. I had nothing to give up because I had entrusted all my things to Meister Hermann. However, others who did not have a hiding place for the belongings they had accumulated over time, from foreign workers and German civilians, had to give everything up, with a heavy heart. Some hurriedly scuffed the ground with their feet as they tried to bury their money in the hope of retrieving it later. Those who were caught were heavily beaten until they collapsed.

After we had been chased around the Appellplatz until midday we were told: "Take everything off, fold your clothes and put them in a pile". We were only allowed to keep our shoes and belts. We stood naked on the Appellplatz on this cold December day. There was a table around which a white circle had been drawn in chalk, and we had to march past it in single file. Here we had to give up our things and afterwards we were subjected to a humiliating body search. Then we were marched in double-quick time to the next table where a commission of ss men were seated. Among them was a doctor who inspected each and every one of us, but only superficially. We had to stand still for a few moments before walking to the next table where the decision who was and who was not fit for further work was made. All those whose final reserves of strength had been lost in the cement works in Markstadt looked as if they no longer had a single drop of blood, and there was no room for them in Fünfteichen. Several hundred of these unfortunates were written off and taken to a special block. Some of them who were then sent to Auschwitz and by extraordinary good fortune escaped with their lives spoke after the war about the final fate of these transports.

Those of us who passed this so-called medical selection were shoved to the next circle where the report-writer, a criminal from Grossrosen, sat at a table. We had to give him our names and we were each given a number. "From now on everyone must remember their number", he impressed on us. "Now you are only numbers, and if you forget your number then you will no longer exist." I became 24131, and I immediately learned it off by heart. Still naked, they chased us into a corner where amateur hairdressers were to shave us. These "hairdressers" were ordinary inmates who otherwise undertook normal work and for these additional duties wanted to earn a plate of soup.

It was their job to remove our head and body hair with implements they had made themselves. Most of us bled after this procedure. We were sprayed with disinfectant lotion. Then we were chased under the showers in the bathing area where we were rinsed under a stream of hot and cold water for a few moments. We were harried back to the exit. As we emerged two Kapos threw each of us a shirt, a jacket and trousers and urged us to dress quickly. Some of us were given trousers that were too long or too short and jackets that were too large or too small. But there was no time to swap things among ourselves. Immediately, we had to line up again in formation on the Appellplatz. So for a while we stood at attention struggling with ourselves to remain silent, fearing even to exchange a word with our neighbour. Those who could not refrain from exchanging comments with their comrades were mercilessly dragged from the line, beaten and trampled underfoot. As a deterrent, people who had not uttered a word were seized and forced to confess things of which they were not guilty. The unfortunates were hideously beaten in front of us as a warning to us all, to learn the new regime of the camp. In order to escape the attention of the Kapos some pushed to the rear or tried to make themselves small and inconspicuous. I was grateful that I was naturally small in stature so I did not have to look the Kapo in the eye. We all wanted to avoid being noticed and so give cause for "special treatment".

We were divided into groups of two hundred men and each placed in the charge of a Block Elder who led us to his quarters. We were brought by a Pole called Karol, the Block Elder of Block 5. He originated from Warsaw and had come from the camp of Grossrosen. When we reached his block he sent half of us to the right and the remainder to the left of the sleeping quarters. He appointed a room orderly for each dormitory. Our search for a plank that was favourably situated naturally caused a certain amount of noise. Immediately Karol and his helpers stormed into the room and wildly beat everyone in range of their sticks. "I will teach you, you sons-of-bitches, you criminals! Who the hell do you think you are? If I hear the merest whisper I will finish you all off!" he screamed angrily. Then he shouted over to the room orderly, "Bring me all those who do not remain silent if it gets noisy again. I will shut them up once and for all, and very quickly. There are too many of you anyway!"

They wanted volunteers to collect the soup kettle but we were so intimidated by Karol's "inaugural welcome", that we all wanted to avoid any contact with him. Then he suddenly bellowed, "I need ten men for the kettle". He chose ten from our ranks with shoves and blows. Then we had to stand around tables in the front room. He appointed a table elder who was made responsible for everyone at the table. He had to share out the bread and make sure that everyone collected their soup without noise or pushing. Karol apportioned the soup himself, hitting a few on the head with his ladle if their plate was not taken away quickly enough or if anyone peered into the kettle to see if the thick soup at the bottom had been reached. However, the content of the kettle at the bottom was never given out. The last few litres remained inside and were put to the side by the Block Elder's helpers. This nutritious remainder was shared out among the "prominenten" (i.e. the camp elite) and those who assisted the Block Elders. Sometimes they swapped this thick soup for cigarettes and other sought-after articles.

We newcomers were subject to curfew when we entered the block, and were permitted to step outside only with the prior permission of the Room Elder. Our Room Elder was a sadistic Ukrainian who would punch us in the face for no apparent reason. If we needed to go out we waited until there was small group of us and then we were led together to the latrine. The Room Elders chose a man who they trusted to hurry us along. I needed to go but I hesitated because some were falsely accused of going to the latrine twice, and were beaten. I hoped that eventually the Block and Room Elders would tire of bossing us around, but in vain. Afterwards, they put us in groups that had to clean the floor, tables and stools. While doing so, the workers chatted quietly, but this infuriated the Block Elder. Suddenly he grabbed a stool and hit out at us with it. With a single blow he simultaneously struck several prisoners because the table had not been properly cleaned. Blinded with rage, his assistants struck out at us and swore at us with utter contempt.

The day seemed endless. We yearned for the night to bring us respite. Until now, we had not found any time to reflect on our new circumstances. At least in Markstadt we had not been so near to death. Here it could confront us at any moment and in a really terrible way; one careless word was sufficient for us to be trampled and beaten to death. Whilst in Markstadt, where there were several thousand in the camp there were only a few men who were permitted to beat us. Here in one block of two hundred men, there was a gang of thugs at work. In despair, we asked ourselves, "How on earth could we stand it?" We were certain even hell could not be as bad as this.

We had no time for such thoughts. We could be kicked in the stomach or punched in the face at any moment. We had to steel ourselves internally if we were to survive this bitter battle for life and not prematurely die.

When in the evening we lay totally exhausted on our planks, the Block Elder Karol made a speech. "You must forget the life you have led until now. Now you are in a concentration camp. I am from Grossrosen Concentration Camp. There, Jews live for only fourteen days. Perhaps you will be able to live longer, but the only way you will leave here is through the crematorium chimney. You have not come here to live. Those who do not want to wait for death can choose the short path to the electric fence."

So we knew our lives were now reduced to barely existing and we just wished to fall asleep and never wake up….

In the morning, the following thoughts of death and final rest were interrupted by reality. With a screaming roar, "Get up!" we were driven off our planks. "Quickly, dust everything. Pick up the straw from the floor" was the command. We knew that we had to clean up every speck of dirt. If we left the tiniest untidiness we knew we would be severely punished. Then we were driven to the tables where we were given a black brew that was described with irony as coffee. Then a rapid sequence of events took place in a great hurry so that we could assemble for Appell on time. First, Karol carried out the block

Appell, to ascertain the exact total number of inmates, both dead and alive. As he did so, he lashed out in all directions, striking anyone in range. Then a sharp whistle called us to the general Appell. Rapport Führer Schrammel again exercised his importance and authority. He warned that anyone deviating from the column while marching would be shot on the spot. Anyone coming within three metres of the fence would get a bullet in the body. Then he tormented us with his cruel soul-destroying and favourite game, "Hats off! Hats On!..." Then he condemned us with the judgment, "It's not working!" Then, "Lie down! Get up!..." He was only satisfied when the slap of our caps on our uniform produced a single sharp sound. When he had finished maltreating us, newcomers were led back into Block Five because they had no work for us. I tried to use this breathing space to search for my acquaintance Otto Schwerdt in the hope that he could help me to change block. If I did not succeed in leaving Block Five in good time I would have to share the unavoidable destiny of those who had already been beaten to death. My plan to search was frustrated because I could not leave the block. Anyone who merely turned to the side was mercilessly beaten. In the block we suffered the same harassment we had experienced the previous day. I was removing a tabletop of broken glass when I noticed that Otto was standing outside the camp building window. I was so overwhelmed with joy that my first impulse was to instantly rush to the window to attract his attention but I tripped. I wanted to signal to him that I wanted him to get me out. (Otto was an experienced camp inmate who worked as a clerk in the factory. When I was an electrician and able to, I had done him a few favours, so he also helped me whenever he could.) Suddenly I felt a harsh blow from behind. My glasses flew from my face and when I bent down to retrieve them I received a second beating. I had no time to turn round because the Block Elder Karol took hold of me by the lapel of my jacket, pulled me to him with a single jolt began strangling me and suddenly shoved his elbow in my face. "What are you looking for out there, you criminal?" he screamed at me. I made a piteous remorseful face and remained silent.

My experience of more than three years of camp life had taught me that every answer would only add to the anger and sadistic lust of this criminal and then under no circumstances would he release his victim. My best strategy to avoid further beatings was not to give any answer. I received an almighty push and quickly ducked back into the tightly packed crowd and immediately recommenced my work.

When the work was being allocated, some were assigned to work in groups outside the camp. The remainder had to return to the barracks to polish the tables and stools that we had previously cleaned. I was in a group that had to dig an area sparsely covered with grass. Others had to move coarse gravel. It was endless work with no purpose.

The inmates had to fill the pockets of their jackets with stones and carry them to a certain spot. When one stone heap had been removed they had to start another pile and carry the stones back where they had started until a new heap was formed, and so it went on without interruption. As always, all conversation was forbidden and the Kapo made sure that no one interrupted their work to stretch their backs. The cycle of work and unthinking, repetitive movement made the inmates appear like beasts of burden.

In the evening we had to be deloused before we were chased onto our planks. At this procedure we had to get undressed and scrupulously examine our shirts for lice for fifteen minutes. We were warned that if a single louse was found we would receive fifty lashes on our bare bottoms, so with considerable trepidation we meticulously searched. After a quarter of an hour we were asked if we had finished, and on Karol's orders we had to respond with a loud "jawohl". It was his stipulated "request" that we must respond to all his questions and orders with a loud "jawohl". We always hoped that this concluded the tortures of the day and at long last we could get some rest on our planks. However, Karol prolonged the delousing procedure with a few extra tortures he invented himself. He grabbed a few exhausted older men from our group and checked if they had obeyed his instructions with the precision he insisted on. Of course he easily found a few more lice because this pest is quick. Karol showed off his great catch triumphantly and instantly ordered that these unfortunates should be laid across the stool. Then he began to beat his victim with the narrow edge of a wooden board taken from one of the bunks. In his rage he also struck the spine and kidneys. Sometimes the victim was beyond screaming and we heard his final death rattle. The maltreated returned to us covered in blood, but his life had actually ended because of the beating he received on the stool. The following morning they would be grossly swollen and could hardly walk. The only way for them was to the sick bay from which they never returned[1].

As we lay on our planks we felt really depressed, and yearned for the morning when we would be led out to work on the building site. We looked forward to the day to escape the curses, degradation and beatings of this hell.

Our hope of escaping to work proved false. We were detained in the camp for a few more days. Whenever we went outside we were in a state of panic because they continuously chased us like trained dogs round the exercise yard. Whenever we saw an SS man we tried to make ourselves invisible. However, sometimes a meeting with our torturers was inevitable. Then we had to remove our hats and stand at attention, and remain so until either the SS man dismissed us with a merciful wink or disappeared from view.

If, in his opinion, we did not stand straight enough he would "help" us with kicks and blows. It was just as dangerous to bump into a Kapo or Block Elder when there was a curfew. One inmate was beaten because, apparently, he walked too quickly and he had committed some offence. The questioning was always cynical, "What's the hurry?" They never waited for an answer, instead just a hail of blows. Others would be singled out because they did not move quickly enough.

The pointlessness of many of the orders issued by those who ran the camp demonstrated their malice; they could only be the product

---

1. The sick bay consisted of a barrack block with a criminal in charge. He had doctors and medical orderlies from among the prisoners at his disposal. Only those with a high temperature were admitted. If the thermometer did not quickly reach a high enough temperature the sick were sent back. The chance or recovery was very limited. The medication was inadequate and the treatment was mostly rough or even ruthless. Dr. Zabranny was reputed to be especially cruel. Immediately after the war he was condemned to life-long imprisonment by the Polish Court for his inhumane behaviour.

of sadistic minds. The subtlety of the regulations and the constant tensions they evoked seemed deliberately calculated to destroy both body and soul. Unfortunately for many, this goal was achieved. When their will to live was broken, they gave in to apathy and finally they bore the features of a "Muselmann". Among those who fitted that description were some who came from our home town.

Many others and I possessed the will to continue living. Even today, this utterly inexplicable will to live still seems unbelievable to me and cannot be analysed. Our spirit of resistance enabled us to continue existing in a concentration camp despite being enveloped in senseless brutality and tortures where human beings were corrupted and died in humility and amidst degradation. An inexplicable instinct enabled us to recognise danger from afar and conditioned us to be constantly vigilant day and night, to patiently await the morning, and not to give in.

Morning broke with the shrieking and noise to which we had become accustomed. Regularly I did not even hear the morning command "Aufstehen!" (Get Up!) because my young body craved sleep. I was finally torn from my slumbers by the clatter of my comrades dressing and finding their way around in the dark and narrow confines of the room. Haste and lack of space made everything difficult. Sometimes in our hurry, people would put their shoes on a neighbour's plank. They were reproached for this nuisance and told not to dirty the space. It would take precious extra time to clean up, and people dreaded this might make them late for Appell. Even worse, if any dirt was discovered, one could be certain of receiving a beating. The list of such small infractions that sometimes led to serious consequences was endless. Nearly every morning someone would shout out that their shoes had been stolen. Good shoes were a desirable commodity. Those who had bad shoes would wait for the opportunity to take a better pair from their comrades. Those whose shoes were stolen had to make do with whatever pair was left in the block. Often they were either too big or too small. There was no opportunity to exchange them during the early morning before Appell. For ordinary inmates the clothes store was only open after the evening Appell. Our shoes were so important to us. We were especially afraid of the torture of having to work all day in shoes that did not fit. If our heels were rubbed raw or we got blisters on our feet it became impossible for us to march in step and remain at the required distance from one another. The slightest deviation from perfect order was sufficient to attract the attention of the Kapo. The smallest injury could easily become infected. Since we were on our feet from early morning till late at night and we had to rush about all the time, a small poor-healing wound could soon become a major problem. So we all knew how important it was to guard our shoes like treasure and ensure that we did not injure our feet. Sometimes it was possible to take a dying person's shoes and later swap them for an extra ration of soup or bread.

Every morning we had a sinking feeling of another day to be endured. Every day it was the same monotonous noise and rush. The sound of my room-mates shuffling feet as they dressed would wake me, and, drowsy with sleep, I rose from my plank. Like all the others, I soon succumbed to a permanent condition of nervously rushing about. We all knew every moment was precious; every missed minute would lead to punishment. Finally, one day we heard that we would be moved out to work. We were all very relieved. Even if it was only for a few hours, at least we would be outside the camp. We would be free of Karol's clutches and the dismal, hopeless atmosphere of the camp.

I desperately hoped to be reunited with Meister Hermann, so that at long last I could talk again freely as one human being to another, and be comforted. He, who I so respected and who so empathised with my plight. I was desperate to tell him the truth of the conditions in Fünfteichen: the terrible atmosphere in which we were forced to exist, an atmosphere in which sadistic torture and beating to death was just part of the normal daily routine and in which it was possible to be attacked in any circumstances.

That morning, Appell took a long time because many of those who worked for various construction firms were now allocated different jobs. Many were assigned to work for Krupp. Their factories were already fully equipped and all they lacked was a workforce. These factories worked day and night, and our camp had to provide two twelve-hour shifts. Until then I had worked for Schallhorn as an apprentice electrician, but I had to leave them and report for work to the firm Krupp. And so my hopes to work again with Meister Hermann were finally dashed. I had lost a helpful friend who had not only fed and protected me, but had also given me the feeling that I was a human being and an equal partner. The way he behaved towards me gave me self-confidence and strengthened my will to live. This prevented me, unlike many of my comrades, from sinking to the level of an apathetic animal and committing unspeakable acts. I had often witnessed how constant fear of ill-treatment had degenerated into indifference to evil, and into a condition in which sympathy for oneself and others was completely lost, in which a person became a vegetating creature devoid of any human characteristics. Our oppressors were intent on extinguishing our human spirit and trampling on our human dignity.

When I finally reconciled myself to being separated from my former meister, it was as if the ground had been taken from under my feet, and I did not know how I would be able to bear the burdens which lay so heavily on my soul. Could I cope without Hermann for long? Only after a long internal battle was I able to force myself to confront my new disgusting circumstances as best I could. The past three years of imprisonment had hardened me so much and sharpened my instincts that I managed to adapt myself again and again in a relatively short time. However, I do not want to do an injustice to my comrades who could not manage to adapt themselves so easily to their change of situation. For one and a half years I had the good fortune to live and work under the shadow of a good person while my comrades at the same time were often beaten and laboured under an iron rod of bad-tempered, often dangerous Kapos. Little wonder that under this regime they were emaciated, had become like skeletons, and were incapable of any kind of spiritual uplift. In marked contrast, my relatively good physical constitution enabled me to calmly contemplate my new situation and I comforted myself with the thought that, "I will not have to endure these circumstances much longer. The bloody regime must sometime come to an end."

In actual fact in the camp we heard all sorts of rumours that the German armies were in hasty retreat on all fronts. These stories sounded wonderful to us and we hoped that we, the only Jews remaining in the concentration camp, would not be exterminated. There were even wild rumours that the Red Cross would try hard to take us under their wing.

We had heard similar rumours in the past but this time they seemed even more real. Even though they had little or no foundation in fact, we were eager to believe them. Like a recurring mirage in the desert, we time and time again embraced the same old illusion of a miraculous liberation that helped us momentarily to forget the present.

Sometimes we found joy in our fantasies of refuge in peaceful Swiss towns or our reception in other neutral countries. We dreamt of people welcoming us with sympathy and love, and supporting us as we tried to heal the wounds inflicted upon us during the years of repression and slavery.

Now I marched with an unfamiliar group, with comrades I had never met, to an uncertain workplace, my head filled with confusing dreams. To our right and left marched ss people, their guns cocked and ready to shoot. Many were accompanied by wolfhounds who, on the command of their masters, fell on us and tore off our clothes together with pieces of skin and flesh. However, I would not and could not believe that this oppressive presence was our ultimate destiny.

We arrived at Krupp and I was assigned to the group that supervised the electrical installations in Hall 4. Our job was to ensure that the electric cables worked efficiently. The man in charge, a certain Schmidt, was a master-electrician from Essen. His deputy was called Krumbach, he came from area of the Ruhr. Schmidt wore his Party emblem with pride and busied himself in pursuit of Party doctrine. In marked contrast, his deputy Krumbach made jokes about the Führer and the Party, and treated us very decently.

Another comrade was assigned to work with me. The group also included a number of other "free" foreign workers – 4 Czechs and 2 French. I was assigned to a Czech foreman and we were responsible for the lights on the ceiling and in the corridors. Since I could speak Polish, I was able to quickly and easily acquire a smattering of broken Czech. Of course, I always tried hard to comply with the wishes of my foreman. As a Czech, he could still obtain sufficient grocery, and, in addition, he was free to return home every eight or fourteen days. He was even able to barter and thus get hold of an adequate supply of food. At lunchtime, my Czech colleague allowed me to collect his soup which he "generously" left for me. In great comfort, he unpacked his bread and nourishing bacon and spread them out before him, not allowing himself to be disturbed by my hungry eyes. Of course I was happy to have the warm soup, but I was irritated by the sight of the crispy farmhouse bread and the thick slices of ham. I hoped that I would be invited to share this meal. I expected this kind of behaviour from anyone who was a member of the Czech nation, who, after all, also suffered under the occupation. However, his cold, indifferent demeanour forbade this contact. He revealed his complete disinterest in me by the haughty way that he gave me my instructions and because he pushed towards me only that which he did not want to eat himself. He regarded me as the lowest of the low because I was a Jew. He was a primitive person. This revealed itself in his superstitious Catholic mannerism, making the sign of the cross at every opportunity in an attempt to deflect troubling thoughts or to ward off temptation. It was impossible to converse with him as one human being to another. I knew he was strictly orthodox and I often tried shyly to ask him theological questions. These fell on deaf ears and from his reaction it was clear to me that he thought our persecution and misery were acts of God. Although he did not actually condone our maltreatment, this was as far as his Christian neighbourly love extended. He even thought of the killing of a pig as a visible intervention by God. He was a stranger to genuinely Christian behaviour. He felt absolutely no sense of duty or obligation to help his fellow man, or to stand by a sick, weak or hungry person, in short, to love his fellow-man.

In the evenings, when we finished work, I marched in my group back to camp. My comrades were mainly "old hands", people who had been sent to Fünfteichen before me. They had all come from Auschwitz. Most of them were skin and bone, and in hardly any condition to keep up with the tempo of our march. They limped and stumbled as they tried to march. I discovered the truth of what was happening in Auschwitz from their conversation.

As I marched back in the evening I was stunned by what I heard was happening in Auschwitz. My thoughts constantly focussed on the same question, "who from my family might still be alive? Maybe my father, or both my sisters who would now be sixteen and eighteen years old? And what had happened to my little brother who would now be only fourteen? Had he been allowed to live or had they murdered him?" I could not bear to think about my mother. I was dominated by the sobering thought, who of all of them had the best chance to save their lives? "Who like me was just marching on a country road guarded by the ss and their trained dogs? If they were really still alive were they still recognisable as people or were they already nearer to death than to life? Had they found helpful people as I had, or had they been irretrievably delivered to the mercy of their torturers?"

We were driven on by shouts and screams, "Move yourselves, left, two, three, four." At long last we passed through the camp gate, and we were counted as we did so. The Block Elders did not hesitate; they beat us brutally as they tried to instill order as they forced us to line up in groups on the Appellplatz. Some comrades sank exhausted to the ground and did not respond even when they were beaten. They had given up their fight for life. Even so, they also had to be accounted for too. We had three different Camp Elders. The man responsible for supervising the count and the Camp Leader Number One then appeared in unique, grotesque, eccentric, absurd uniforms. With military precision he then announced to the Report Leader the number of prisoners standing and the number of sick in the sick quarters. Following that, everyone was carefully checked once more by the ss Block Leaders, after which our group was returned to our block. We were not led there by Block Elder Karol of Block Five, instead the Czech Watzlaw of Block Three took over. As I heard his screams I asked myself if he was a murderer like Karol. We tried to read his character from his facial features and we were reassured that he did not share Karol's sadistic nature. Unlike the previous day in Block Five, only a few of us were beaten when the food was distributed. So here was at least one thing that had changed for the better. After eating, we were allowed to leave the block. I immediately left in search of my uncle and friends. Uncle Leon was in a group that peeled potatoes.

When I appeared, he welcomed me with a kiss on my forehead and immediately pushed some potatoes towards me which he had saved for me. I was grateful that I had been able to improve his circumstances, albeit only slightly. He was no longer forced to work for Grün & Bilfinger. In the long term he did not have the strength to endure the twelve hour shift, not to mention the terrible food and the harsh regime. I also met a few friends who worked as stokers in the kitchens or bathhouse. I was encouraged and drew strength from their friendship as I returned to my block. As I returned, I was horrified to see an inmate being beaten with a board by an elder. I immediately crept to the sleeping quarters. The unpleasant procedure of delousing was followed by the long-yearned-for order, "Lights out!" It was the signal for us to fall asleep on our planks.

I had lost contact with Meister Hermann so I tried to make contact with him through acquaintances who still worked at Schallhorn. Hermann knew that I worked in hall 4 and could not leave because the exits were guarded by the SS. Despite the fact that it was dangerous for him to do so, he visited me a few times. Although I was very attached to him, I had to come to terms with the fact that we were now firmly separated. He gave me to understand that in the unlikely event of some shattering occurrence or revolution that might end the war (we hoped a revolution or some other event would end the war) I could still count on his help. The parcel that contained my civil clothes and underwear was still hidden in his hut. This also concealed the false passport with which I hoped to cross the border if I was able to escape.

However, I now had to get back to reality and concentrate all my efforts on my work in hall 4. I had to grasp every opportunity to improve and secure my situation. I had some freedom of movement and in the stores I was permitted to complete requisitions for electrical equipment and spare parts for machinery. Despite language difficulties I got on well with the French who worked in the electricians' commando. Every morning I would greet them with the words, "Vive La France," and they responded, "Vivent les Juifs". With that they even dared to show with their fingers the famous "V" for victory sign. This certainly added a little to my self-confidence, my inner peace returned, and I was full of confidence that I would survive here too.

My comrades and the Kapos liked to "visit" me because I was permitted without supervision to draw electrical equipment from the stores. It was 1944 and by this time electrical goods were a scarce commodity. Time and time again I was handed "orders" requesting electrical equipment, especially by the Kapos. At first, I was anxious about stealing these sought-after items, but very quickly I set aside these doubts. When, for example, I did not quickly deliver to Kapo Wilhelm the things he had demanded, he took me aside and searched me. There were some things that, as an inmate, I was forbidden to have in my possession, and he found them. He did not beat me but he strongly advised me that it would be in my own best interests to comply with his demands, otherwise he would report me to the ss for being in possession of contraband. So, in order to placate the Kapo, I began to steal unbelievable quantities of electrical equipment. I was also approached by the ss, who presented their own demands. Some rewarded me with bread, others only with their "honour". They believed it was sufficient that they had lowered themselves by accepting stolen valuable war material, and even more so, from a Jew.

As time went by my ss "clientèle" became more and more greedy. They pressed their demands for rubber cables and electrical equipment with increasing urgency. They bartered these contraband goods with farmers who lived in the neighbourhood, and typically would receive bacon and home brewed spirits in exchange. Although they were provided with canteens for coffee, these were almost always filled with spirits, and they stunk of drink from a distance.

There was one order that was so outrageous it caused me a great deal of anxiety. An ss Block Leader demanded a large motor he wanted to barter with a farmer. I discussed how this might be "organised" with a Kapo who said he was willing to help me. The first thing I did was to busy myself with the ceiling light and pretend to the storeroom attendant that I had more work to do. I took advantage of his absence and removed a motor when he had to leave the room for a few moments. With a great deal of effort I was able to conceal the motor under a big lathe. There remained the challenge of how to get the motor out of the machine hall, in itself no mean task when one took into consideration how closely the factory security service watched over the workforce; however we were the exception only because we were under the supervision of the ss. But even the ss was closely watched because it had become known that they too were interested in "scarce commodities" and had already successfully "organised" some items.

A few kettles of soup were brought into the camp and distributed among us at lunchtime. What I had in mind was to hide the motor inside a kettle when they were returned to the camp. Obviously I could only do that during the lunch break when everyone was eating. The Kapo helped me by keeping "guard" and so we hid the heavy motor in a kettle. It found its way back into the camp in its unusual casing.

However, the camp management and ss needed other supplies besides electrical equipment and we were expected to "organise" them. They sought out a few experienced inmates to act as middlemen. A young Hungarian called Miklosz worked alongside us in Hall 4. There was nothing he could not get hold of. Miklosz promised to obtain a transmission belt for the Kapos and ss. The transmission belt consisted of a leather band a few metres long. It was essential for the operation of various machines. Once again the question of finding the ideal hiding place arose because as soon as such an object went missing they would search everywhere for it. My job was to find a hiding place for it.

In the basement of the hall there was ducting for electric cables and other purposes. So I suggested that the stolen band be hidden in a distribution cables cupboard. During the lunch break, when the machine was stationary, we set to work. Miklosz cut through the band and pushed it through the ducting while I waited at the other end to hide it in the distribution cupboard. When the lunch break ended and the machines should have started again the machine-minder noticed that his machines were idle and the band had disappeared. There was great alarm in the hall. Work was stopped. All inmates had to stand to attention and the ss began their search. The theft of a drive belt was regarded as an act of gross sabotage. The factory security service threatened that ten of us would be hanged if they found we had any suspicious material on us. We were strongly urged to confess our theft, in which case we would be subjected to a less severe punishment. I glanced across to Miklosz furtively. He stood there calmly and unmoved as he observed the ss man rushing around and signalling that we should be searched.

Since the security alarm had been activated we had to conceal the band for much longer than we had originally intended. Later Miklosz obtained a sharp knife and used it to cut the leather into strips that could be used to make soles for shoes. The ss man and the Kapo took most of this leather for themselves, and I also received a piece that I could barter. After a few days the Kapo called me over to his table where he sat with the ss Block Leader. They complimented me on my organisational skills and the resourcefulness I had shown in finding a hiding place for the band. The ss man turned towards me, opened his canteen and poured some schnapps into a cup. "Have a drink", he said. So for the first time in a very long time I drank schnapps and ate the salami sandwiches that the ss man also gave me. An ironic question of our relative rank then occurred to me: were we of equal standing so long as we were involved in thieving and drinking schnapps?

This incident strengthened my position, even though my official "status" remained unchanged. I was allowed to move freely about the hall, to talk to others, and occasionally allowed an hour off to rest or sleep. I would climb into the cab of one of the cranes in the hall and disconnect the electric cable when I wanted to sleep without being disturbed. There was one occasion when quite by chance a crane was needed but I had fallen into a deep sleep. They searched for me and called my name but I heard nothing. The foreman of the electricians' commando climbed into another crane to look for me. He quickly discovered me in my hiding place. He rudely woke me from my sleep. He immediately took me to the ss guard and Kapo and informed them of my offence.

On the way to the ss guard and Kapo, he could not contain his rage. He kicked me with his boots and screamed, "You dammed Jew! You lazy dog!" He swore at me, but strangely continued to address me respectfully as "Sie", not the contemptuous "Du". Clearly he had the benefit of a genteel upbringing and could not quite bring himself to address a stranger as "Du".

The ss man and Kapo heard his report but did not pass it on. Thankfully they felt they were obligated to me and I was therefore spared the beating that would otherwise have been my due. The master electrician threw me out of his commando and I was transferred to the commando that was responsible for cleaning the halls. He also told the foreman of the cleaning commando to keep a special eye on me.

Fortunately for me the Kapo of the cleaning commando was Abram Hellmann, a young lad who then was not twenty years old. He was a distant relative of mine and he had already spent a few years in camps, so, like me, he already had the benefit of a thorough camp education. He had already learned to behave like other Kapos, oppressing the weak ones with unpleasant duties. When he could, he would favour the stronger ones, giving them lighter duties and allowing them breaks so they could keep warm. He was a total arse-licker to all his superiors. He had quickly and certainly grasped the essentials of how to survive in such a "community", and after working for a short period as assistant to a Kapo he was promoted to a full Kapo in his own right.

He was visibly pleased with himself when he was put in charge of me. Immediately he gave me special duty: namely to supervise a small group of prisoners whose work consisted of collecting the large quantities of steel waste produced when the barrels of cannon were machined. I had to ensure that the speed of production was maintained and the whole process ran smoothly. Inevitably Hellmann and I had our differences. On one occasion he instructed me to choose a group from his commando to unload wagons: that meant he very generously put at my disposal those prisoners he considered were suitable for this task. This selection was conducted in accordance with the usual tried-and-tested camp procedure: whenever prisoners were transferred from one commando to another, it was always the weakest and the most unsuitable who were chosen. So, in this case, Hellmann also chose the poorest performers, mainly Hungarian Jews who were far less capable of withstanding the physical and psychological burdens of camp life and who quickly became dishevelled and frail. Until a few months ago, these Hungarians had a comfortable life; many of them had been respected academics in their home towns. Now they were completely helpless in the face of their new circumstances. They could not adapt to the conditions of "life" in a concentration camp, unlike those of us who had already been interned for so long. Moreover, many of them made themselves unpopular because they did not understand how to conduct themselves in the camp. They wore crosses and Madonnas visible at the neck in the hope that this ostentatious display of Christian symbolism would win them preferential treatment, a disastrous error which only incurred the suspicion and contempt of other inmates. Their clumsiness, like their poor adjustment to difficult situations, often reduced them to figures of ridicule rather than evoking our sympathy. They were ruthlessly allocated to the heaviest work.

When Hellmann began choosing these poor weakened figures to unload wagons I protested at his "selection". I suggested that he take strong people because those who were weak would soon end up as "Muselmänner" in the sick bay. Hellmann vehemently contradicted me and when I did not immediately submit to his demands he gave me to understand he would denounce me to his friend the Camp Elder and I would be transferred to the punishment commando. So once again I was exposed to the merciless regime of existence in the concentration camp system. In order to save our own skin we had to learn to be silent to every injustice and had to avoid the risk of punishment, even for unforeseen accidents. This severe self-discipline also obliged us to refrain from irritating or contradicting our superiors.

A few days later, when we were due to depart, one of the junior Kapos failed to appear. I was appointed in his place by the

"Oberkapo" (senior Kapo). I was allocated a group of eighteen Hungarian Jews. They had to unload several wagons of iron bars. Among this group was a young man who had been a member of the same Zionist organisation to which I had also belonged. I was very keen to find out from him what was happening in the "free world" because for more than three years I had been forced to rely on rumours, but these distorted everything, whereas my new Hungarian friend had only been deported a few weeks ago. We had an animated conversation[2]. Most of the group seized the moment to absent themselves from the work site and organise a little food or a few cigarettes. Those who remained moved idly and sluggishly around the wagons. Unfortunately, all this was observed by an ss Block Leader who happened to be on a tour of inspection. Suddenly I heard a bellowing voice, "Where is the Kapo?" I tore myself away from this conversation. I immediately assumed a military posture and marched in the regulatory manner towards the ss man. In a curt military voice I reported, "Eighteen inmates for unloading wagons!" Whenever called upon to do so we were obliged to give the exact total of inmates and a precise description of their work. "Quickly assemble, group!" came the immediate order of the ss Block Leader. I tried to line up the group and then I had to count them. To my horror I discovered that only twelve of the eighteen were standing in line. "False report!" screamed the ss Block Leader. He struck my head so hard that my hat fell to the ground. "Where is the Oberkapo?" he screamed. Oberkapo Helmut duly arrived in great haste. Then I had to search out those who were missing. Finally, when they were all present the ss Block Leader ordered the Oberkapo to punish me for neglecting my supervision duties, so I received twenty-five lashes on my naked backside. Helmut, who would like to have spared me, was forced to march me to the toilet in the presence of the ss man. The doors of the toilets were all closed and locked so that the civil workers would not hear my screams. When the few civilians who were working in the vicinity of the toilets saw our small group approach, they recognised the

---

2. My Hungarian-speaking friend survived and at the time of writing (1967) was Chairman of the Concentration Camp Invalid Association in Tel Aviv.

"important gentleman" (i.e. the Block Leader) and cast compassionate glances in my direction. The all too familiar routine began when we arrived in the toilets: under the supervision of the ss Block Leader. I had to bend over, the Oberkapo began to beat me with a rubber truncheon, counting each blow out loud. The first few blows were brutal and the pain was terrible, but the next few were more merciful. As he counted, Helmut shouted loudly and over the noise of the beating in order to deceive the ss man of their force. I also continued to scream loudly. After that we were ordered back to work, but this time at the very fast pace set by the Block Leader. With my truncheon I was compelled to urge on all those who failed to keep up. This "work" left me with a very bitter taste and I felt troubled for a long time after as I remembered the day when I was forced to act like a Kapo. Not only did my body have to bear the consequences, I could not get out of my mind the indelible, hateful memory of the hours when I was forced to oppress my comrades.

As I worked on the waste collection commando the weeks passed quickly. Then I returned to the electricians' commando where I resumed my former duties as an electrician. Even though we had to work very long hours and the march to and from work was also long, the time seemed to fly by. As we marched back to the camp from work each day we shuddered at the unbearable prospect of returning to the camp, even though we were there for a relatively short period of time. These few hours were filled with countless unpredictable, absurd and monstrous events, with the inevitable result that we were in a state of constant anxiety. The Lagerkapo (Camp Kapo) was a "model" of atrocious cruelty. He was a natural sadist, who was brutal at the slightest offence. With his truncheon, he would ruthlessly beat anyone who failed to meticulously follow the minutiae of camp regulations to the point that they had to be taken to the so-called sick bay. Such was his lust for blood, that his victims did not receive any help or care; instead they were abandoned to a quick and deadly fate. He wished for a quick transformation from life to death. They did not waste medication or medical care on anyone who was no longer capable of work. That is why all those who could barely walk or stand avoided the sick bay at all costs. It was an open secret that most patients left the sick bay dead. Only a few patients who enjoyed special protection received medical care or treatment by the medical orderly.

This "education through beatings" struck most cruelly those inmates who were so weakened they were no longer able to focus all their attention on the complicated details of camp routine. It was almost impossible for these people to control their bodies. They were incapable of complying with specific rules of personal hygiene, and this attracted the attention of the Kapos. They would instantly resort to their truncheons if we failed to comply with their insistence upon cleanliness throughout the camp.

We thought that our Block Elders were expected to achieve a weekly quota of at least ten dead prisoners. We had no doubt about the correctness of this claim. The evidence was irrefutable. However, we could never discover whether this was part of a planned process of destruction or merely the initiative of the local camp leadership, i.e. the Kapos. In any case, it would have made little difference to us even if we had known the origin of these measures. Resistance was impossible; all we could do was to continuously strive to avoid the worst of the slavery torture that lay in wait for new victims.

In this camp we had to take the greatest care to avoid being beaten, and it was equally difficult for us to "organise" additional supplies of food. It was always a big risk to get involved in bartering; we did so only when our hunger became unbearable.

Without an extra ration of bread and a few potatoes we could not survive; occasionally we managed to barter for these precious essentials of life. Some of us had the misfortune to be caught with a few raw potatoes or carrots; for a while they were struck a few well-aimed blows which were accompanied by the cynical question, "Do you understand why you are being beaten?" When the beaten one replied, "Because I organised potatoes", he would receive further blows and a stern lecture, "No, you are being beaten because you allowed yourself to be caught".

As always and everywhere, the "Muselmen" were easy prey for the Kapos. Their attention span was such that they could only just grasp the imperatives of the moment. When they felt severe hunger they were no longer capable of taking any precautions that might otherwise ensure their survival when stealing a few morsels of bread. They no longer cared and were completely indifferent to the consequences of their actions. Their senses and responses had become so dulled that they no longer appeared to show any fear of being beaten. For the others, who had not yet reached this apathetic vegetative state, the images of beatings had such an impact that it severely inhibited their ability to "organise". An unforgettable impression was etched into the memory of all those who witnessed the punishment inflicted on a starving prisoner for devouring a bit of raw potato or cutting up a camp blanket to bandage their sore feet. These pitiful people were shown no compassion or mercy, very often they were just beaten or trampled to death on the spot.

Those still capable of work who were caught pilfering were dealt with in a different way. They were sent to the "Strafkommando" (Punishment Commando), which was commonly known by the abbreviation "SK" and the Camp Kapo who had the reputation of being a notorious criminal. The Camp Kapo had come from Grossrosen concentration camp. He had won for himself a reputation as a genius for inflicting sadistic torture. Poor camp nutrition and housing, freezing winters and numerous sources of infection caused frequent gastric illnesses. Many inmates suffered with diarrhoea. Many were overcome with stomach cramps while standing during the long Appells. We were strictly forbidden by camp regulations from absenting ourselves from Appell. Those who were sick had either to soil themselves, or, despite the ban, to run to the latrines and hide themselves until Appell was completed. Breaching the regulation made a great deal of sense because we were all afraid to soil ourselves and our clothes. We never had a change of clothing, so what we wore was literally irreplaceable. Despite the fear of punishment, some prisoners dared to absent themselves from the Appellplatz, and sometimes they were caught. They were dealt with by the Camp Kapos who would inflict their personally preferred torture on any prisoner discovered in the latrine during Appell. First he would give his victim a few kicks in the stomach until he lay doubled up on the ground, then he would stamp his heel on the head a few times. Finally, when they lay on the ground unconscious, he placed the handle of his favourite shovel across the neck of his victim and stood on both ends until there was no more sign of life was extinct. If this occurred in the vicinity of the bathhouse the Kapo would pull his victim inside, stuff the end of a hosepipe into the victim's mouth, and pump him full of water until he drowned.

So the Camp Kapo made sure that the lorry that came every week to collect corpses to be cremated in the main camp at Grossrosen was fully laden. Those of us who managed, by some miracle, to apprehend the danger that threatened us all at any time had a permanent fear of falling into the hands of that particular murderer. What was truly remarkable was that some of us had an apparently innate instinct that enabled us to sense his closeness, and to flee. I also did everything I could to ensure I did not attract the attention of that particular Kapo. Even now, to this day, I continue to be plagued by nightmares and haunted by these awful memories of being persecuted by this Kapo. Many Block Elders, who at first treated the inmates fairly, were corrupted by his devilish example. Such was the impact of this brutal violence they no longer had any inhibitions. Their moral scruples were by this time entirely forfeit.

We had personal contact with members of the ss because some of them used us as middlemen for their bartering. Around this time, news reached us, in part from some of the ss, of an uprising in Auschwitz concentration camp. It was clear that this was a source of anxiety for the ss. However, we had no other means to determine the accuracy of these conflicting rumours.

At the end of July, after a delay, news reached us of the failed attempt to assassinate Hitler. It really seemed to us that the fates were conspiring against us and shielded the evil dictator and his henchmen. After the initial excitement had abated, and our disappointment that the defeat of the forces of good had passed, we came to realise that we still had reason to hope. We could believe that eventually the Nazi regime would be eliminated because opposition to it had been able to establish itself in the highest echelons of its leadership.

The first month of our stay in Fünfteichen concentration camp claimed many victims, creating space for transports that continued to arrive. A new batch of Poles who had been captured during the

Warsaw Uprising arrived in the summer of 1944. They were members of the Polish underground who had fought under the leadership of General Bor-Komorowski. A prisoner from this transport slept on the plank directly above me. My new companion was an intelligent boy from Krakow. We became friends. I enlightened him about the complex conditions of camp life which at first glance defied any logical explanation. I drew much comfort from this encounter. It was in marked contrast to many Poles who had been transferred from Grossrosen to Fünfteichen. It was their bestial behaviour that convinced me that most Poles had chosen to become accomplices of the despotic national socialist ways of the ss in the process of our destruction. However, I was relieved to discover that this was a misleading generalisation. The fighters of the Polish underground did not fight on the side of the conquerors. They belonged to that large majority of Poles who hated this oppression and forcibly rebelled against it. They had felt compelled to totally commit themselves to years of underground resistance. They were united by a strong sense of comradeship that enabled them to commit themselves to a trail of strength with the apparatus of destruction of the ss. I had been able to glean from Hungarian prisoners a very limited understanding about the incredible events that had taken place in the outside world during the three years of my incarceration. I was finally able to confirm my understanding of these events in conversations with many Poles. I heard about the economic and political conditions that prevailed in occupied Poland and the assumptions the outside world had made about the concentration camps.

Everything they (i.e. the Poles) had previously known paled into insignificance as they had to come to terms with the stark reality of the concentration camps. Soon after these Poles had been inducted into camp life, they frequently acknowledged their preference to continue to engage in a hopeless battle and death with a bayonet in their hands rather than to succumb to this existence.

My neighbour enquired about my personal experiences and impressions of the years I had been imprisoned. He also shared with me an account of the bestiality with which the Nazis had liquidated the Warsaw Ghetto. Polish members of the Underground movement were well-informed by foreign radio stations and press about the aim of the National Socialists (i.e. Nazis) to encompass "the Final Solution of the Jewish Question", which was to bring about the physical destruction of our people.

Whoever had to fight to sustain their life could not know for how long they would have to battle, nor could they know whether their sacrifice and struggle would ultimately prove futile. Every danger and risk seemed insignificant because there was no hope of a positive outcome. As we witnessed the ultimate destiny of so many, so we, the persecuted ones, resorted to the most astonishing strategies to maintain our lives, even for a limited period.

My Polish friend told me how young people had been affected by the occupation. He said that the general morale was low because of the foreign rule and associated corruption. In the new chaos some youth found that their traditional morals and values were superfluous, and they had to adapt to a new and permissive immorality. I told him of the strict moral standards my parents had taught me and that they would never have tolerated the kind of behaviour he had just related to me. My neighbour commented on my lack of experience and commiserated with me because I had been denied the experiences that he thought should be an integral part of every fulfilled life. His words had a tremendous impact on me and I thought about them at great length. Time and time again I asked myself whether it really made any sense to fight for the continuation of this life. In the eyes of this friend, I could see he had already concluded I was already condemned to die. According to him there was not the slightest hope we could escape this hell alive. We knew that the ultimate conclusion of our suffering would be in the extermination camps where millions had already been murdered.

Although it was forbidden, many of the camp personnel, Block Elders and Kapos had girlfriends among the women and assistants who worked in the ss laundry. This was silently tolerated, particularly because a few ss people and camp leaders imposed themselves on Jewish girls. In Fünfteichen concentration camp contact with women was impossible. Some camp personnel were favoured because they lived separate from the other inmates in another part of the camp in a block that was comparatively well-equipped. It was not always occupied because the personnel worked in shifts in the kitchen, bath area, etc. The shower room was at the disposal of the night shift when they returned each morning from their work. There was nothing to obstruct contact among the men in the showers or the sparsely-occupied dormitories. Homosexuals were able to pursue their inclinations without being disturbed. I learned about this from some of the inmates who enjoyed a comparatively more favourable position in the camp. They chose young boys from among the inmates and allocated them to positions in the camp that secured for them a tolerable life. Some of the Camp Elders had favourites who had been appointed to these posts in this way. It was only in the grounds of the factory and very rarely that we caught sight of a woman. Sometimes the inmates resorted to curious ways and detours in order to approach a woman with being disturbed. This is how I came to witness one episode of lovemaking. A Kapo from our hall who was a gypsy made a rendez-vous with a Belgian girl. He took her into the ducting for electric cables that was located beneath the factory floor. Here he confided his secret to me and asked me to stand guard at the entrance to the ducting. If anyone approached I was to quickly switch the light on and off. All went extremely well. Occasionally he would use me as an intermediary to give the girl parcels of bread in gratitude.

There were only a few such brief, "private" moments. Of course most inmates did not give a moment's thought to problems of this kind. Whoever was hungry or weak had plenty to worry about: to calm a rumbling stomach and to take care he did not get caught "organising" food. They needed all their strength to secure their most basic needs. The only plans we made were to escape, we were not interested in lovemaking.

In the summer of 1944, two Russian prisoners tried to escape. On a pre-arranged signal they suddenly ran away from the marching column and disappeared into a field of com that waved in the breeze. Immediately the ss guardsmen shot at them, but missed their target. The escapees fled like rabbits and at first the pursuit seemed hopeless. We were ordered, "Lie down!" Wherever we were walking or standing, we had to throw ourselves to the ground. The ss quickly organised a large group to undertake a systematic hunt for the escaping men. They were soon surrounded and shot at, and their escape became a hopeless race with death. After a short while, the shooting stopped and some inmates had to drag the shot Russians out of the cornfield back to the column. That evening they were laid naked on the ground of the Appellplatz as an example and warning: their terribly distorted faces were turned upwards and a board announced in big letters, "Anyone who tries to escape will end up looking like this!"

After the evening Appell we had to form a single file and slowly march past the two mutilated naked corpses.

As the shortage of ss guards became more obvious the camp administration decided to create a passageway to prevent any more escapes attempts. The route was enclosed on both sides by high barbed wire fences, but the top was open. It stretched for miles from the camp to the factory and made it very easy for the guards to supervise our daily progress. This made it easy for just a few guards to detect any attempted escape in good time.

Many rumours circulated about acts of sabotage committed by Partisans in the vicinity of the border between Slovakia and Bohemia. There were many among the thousands of foreign Krupp workers who had contacts with the Partisans. We believed that the ss were afraid that if we had the chance to conspire together they might secretly equip us with weapons. The ss took advantage of the opportunities to exploit the differences between the many distinct nationalities inside the camp. The grievances that preoccupied individual groups were partly due to the way the camp was organised and partly historical in origin. These had a very detrimental impact on daily life in the camp so that, for example, a Kapo of Polish extraction would not hesitate to beat a Russian or Jewish prisoner, and vice versa. So it was easy for the ss to recruit informers from among the ranks of these feuding groups. We were all mixed up together because were we not segregated according to origin and nationality. We were constantly fearful we might be betrayed, and this made it almost impossible for us to attempt or even make plans to escape. Nevertheless, some like-minded people formed small groups and they occupied themselves with these kinds of plans. It had become increasingly clear that the collapse of the Third Reich was imminent. From the conversations we had with civilians at work we could deduce that the German front lines were disintegrating and the war could not last for much longer.

Camp patrols were intensified. The ss and Kapos would suddenly appear where we worked in order to sniff out any escape plans or suspicious bundles or materials we might have hidden away. Despite these precautions, some managed to escape. Jakob Osterreicher and Hermann Wiener were both prominent camp officials. Hermann Wiener had been transferred from Auschwitz to Fünfteichen and had worked himself up to the position of chief administrator for Krupp. He was highly regarded by both the ss and the Kapos. He had to complete a report of the exact number of all those who lined up for Appell each day and those who were sick. So he had some freedom to move about in the various factory buildings, workplaces and also among the guards. Osterreicher, who had also come to Fünfteichen from Markstadt camp, was promoted from Kapo to Oberkapo (Senior Kapo). He was responsible for various groups with the exception of those who worked for Krupp. He enjoyed freedom of movement within the factory premises because of his rank of Oberkapo.

One evening when we were again counted prior to our march back to camp, Wiener and Osterreicher were missing. The ss searched the entire area, but in vain. After a lot of to-ing and fro-ing, we finally marched back to the camp where we were detained for hours on the Appellplatz. Time and time again they demanded we should give them any clue or information about their whereabouts. Those who shared a room with Wiener and Osterreicher were taken away to be cross-examined. They were threatened with severe punishment to compel them to disclose how they might both have prepared their escape, or even any suspicious remark they may have unwittingly uttered. These efforts failed to yield any worthwhile clue. We were not released until past midnight, when we laid down, utterly exhausted. A few days later my friend Jakob Bloch told me that he was a lookout for both of them. He had seen exactly how they had dressed in civilian clothing in a shack. A German foreman who was favourably disposed towards us had supplied work permits and bicycles. Thus equipped, they were able to pass the factory security service unchecked and make good their escape.

The next day the camp administration informed us that they had both been captured and shot, and their corpses had been transported to the crematorium in Grossrosen. This announcement was a pure lie intended to destroy any yearning to escape. In reality they both found a hiding place fifty kilometres away that a German farmer had prepared for them, and they survived. In January 1945 they were liberated by the Soviet Army. Today (in 1967), one of them lives in Munich.

The atmosphere in the camp was filled with excitement as we anticipated the long- yearned-for prospect of the end of the war. The first changes soon made themselves felt. Suddenly the beatings and killings stopped. Confident voices assured us that the Block Elder was no longer obliged to produce a daily quota of corpses. The routine of daily camp life seemed to ease and the prospect of survival grew. There was growing hope for the future for those able to "organise" extra food. However, at the same time we were even more close-watched than before. Painstaking care was taken to ensure that twice a week a two finger-wide strip from our forehead back to the nape of our neck was meticulously shaved. In the vernacular of the camp this was known as "lice street". This was done to make us conspicuous if we were to escape. The quality of our daily ration of food also improved. We even received preserved meat; it was partly horsemeat, but we did not care because we were happy to assuage our hunger. The soup also became better and thicker, and sometimes even contained diced ham.

We were never able to discover the reason for this transformation. Some claimed that Krupp had complained to the highest ranking officials in Berlin that our efficiency had fallen substantially, leading to the fall in production. They strove to fulfil their war industry production targets, but it was impossible to demand maximum performance from the undernourished inmates who operated the machinery. The management finally had to admit that the constant pressure was unproductive. The inmates were subjected to such intense and sustained pressure that they wilted and collapsed, and instead of increasing production all that was accomplished was the accelerated decline of the workforce.

Since we had to work a hard-labour twelve-hour shift, quite apart from the twohour march to and from work each day, we were all entitled to a hard-labour bonus, but this was never distributed in accordance with the camp regulations. A new commission was established to monitor this distribution and eliminate any irregularities, and one consequence was that large-scale corruption was discovered. The camp management was warned and ordered that they must carefully supervise the distribution of the heavy-labour bonuses and ensure that each inmate received the ration to which they were entitled.

This easing of camp life gave a new impetus to those among us who had thoughts of escape and freedom. Thanks to our contacts with foreign workers and civilians we were sometimes able to circumvent the regulations which forbade us to read newspapers. We would roll newspaper cuttings so small that we could conceal them in the hollow of our fist and furtively pass them from one to another. Thus we had some information about the Second Front and the successive advances of the British and American forces. We were enlivened by this encouraging news. Our spirits, which had been dulled by the hopelessness of our situation, were resurgent. However, it must also be admitted that there were many inmates who were unmoved by this news. They were paralysed by a deathly lethargy, bereft of wishes and hope, incapable of functioning even as animals. The rest of us were still preoccupied and afflicted by the apparent bleakness of our destiny. We tenaciously devoured news of both the developments on the fronts and the destiny of the concentration camps in the occupied territories that the German troops were forced to evacuate. We received terrible news that as the ss retreated from Poland they had obliterated concentration camps and inmates in the vicinity of Lublin. So we fell once again into a state of submissive despair. We lived with the fear that we were condemned to death and that our execution was imminent. Those amongst us who were not yet completely dulled by hunger suffered a period of deathly fear. We knew that millions of European Jews were already dead and we were conscious that we would not be spared. Every day we were consumed with endless discussions about this dominating preoccupation, and we were all convinced that the ultimate outcome would be that we would share the fate of our brethren.

One Autumn day when I returned to the camp I discovered that a group of one hundred men had been assembled and transported to the neighbouring Kittelstreben Camp. My Uncle Leon, who had worked for a while in the potato-peeling room, was among those who were deported. Until this time, Uncle Leon had remained the only member of my family with whom I still had contact, so I was shocked and bewildered by this news.

When I first arrived in Fünfteichen, I had several relatives there. One relative, Uncle Zimmermann, suddenly disappeared. Before I was dispatched from Markstadt to Fünfteichen he was beaten, then sent to the sick bay where he died of his injuries. Also, my Uncle Meisels did not survive the cruelty he suffered in Fünfteichen. He was a lively character with a very gentle nature but he could not withstand the harshness of camp life for long.

So I remained alone. I tried to discover why my Uncle, in particular, had been sent away on this transport, but in vain. Nobody knew the reason. However, I was assured that this transport was not destined for extermination; instead he would work in the munitions bunker in Kittelstreben. This concentration camp was about fifty kilometres from Fünfteichen. They urgently needed them for their workforce and had requested them from our camp management.

At first I found it very difficult to come to terms with this separation from Uncle Leon, but camp life allowed me little time to dwell on it. I knew that I was utterly reliant on my own resources, as I had been at the beginning. If I wanted to survive I would have to carry on my fight for life alone.

The air raid warnings became more frequent in the final weeks of 1944. During these attacks we sheltered in small trenches that were only a metre deep and arranged in a zigzag pattern outside the barracks. With a tremendous effort we had excavated them on our "free" Sundays.

When the sirens wailed we found it difficult to lift our tired bones and painful muscles from the planks. We were utterly exhausted and would have preferred to remain asleep and undisturbed. However, each of these nightly disturbances signified the continuing advance of the Allied Forces that we hoped would bring about our liberation. The war had already lasted more than five years. We were tired of the recurring rumours of an imminent end to the war. We were resigned to what was in our eyes the irrefutable fact that we would not survive the outcome. We lived in the knowledge that our parents and siblings together with hundreds and thousands of other Jews were taken to Auschwitz and that we belonged to the last remnants of Jewish workers whose lives had been spared because we were producing the war machinery.

At this time most of us had reached a stage at which our last inhibitions fell away. Ruthlessness and a lack of compassion seized even those who had known certain limits until then. We had ceased to be human, in the true sense of the word, long ago. We were instruments of skin and bones, which, more or less day in day out, fluently worked to a schedule which had been drilled into us. All our thoughts were solely aimed to adapt to the forced labour and avoid any disturbance of this process. Any interruption was cruelly punished. The all too hungry and the "Muselmänner", who were no longer sensitive to physical pain, could no longer find their way in their state. They hung about just to catch a few potatoes or a spoonful of soup. The range of human emotions had become strangers to us all. Only the air raid alarms tore us from our lethargy. When we saw how the civilian workers ran to the air raid shelters and the seemingly fearless ss, disappeared from the factory trembling, then we woke up to the fact that we were left behind in the hall, and we had a trace of elation and hope. The alarm siren was for us a wake-up call, a reminder. You can still hope that you are not yet forgotten and you are still human. Shortly after the wail of the siren died down, there followed heavy detonations leaving aftershocks and dust clouds. We were pleased about every bomb attack that lessened our path to death, but gave us hope for a new life.

The noise of the engines overhead and the bomb drops from the "enemy" aircraft did not scare us, even though we were helplessly locked in the factory hall. All our fear seemed wiped away and on each detonation our faces lit up joyfully. I will never forget the sight of the emaciated faces, existing only of literally skin and bone, twisted into a ghostly grimace of pleasure. It was as if a dead face smiled suddenly.

Even the most worn out among us seemed to be capable of rare moments of expressing human emotion and shared, for a short time, the feelings of all those who now eagerly waited for a further attack.

In the first days of 1945 the Allies' air raids continued unremittingly. The planes flew over the camp and the nearby factory, but dropped "Christmas trees", bombings occurred all too rarely. Our desire that the camp should be destroyed was not fulfilled, but there were signs of some changes in the camp. The ss guards as well as the civilian workers showed clear signs of worry which they had difficulty hiding from us. It was no longer a secret that the Red Army advance was unstoppable and they had already entered into Upper Silesia. The roads were apparently clogged by the treks of fleeing civilians and the battered units of the retreating German Army.

In the night of 20 January 1945 the heavy thunder of artillery woke us from our sleep. At first we were unclear as to whether the fighting was being played out at a long distance from us. However, each of these muffled noises made our hearts thump and brought tears to our eyes. Yes, you saw tears in the eyes of burnt faces, transformed for but a few seconds, bringing hope of life.

The camp was becoming more and more restless and the news kept changing about the location of the battle fronts. The civilian workers whispered to us that the Russian army was only twenty five kilometres away from our camp, a rumour even claimed that it was only ten kilometres away. The joy on hearing this news was tempered; as at the same time there arose the anxious question: "What will the ss do if it is in imminent danger from the enemy?"

On Sunday 20 January 1945 we gathered together in small groups. We speculated about what the ss would do to us next and how we would fare. We had not failed to notice that new higher calibre machine guns had been installed in the watchtowers. Would the whole camp really be shot and burned? As we shared our severe anxieties, other prisoners joined our group and told us about the preparations for the evacuation of the camp inmates, with the aim of establishing a new camp in the central region of the Reich. I clearly remember how Bloch, Scheyer, two other friends and I were huddled together on the bed planks as we tried to figure out how we could save ourselves. Jakob Bloch, who was a strong man and a butcher by trade, proposed we should excavate a bunker behind the latrines and conceal ourselves there. This plan was really quite impractical because it would have taken several days to dispose of the earth without attracting attention.

Meanwhile, it became dark. After the evening Appell we were not allowed to disperse, instead we had to remain. The uncertainty became unbearable. We were transfixed and felt menaced by the large machineguns that pointed directly at us from the watchtowers. Suddenly we were alerted by a shrill screamed command, "March in step! March!" The spell was broken; slowly our group marched to the food store where each of us was given half a loaf of bread and a bit of margarine. After we collected our food ration we returned to our hut to collect our blankets. In response to our questions the Block Elder explained that soon we would have to embark on a long march on foot. Those who were weak or sick and thought they could not cope with a long march were advised to go to the sick block. They were given permission to remain behind in the camp.

Meanwhile, because they were mortally afraid to remain behind, many of the sick mustered all their strength as they tried to mingle among us. We heard whispers that the Camp Elder had confided to one of our comrades that all those left behind would be shot without mercy. We finally received the command, "Line up! We are marching out of the camp!" Once again we were consumed with all the anxieties that had obsessed us for days. Now we knew that the rumour was also fact. The Red Army had penetrated deep behind the German lines and our camp, which was situated west of Oppeln, had to be cleared from the path of the invading Russians. Oppeln, the largest town in Upper Silesia, was apparently already in Soviet hands.

We marched out onto the snow-covered country road. Now we knew we had been released from this camp, out of the gates that we had believed would never open for any of us.

I had spent almost a year behind its wired fence. Often in desperation I had wondered, would I ever be able to live again in freedom? Now my thoughts were with my relatives and acquaintances who had been forced to abandon life here. However, I still wore an inmate's jacket and was flanked by ss guards who marched alongside me with their weapons at the ready.

News reached us that my home town had already been liberated by the Russian Red Army, but I found this even more depressing. I was overwhelmed by memories of my family. I was tormented by questions: what had happened to them following their deportation to Auschwitz, which of my relatives might still be alive? Parts of the march became little more than a daydream. I could not easily relinquish this chain of gloomy thoughts and I was for some time totally distracted from reality.

For a while, our hopes were nourished by the fantasy that partisans would attack our marching column, fight the ss, liberate us and secure our freedom. There were thousands of us. We would have relished the chance to join the partisans and fight with them, but no matter how hard we scanned the horizon they were nowhere to be found. We had absolutely no information about partisan activities in the area so all we could do was to furtively speculate among ourselves about the vigilance of our guards.

During the march my thoughts frequently turned to my good friend Meister Hermann[3]. Had he remained in the hope of being liberated by the Russians? Had he fled as I had once hoped to do if a favourable opportunity had ever presented itself? I had left my foreign passport and civilian clothes in his care, and perhaps he had been able to make use of them.

We were in the midst of a bleak and monotonous winter landscape. We could clearly hear the sound of exploding heavy artillery

---

3. In the course of research for this book, the author discovered that Hermann had remained behind until the Russians arrived in the mistaken belief that they would treat with sympathy and understanding anyone who opposed or was oppressed by the Nazi regime. He was probably seized by front-line troops, but there remained no trace of him.

punctuated by small-arms fire. We could not tell if the noise was enemy action or a harmless military exercise. All I knew was that we were ordered to march more quickly. With the butts of their rifles the ss kept chasing and forced us to go faster and faster until we were almost running. Invalids in the march could no longer keep up with this more rapid tempo. Moreover, some of them wore wooden clogs that were more and more heavily encrusted with snow. They looked as if they were walking on stilts and it became more difficult for them to keep moving forward. In order not to fall behind some of them threw their clogs away and tried to march through the ice and snow with bare feet. No one could drop back. Anyone who faltered for a moment was pushed onward by the man behind, and if his pace slackened he was pushed on in turn by those behind him. The pace kept quickening to such an extent that we even had to attend to our bodily needs as we marched along. Our anxiety mounted as we felt our way in the dark. We completely lost our sense of direction and kept tripping over one another's feet. It was the weakest who fared the worst. They were pushed and shoved from every side, but had to drag themselves along no matter how badly their feet were injured from being stepped on by others.

Within a few hours many were so exhausted they had to remain behind. Others who been forced to dispose of their wooden clogs in order to continue complained bitterly; they had lost all feeling in their feet and were unable to control them because they were absolutely frozen.

From time to time we heard single shots that were quickly swallowed by the darkness of the night. We did not want to think about their meaning or what was happening around us. However, some inmates who were marching toward the rear of the column noticed that ss officers shot all those who could not keep up. These inmates pushed to the front and begged us to warn everyone that anyone who could not keep up would be shot. We had to muster our final strength in order to maintain our position in the marching column. We made every effort to support the weakest under their arms and so help them keep pace. Those at the front were driven at such speed that those in the rear were forced to run. They could not maintain this pace for long. Even the ss who were guarding the rear became exhausted and finally gave the order to slow down. Hardly had the inmates heard this new ss order to slow down the pace of the march when hundreds of us erupted with mutinous calls, "Slower, slower!" We had been chased along so hard that we were all absolutely shattered. Whereas the ss was normally able to exploit our national differences, now we were united by a revolutionary atmosphere.

It became more and more dangerous to make the slightest deviation from the column. Many who up until now had been able to attend to nature by running a very small distance ahead and then rejoining the column as we marched by, became reluctant to leave the row. Now, we all knew that those left behind would be shot on the spot. Even those who momentarily stepped to the side in order to attend to their needs met the same fate because the ss assumed they could not continue.

As we struggled onward those whose bowels ached with pain groaned, "Slower, let's have a break!" Slowly this mutinous chorus grew. The ss were infected by the growing tension and began to panic. A new command was issued; anyone failing to obey any order would be shot. In their confusion many ss started wildly shooting, sometimes into the air, sometimes into the inmates whose plaintive cries and pleas terrified the ss still more. The shooting quickly suffocated our desire to slow down or rest.

The old instinct to fight for and preserve human life no matter what the price or circumstances prevailed once more. It overtook the paralysing tiredness and bitterness that had fuelled our dangerous and mutinous mood. Somehow the march resumed its former rapid tempo. We could no longer help the weak ones, so they remained behind and were shot by the ss.

We had already marched about thirty kilometres and it was past midnight when we were ordered into a farmyard. We had to lie down under the open sky on snow blanketed, hard-frozen ground. Three times we were expressly warned that if we got up we would be shot immediately. Then most of the ss disappeared so they could search for somewhere to sleep. Some remained to guard us. We were ordered to remain motionless so that the smallest number of guards sufficed.

We put our blankets on the snow, obediently stretched out, and almost immediately fell into a deep and exhausted sleep. It did not take long before we were woken by the penetrating dampness of the snow which had been transformed into ice-cold water by our body heat. We tossed and turned restlessly on the wet ground as we impatiently waited for dawn when we would be allowed to move. Many were tormented by the need to relieve themselves but they were not allowed to get up. Finally, we requested our Kapos to ask the ss to allow us to go to the toilet. They did as we asked, and in groups we were permitted to do so, always accompanied by a guard.

As the next day dawned, we were finally allowed to get up. At first we were relieved to be able to get up from the wet snow, but quickly we realised how painful our limbs had become. We feared we could not bear the strain of continuing our march.

When we were finally assembled five abreast in a single column we were carefully counted several times. This was the moment when it was discovered that two inmates were missing. They were two Kapos, the gypsy and Horn. Sniffer dogs were immediately used to search for their tracks, but without success. After this, the ss remembered their tried-and-tested method of collective punishment, and beat us blindly with their rifle-butts until we had re-formed into a marching column.

We later learned that both escapees were denounced by civilians and shot on the spot.

We were not given any food at all but had to continue with our march nevertheless. We asked the Kapos if we would get any food today. They comforted us with the assurance that we would be fed when we reached the next village where we were expected to arrive at lunchtime. For some time we were not the only ones who marched along our route. It overflowed with a pushing, shoving, heaving human mass. Women were burdened with heavy bundles of clothes. Men and children pushed overloaded handcarts before them. It was only with considerable difficulty that hooting cars were able to clear their way through all this confusion. German army demolition squads also marched alongside us. All shared a common goal: to escape to the West. The street was completely overcrowded and we were merged into an unmanageable mass. So, guards diverted our column onto a path that crossed fields to eliminate the risk that we might otherwise make contact with civilians. So once again we were completely isolated. No one took any notice of us, they were utterly indifferent to our fate. From time to time the muffled sound of rifle shots punctuated the silence, and it was as if each time our hearts were pierced. Again, a comrade became detached from the column. Again, another human life was extinguished and lay mute at the wayside. How often, and for how long had he been tortured before he was struck down with a single shot in his neck, and pushed like a piece of rubbish into the ditch which became his grave?

I marched alongside Scholem Gemeiner. He had previously worked in the kitchen, and had managed to fill his pockets with sugar. Even in these circumstances he retained his scruples, for he did not eat alone. He shared this with his brethren, pouring a small pile of the sweet dust into their palms. It was as if I had partaken of the finest food, and I was strengthened by it. Slowly and carefully I licked the sugar from the palm of my hand. It was with the greatest pleasure I allowed the last crystal to dissolve on the tip of my tongue. Most of us had already eaten the ration of food distributed the night before our march began. We had been on the way for twenty four hours without nourishment. We were exhausted and frozen. We moved forwards as if in a trance. If, in our shattered state, we briefly succumbed for a fragile moment and inadvertently staggered from the path, one of our well-meaning colleagues, whether in front or behind, would shove us back into line.

Like other long-term prisoners who had come from the work camp of Markstadt, I had the good fortune to have been allowed to retain my leather shoes in Fünfteichen. It was on that march that I really came to appreciate their value. Some inmates wanted to exchange their clogs for shoes. They offered bread, even tobacco, for my leather shoes. However, I chose to keep my shoes and carry on marching with an empty stomach.

The ss had arranged large sledges which they loaded with their rucksacks and the rest of their luggage. They sought volunteers to pull the sledges, and offered additional bread rations for those who agreed to do so. Those of us who were long-term prisoners knew that this "voluntary" service was usually only poorly rewarded; any disappointment we showed became a source of their amusement. Each one of us longed for a piece of bread to silence our growling stomachs. Slowly the news trickled that the ss had not received any food on this march and a patrol had been sent on ahead to obtain food. We desperately hoped that these supplies would be sufficient for us as well.

We were fixated on knowing exactly where we were marching to. The Kapos told us that our destination was the main camp of Grossrosen, but many inmates doubted the accuracy of this information. However, we had no choice but to continue marching, regardless of our destination. Would we reach Grossrosen before the day's end? No matter how hard we tried to avoid it, this was the question that preoccupied us all.

It went on and on and on. We left the main road and continued on side streets. After a few hours some comrades fell behind once again and they gave up the struggle. We tried to support and encourage the weak ones to continue, but to no avail. They refused to accept our help. Their weak gestures expressed so much more eloquently than any words could the futility of the march, and of life. Full of dread we watched how many silently stepped from the column and sat on the roadside. They were without expression, their eyes glazed over, incapable of any understanding. Their heads slowly slumped forward as if they were waiting for a sleep-filled deliverance, not a deathly bullet.

None of us wanted to come to terms with the march's true purpose. We were strongly convinced that when we came close to the Russian Army we would either be released, or shot. It never occurred to us that when the German Army retreated the ss would drive us deep into the German Reich. We asked ourselves why the weak ones among us were exposed to this ordeal when they were destined to be cold-bloodedly shot on the roadside anyway. Was the purpose to keep us alive so we could be evacuated? Or had the ss found a new method? Was their plan that we should be so weakened by marching that this would serve as the pretext for shooting us?

To our astonishment and disgust, one of the ss who had so far distanced himself from such murderous actions now willingly participated in these shootings. They appeared to be able to commit these murders without any difficulty. Just as liberation became possible, row upon row of human life was extinguished. A shot in the neck, and a human being sank to the ground so quickly, so easily, as if pushed by an invisible hand. The January day grew dark early. We finally stopped in a small village. We were divided into two groups. My group was led to a farm. Everyone received a few cooked potatoes. Then all of us were crowded into a barn, but it was too small to accommodate all of us. The ss used the butt of their rifles to press us all in, but even so a group of inmates remained outside. Suddenly the ss shot into the air several times. They threatened that anyone who remained outside the barn would be shot. Inmates shoved and pushed one another desperately, and using all their strength, some managed to force their way into the barn. As the ss applied more pressure those who remained outside were desperate to get in. They pushed forward with such force, even stepping on the bodies and heads of others to save themselves. Finally, the ss closed the gates. We fought for every inch of floor, such was the lack of space. I had managed to remain in the group with whom I had marched. We searched for strong beams we could pull ourselves up to in order to escape the crush on the floor. However, we could not make ourselves comfortable as we struggled to rest our weary bodies with our legs dangling in the air but here at least we could breathe freely, and we were not hemmed in on all sides. We were all in a state of turmoil as each of us fought our own personal war for every inch of space. There was no end to the quarrels and pushing. Gradually the cries of those being crushed and trampled became louder and louder. Finally, to contain the tumult, the ss on guard in front of the barn shot into the crowd through a gap in the door.

After this hellish night we were all grateful to leave the barn and move about in the courtyard. We rubbed our hands and faces with snow and greedily sucked in the icy morning air. Our strong muscle pains diminished in the clear cold morning air. As we waited again for the signal to commence marching, many of us ran from group to group begging for old rags to bandage our wounded feet.

The shrill blast of a whistle sounded suddenly, and we were ordered to remain where we were. The Block Leader and Group Leader searched our jacket pockets and the pleats in our clothes. It emerged that some of the inmates had torn open a number of sacks and had removed some of the grain stored in them. The farmer had complained to the ss and demanded that we should all be searched. And in truth some of the inmates had tied the bottom of their trousers and filled them with grain. Others had concealed the grain in their shirt-sleeves. All inmates found in possession of this corn were immediately stood against the barn wall. Then the whole group were all ordered to face the wall. They fell to the ground as they were each shot in the neck by the Group Leader.

Our group was searched by Group Leader Morhard, an ethnic German from Bessarabia. He found a handful of grain in my neighbour's pocket. The poor fellow had not even taken it himself, it had been put there by a comrade, "Crouch down!" ordered Morhard. The inmate assumed a squatting position as if he was waiting to get a kick up the backside. However, Morhard took the blanket that we each carried on our shoulders, pulled it over the head of his victim, calmly removed his pistol from its holster, placed it with precision on his neck, and shot him.

This entire scene took place less than two metres from where I stood. I stood there, rooted to the spot, absolutely petrified. I had thought Morhard would beat my neighbour with his pistol-butt. The breath caught in my throat as the unsuspecting victim was shot in cold blood. A small hole, its edge scorched, appeared in the blanket. The shot one slumped forward and collapsed on the ground. A thin stream of blood ran slowly onto the snow and formed a dark rivulet in the glistening white. I stood there, severely shaken, unable to remove my gaze from this horrific scene. Was it possible that a human being had just been murdered here for a handful of grain?

Meanwhile, with total indifference, Morhard continued to search us for grain. I felt sick. One of my friends noticed that all the blood had drained from my face. He took me aside, but I was so numb that I neither saw nor heard how Morhard, with ease and precision, shot more victims.

At last the order came for us to continue our march, and we lined up. We had already marched for three days. We no longer felt any pain. Our nerves had been numbed with exhaustion. Our awareness and understanding of our circumstances were diminished. Our senses were so paralysed that a veil of apathy overlaid our grasp of reality. The muscles of our legs moved automatically. Occasionally we asked the Kapos how much further we still had to march, and would we reach our destination today? As well as that we wanted to know if we dared hope for a piece of bread or a bowl of soup, but we were constantly fobbed off with vague answers. We resigned ourselves to continue trudging without any apparent purpose.

The pace of the march became noticeably slower. It was likely that the ss were also exhausted. We learned from the Kapos that the previous night the remainder of the ss guards from Fünfteichen had been dispatched to join us. These guards later told us that the day after we left Fünfteichen Camp it had been heavily shelled by Red Army artillery. The following morning the camp was quickly occupied by units of Russian infantry. The ss were taken completely by surprise and able to save themselves only with great difficulty. Fortunately for them, those of our comrades whom we had left behind in the sick bay escaped the grasp of the ss at the very last moment only because they were liberated by Russian troops.

As we were forced to continue dragging ourselves along we bitterly regretted our decision not to remain in the camp. However, there was no point in brooding over missed opportunities. We were overcome by extreme tiredness and could no longer think clearly. Those in whom the last spark of life had been stifled, who were suffused with numbness and whose limbs were paralysed, wished only to rest, to step out of the human chain that continually pressed them forward, and against their wishes, compelled them to keep moving. But those who chose rest chose death.

I was approached en route by my relation, Avram Hellmann. Avram was an assistant Kapo and hence was able to ask for help. He asked if I would carry his bag, and promised me a piece of bread as a reward. I took the bag, and from that moment I had to march alongside him in the last row. As Assistant Kapo, it was his job to keep a record of concentration camp numbers of the inmates who had stayed behind and those who had been shot en route. The Group Leader also marched in the last row, and I personally witnessed how he shot the inmates who could go no further.

All that we could do was talk to those who stopped and try to persuade them to keep going. Some of us tried to support those who were staggering. We pulled and dragged them along until they got their second wind, and could continue independently. For others, any help was too late.

The day was cold, but despite our dreadful tiredness we could still appreciate how the bright sun illuminated the winter landscape. In this beautiful, quiet, still world, murder happened with monotonous regularity. The ss henchmen marched alongside me, and from time to time, in a very casual way, cocked the trigger of his pistol. Hellmann wrote down the number of the human being chosen for death, sometimes before he was shot, sometimes after.

I viewed the trail of death with neither fear nor excitement. When they fell back and rejected the support of those close to them, they were so apathetic that they were not even touched by the fear of death. Some of them closed their eyes, as if the world no longer had any meaning for them.

Twenty-two years[4] have passed since these events, but the memories are so clear, it is as if I had lived through them only yesterday. Often, when I am half asleep, I wake with a start. They frequently appear before me: grey, shaven figures with sightless eyes staring into the distance, waiting for a bullet to the head. I see how they sit at the roadside, the small dark hole at the temple, the thin hesitant trickle of blood. I wait for them to speak, to moan, but they sit there motionless, and then silently fall forwards.

In my memory I can still see a young comrade, who, like many others, had remained behind, but could not surrender himself to his inevitable fate. His feet could no longer carry him any further, but with a superhuman effort he dragged himself onward. Finally, his legs no longer responded to his commands. He staggered and

---

4. At the time the author wrote this book – 1967.

crumbled. A cross stood about ten metres away from him by the road. The figure of Christ was suspended on it. His glance strayed towards the cross. Once again he wanted to raise himself up but his muscles failed him, so he crawled with his elbows towards the cross, dragging his body across the ground. The ss man, gun at the ready, pulled the trigger, but no shot was fired as the magazine was empty. While the ss man reloaded, the inmate made an unbelievable effort to crawl towards the cross. He stopped before the figure of Christ on the cross. A bright glow appeared to emanate from his eyes, which now appeared large and glassy. With a final effort he leapt towards the cross and embraced it with both arms. Exhausted by the effort, his face relaxed. Peacefully, and as if relieved, he let his head hang to one side. His foam-covered lips moved as if in prayer. The crucified Jesus, with outstretched arms, head bent to one side and with staring eyes looked down upon him: the half-dead inmate who at the moment of death prayed to him. I stood transfixed, mesmerised by the appearance of my young comrade, and it was as if we were connected by a moment of unbreakable unity. The crucified Jesus hung over us. At his feet the victim waited for the bullet. I stood beside him; alive, but shrouded in a veil of death. Suddenly the silence was pierced by a rifle shot.

I continued to march alongside the murderer while carrying the Assistant Kapo's rucksack, always with the hope uppermost in my mind that he would remember me and give me some bread. It seems unbelievable that so close to death one could still plead for bread, that the horrific atmosphere did not stifle all other feelings except fear. As I gratefully and slowly chewed each piece of bread I felt a strange contentment, as if the act of chewing banished every other worry.

We did not reach our destination before evening. I enquired of the Group Leader whether we would reach our destination that night, but he indicated we would not. So the best that we could hope for was that at the very least we would find shelter in a warm barn.

Just before nightfall we reached a farm. We were forced into a barn once more, but this time we received neither potatoes nor bread. The fight for a place to sleep began immediately. My group forced its way to the top end of the barn. We even managed to rest our weary limbs and the burning pain of our muscles slowly subsided. A group of Hungarian Jews lay next to us, but they remained aloof and kept to themselves. Next to them was a group of Ukrainians. On his way in to the barn one of the Hungarian Jews had managed to "organise" a carrot which he wanted to share with one of his companions. One of the Ukrainians fell upon him as he tried to seize the carrot. The Hungarian defended his treasure with courage born of despair, but the Ukrainian pulled him into the circle of his friends and pushed him to the ground. Then he sat on his head so he was free to complete the theft at his leisure. The victim was completely overwhelmed, and his Hungarian friends were too weak to help him. It was impossible for him to break free, so he just lay on the floor, groaning and fighting for breath. Some of us watched, unable to contain our mounting anger but, without weapons, we knew that we were no match for these Ukrainians. We were very wary because we feared they might start on us. It was not long before one of them sneaked towards us and began grasping at our clothes as he tried to discover if we had any hidden food. As he got closer, suddenly and without any warning Bloch turned around. He seized him using all his strength and struck him with several well-aimed blows. The Ukrainian lashed out with his fist. Then Jakob took off his shoe and beat the Ukrainian until he lay motionless on the ground, by which time the sole of the shoe had become completely detached. The other Ukrainians attacked us like a pack of wolves, but we huddled closely together and called for help from other comrades. The Ukrainians were forced to beat a retreat when they realised our group was getting larger and stronger by the moment, and only then were we able to lie down and rest.

During the night some inmates made a hole in the wall that separated the barn from the stable and tried to hide there. The ss with their sniffer dogs soon discovered their hiding place and shot them there and then. By this time some of our comrades were so exhausted and weakened that they were at the end of their strength. They were unable to take their place in the marching column because they could not even get up from the ground. They were unmoved even by the threats of the Kapos. They were completely done for, their grasp on life was slipping away fast. All those able to march took their place in the marching column, waiting for the signal to start. Those who remained on the ground were unceremoniously herded into a comer and shot.

With blistered feet, tired and hungry, we began the day's march. It was the fourth day. The ss and Kapos were much fitter than we were, and they had not been starved as we had, but by this time even they were very tired. We no longer marched in step, and no one appeared to be bothered. Each of us struggled onwards, shrouded in our black camp blankets, bent forward with tiredness and hopelessness.

We were just thirteen kilometres from Grossrosen. Normal people could have walked this distance without difficulty. However, the days and nights of terror and unremitting hardship had taken their toll and we could only keep going by mustering our last strength. After about two hours there were rumours that in another hour we would arrive at Grossrosen Main Camp. But for many it was too late. Without a word they fell away from the column. In a state of total apathy they sank down to the roadside. No one turned round, they remained, unlamented. We were devoid of all feelings except hunger. We were united only by a single fantasy: a steaming bowl of soup. In our imagination we stood in front of the camp kitchen, hands grasped around a steaming hot bowl…

But still we marched on. Our Camp Leader rode on ahead to announce our arrival and to organise some food. Finally Grossrosen was stretched out before us. Our march had come to an end. But what life awaited us beyond the camp gates? When we marched into the camp we saw a familiar spectacle; a barbed wire double fence, the inner part of which was electrified, watchtowers and machine-gun posts. We were surrounded by camp functionaries and Kapos who busied themselves in a show of self-importance. With our final strength we scaled the last snow-covered hill where the camp lay before us. We hurried up the hill, panting and stumbling. We were little more than a group of disorganised, lifeless, tumbling statues. Some Kapos and officials made it their business to restore "order" to our ranks, beating us with their rubber truncheons.

We were soon called to Appell and the customary counting began. We were so weak we could no longer stand upright. Some who could no longer stand were tormented by Kapos who kicked them. Those who could not immediately get up were mercilessly trampled underfoot.

For us Jews, Grossrosen was the epitome of terror. In Fünfteichen we had heard rumours that in Grossrosen no Jew survived more than two weeks. The majority of the camp guards consisted of Polish and Ukrainian criminals who tortured and persecuted the newly-arrived Jewish prisoners until they were dead.

The atmosphere in our ranks and among the non-Jewish prisoners had clearly changed. In Grossrosen we knew that the Red Army had penetrated deep into the German Reich and that the Western Allies' advance was unstoppable. It was only a question of time before these advancing armies would meet. We all hoped and expected that this would happen very soon.

Chapter Five

Grossrosen

The main part of Grossrosen Concentration Camp had been established for a long time. The barracks were crowded alongside the tarmac road. The huge Appellplatz was not far from the main gate. The crematorium was close to the rear exit of the camp. The newer part of the camp did not have any streets and was located on an adjacent hill. We had to wade through deep clay to reach the barracks which had not yet been completed. On closer inspection, it transpired that many doors were missing and black holes gaped in the walls in place of windows. In many cases the floor had not been laid and there were large puddles of water had built up inside these barracks. Our group was put into four barracks. Thankfully these had in part some doors, windows and a wooden floor. There were no other planks or bunks, so we had to sleep on the naked floor. The Block Elder and the Kapo used blankets to partition off a large corner for themselves, so very little room was left for the rest of us ordinary inmates. Naturally, each of us tried to claim sufficient space to sleep. As friends, we clung closely together and searched for a place where we were less likely to attract a beating by the Kapo.

We were not able to rest for very long that first night. We were woken while it was still pitch black outside. We were chased into the cold night air without any explanation. Despite the difficulty, we had no choice but to stand in the pools of clay and mud that stretched out in front of the camp, uncertain what we should do. We were forced to wait around for hours and were soon drenched with rain and snow. Eventually the Block Leader emerged and deigned to count us for Appell. The original part of the camp was counted first, so we had to wait our turn. It soon became clear that as soon as the original part of the camp was called to stand at attention the camp "regulations" obliged us all to do so. Freezing, we stood around until morning dawned. We waited for the Appell in other parts of the camp to be completed before it was our turn. Only then were we assembled in columns and counted. The same procedure was repeated when coffee and bread were distributed. First, the original camp was "fed" directly from the kitchen. Since the kitchen and kettle had been designed to serve only the original camp they had to have a second shift to cater for additional prisoners.

They could hardly cope with the prisoners in the original camp, therefore many times we, as newcomers, had to wait around for our soup until midnight. This highly desired brew was not shared out fairly. Our bowls were always half empty because the Block Elders and "Prominenz" (Camp Officials of various ranks) received a few kettles for their exclusive use. First they served themselves and ate as much as they could; the rest went to the highest bidder.

By this time I still had 300 marks that I had managed to keep hidden. Though it was illegal, this had been sent by my Uncle to Meister Hermann for me when I was in Fünfteichen. I was sorely tempted to part with it in exchange for a bowl of soup, but I managed to resist this temptation. I had learned from four years experience in concentration camps that there are some life and death moments. I clung to this modest sum so that I would have the option to use it to purchase some help later on.

New groups from Auschwitz and its satellite camps kept arriving. We scrutinised these new arrivals in the hope that we might discover friends or relatives among them, and to learn anything about the fate of our families. The groups from Auschwitz and Blechhammer were accommodated in half-built barracks. Inmates had to lie on the soggy clay. Whoever had the good fortune to get bricks was able to lay them in the puddles to provide a dry place to rest for the night, even if it was hard. To get from one barrack to the next we had to jump from stone to stone, otherwise we sank to our ankles in mud. In my search for friends and relatives, I actually discovered a friend from home, Josef Habermann, who had arrived from Blechhammer. We examined one another up and down and with delight discovered that we had both managed to survive the trauma of recent years. We had both been forced to slog along by foot on interminable marches and were exhausted by our efforts, but in comparison to others we were better off. Habermann had also been able to obtain extra bread in Blechhammer so he was not yet as frighteningly emaciated as many others. We were delighted to see one another again and described our experiences to date to one another in great detail. We parted with the firm intention that from that moment we should not be separated.

Among a group from Auschwitz was Rabbi Shlomo Elimelech Rabinowitz whom we revered from our home town. I had always held this patriarchal figure in the greatest respect. He appeared before me sunken and slender. His unwavering gaze and fearless voice were the only clue to his still-strong personality. My parents had been transported with him to Auschwitz, but he was evasive when I asked him about them. He was so weak that he had to lean on me when he walked. Despite his weakness he was extremely optimistic about the imminent end of the war and was even confident that we would survive those who had persecuted us. He told me in moving terms about the many acts of kindness he had so often experienced. His strength of will remained intact despite the fact he was starving and emaciated. Selections by Dr. Mengele at Auschwitz were designed for the sole purpose of consigning the "Muselmanner" to the gas chambers. So the fact that he had survived, despite his poor physical condition, was a miracle. Tragically, his burning desire to witness the end of the terror was not fulfilled. When we continued our march from Grossrosen he was among the many prisoners who fell by the wayside and were shot. We continued to revere his blessed memory.

The survivors grieved that he and his highly respected rabbinical family shared the fate of countless other families whose destiny it was to be wiped out for ever.

Even in Grossrosen some of my acquaintances were able to assert themselves in the most adverse circumstances. Some were able to secure promotion to kitchen personnel so that they could "organise" extra food for themselves and for others. These posts could only be purchased with gold. Gold opened all doors, and even the most brutal became much more approachable. Even when in the direst of straights, with gold one could bribe some of the camp functionaries. However, my acquaintances could only provide for themselves and their closest relatives. So for the time being I had to be self-reliant. My faithful friend, Jakob Bloch, was the only one who looked out for me. From time to time he was able to pass me a bowl of soup or a piece of bread. Although he did not work in the kitchen, occasionally he did jobs there and was able to obtain some leftovers. On one occasion I bumped into Bloch as he rushed between barracks. Quickly he passed me a quarter of a loaf of hard, dried-out stale bread. I quickly hid it under my jacket so that later I could soften it in the watery camp soup. As I walked with my hidden treasure along the camp path I encountered an ss Block Leader. The camp regulations obliged us to stand at attention and doff our cap whenever we met an ss man. As I stood in front of him he noticed the bulge in my jacket and his curiosity was immediately aroused. Full of suspicion he stopped and asked me in a loud voice, "What are you hiding? Come with me!" He led me behind the barrack and began to search me. I had no option but to show him the bread. He immediately removed his pistol from its holster, released the safety catch and pointed it directly at me. He asked, "Where did you steal it from?" I struggled to maintain a calm appearance while I trembled with fear as I stared down the barrel of his pistol. Nonchalantly I replied that I had not stolen the bread, I had swapped some tobacco for bread with a stranger. I was extremely well-advised to withhold the name of my friend. He persisted with his accusation. "You are lying! You stole it! You will be shot like a dog!" I was so fearful I could barely breathe. Just for a moment I grappled with the idea that I should throw myself on the ground, grasp him around his gleaming boots and plead for mercy, but only for a moment. Instinctively, I stood absolutely still and stared directly into his eyes. It may be that he saw in my eyes a silent plea to end this gruesome cat and mouse game, and it may be that he lost interest. He remained motionless as I waited breathlessly for his reaction, and when he said nothing I shyly stammered, "On my honour! I have not stolen it!" I was stunned when without warning he struck me across my face with his pistol. The blood throbbed in my temples as I staggered and struggled to remain upright. Somehow I vaguely registered the command, "Disappear! Get out of my sight!"

Stunned, I moved from my position and disappeared to the next barracks. I did not dare to look back even for a moment, fearful that a careless movement might prompt increased pressure on the trigger. Had I not been pistol-whipped I would have dismissed the whole episode as a nightmare, a nasty nightmare. They taunted and tantalised us, keeping us in fear for our lives. Thankfully, I realised that my senses and instincts had served me well. If I had fallen on my knees and pleaded loudly for my life, that would have been the end. Often it was the victim's growing fear of death that further provoked the lust of the murderer. He would continue to toy with his victim and increase his despair until a bullet finally ended this gruesome duel.

Many of the transports that arrived in Grossrosen moved on within a few days, but our transport remained for a few weeks. However, we were not allocated to working groups like other prisoners in the old camp. We spent the cold February days standing for hours freezing in front of our barracks. Others cleaned the rooms inside the barracks. From time to time we were made to work, and if we were lucky we got a bowl of soup or a piece of bread.

Some jobs brought unexpected danger. We were beaten indiscriminately and at random. We were closer to death than to life. It was impossible to take any precautions because we were allocated to the working groups and taken to do these jobs without any prior warning by the Kapos. On one occasion I had to report to the crematorium for work. The crematorium was incapable of disposing of all of the many corpses that were left behind by the transports that passed through the camp. In the deep frost, in front of the crematorium there was a towering pile of corpses that were frozen and rigid. This was the first time I saw human beings horribly distorted. Emaciated, skin-covered skeletons, all piled up and higgledy-piggledy, naked and exposed, lay there with staring eyes and gaping mouths, as if they wanted to scream. Until this time I was always conscious of our proximity to death and was deeply moved and disturbed whenever I witnessed the demise of an individual. I suffered with them and I gave them a special place in my memories. However, what I saw now filled me with naked horror. Piles of entangled bodies, naked, hairless skeletons, just skin and bone, covered with mucus and faeces, maybe forty or fifty in number, lying on the frozen earth, waiting to be burnt in the crematorium. As I went about my work carrying wood and removing ashes, my eyes kept returning again and again to the mound of bodies. Was this to be our fate, was this also to be my destiny?

I was haunted by this image of the soundless, screaming dead. I was utterly bewildered. I had lost the will to live. After a few hours we were sent back. A piece of stale bread was our reward. Some devoured it ravenously. Others, myself included, put it aside, we could not eat a thing. Those of us who had been together in Fünfteichen had until this time been spared the direct encounter with the crematorium. It was only here in Grossrosen that we were unambiguously confronted with the grim and stark reality of our own destiny. However, gradually our emotions were dulled and eventually gave way to the indifference to which we were much more accustomed.

By this time I had already been in Grossrosen for ten days. Looking back then, my time in Fünfteichen seemed almost bearable in comparison. There, my work had been tolerable and sometimes I had been able to obtain extra food. In Fünfteichen we sympathised with anyone who was abused and we cursed their torturer. Here, death was at home and the victims showed hardly any response, they did not appear to be horrified, repulsed or even disturbed. We felt almost suffocated by our inability to escape this camp of death.

Despite everything, I knew I could not give up. Time and time again I told myself that I still had some strength left, so, in comparison, I was better off than many others. My spirit and will to live was still stronger than many of my companions who arrived in Grossrosen emaciated and broken in body and mind.

I volunteered to collect food because it offered the prospect of an additional portion of soup. The heavy soup kettles had to be carried from the old camp into the new, a difficult job for us because we were too weak and lacked the strength to lift the kettles, so we dragged them uphill across the partially frozen clay soil. As we did so one of us stumbled and let go. To our horror almost the complete contents were spilt on the ground. Immediately some of our comrades threw themselves on the ground and tried with both hands to scoop up the remnants of the spilt soup. Instantly the Kapos began to beat them to stop them completing their "free meal". Our punishment for this "carelessness" was that we were denied our extra ration.

On another occasion, I volunteered to unload bread because I had heard that the reward for this was a big piece of bread. We were taken to the SS stores where the trucks of bread were waiting for us. Eagerly we unloaded these trucks, but when the store man counted the bread after unloading, there were some missing. We were all individually and carefully searched and threatened with severe punishment, but even so the missing loaves could not be found. We had to stand in rank and file and were given a final warning to give up the stolen goods, but in vain. Even with the threat of twenty-five lashes on the backside if nobody came forward, nothing happened. Then the front rank had to lie on the ground to suffer the promised beating. They protested their innocence but their pleas did not make the slightest impression on their beaters. As luck would have it, I was stood in the back rank. By the time these "heroic beaters" got to us they were already exhausted by their efforts, so I got off with a fright and just a few lashes.

Then, I firmly resolved that I would not allow myself to be tempted by such jobs despite the agonising torment of constant hunger. Naturally, it was difficult to watch others returning with extra bread or soup for such extra work. I was deterred from continuing these high risk experiments by my fear of the potentially disproportionate and dangerous consequences. Although it was good to eat warm broth, all too often the reward of soup gave way to a murderous beating that only led to illness and death. In order not to diminish my chances of survival I had to forgo some comforts. If I had chosen otherwise I would have exposed myself to unnecessary danger. Some of my colleagues and, perhaps, I also owe our lives to the fact that we observed this self-imposed rule.

One evening about three weeks after we had arrived in Grossrosen all of the lights in the barracks, and the searchlights on the watchtowers and on the electrified fences suddenly all went out without warning. By that time, particularly at night, we had become accustomed to the howling of artillery shells. These sounded very distant to us. However, we could not tell whether this was the sound of slaughter as the battlefront came ever closer, or the sound of flak batteries putting up anti-aircraft barrages intended to counter nightly bombing sorties. In the impenetrable darkness that so unexpectedly enveloped the camp, we could no longer see the ss moving about. This unprecedented experience soon gave way to the hope that this strange change signalled the imminent end of the war. The Block Elders and Kapos appeared similarly affected by this general confusion. For the very first time in our experience of camp life they attempted to restore order without resorting to beatings. We were aware of these signs of unfamiliar humane behaviour. I concluded it was borne of a combination of fear and cynical calculation. The conduct of our superiors confirmed our suspicion that the war was coming to an end. Naturally, all these events gave way to new rumours of invasion and sabotage. Some prisoners overheard the Block Elder discussing the invasion of the ss camp by partisans. We were only too ready to believe this version of events. The nearby clatter of machine-gun fire seemed to provide confirmation for our suspicions. We were filled with a mixture of hope and happiness that one of these rumours might be true. However, within a few hours our hopes were dashed. We got very little sleep that night, and when it ended we were driven out to the morning Appell which, as usual, lasted for hours. So our gloomy days continued as the prospect of being liberated from the pandemonium of Grossrosen diminished.

The sanitary arrangements in the new barracks were catastrophic. It was impossible to wash oneself or keep clean. Even the supply of cold water was severely limited. There was only a sparse trickle of water from the tap, and everyone pushed and shoved to use it. If we were not quick enough we had to forgo the all too brief opportunity of a cursory wash. Since we had to live on the floor we quickly became dirty and infested with lice. These pests multiplied without interruption. They tormented us through the night. Some barracks did not have glass in the window frames so the rain and snow blew in; then boards left over from the construction of the barracks were used to for an improvised floor covering. Walking on these boards became a balancing act. No matter how careful we were, it was almost impossible to prevent the filthy water splashing around each time we stepped on a board. Infectious diseases took over, and it was only a question of time before each one of us succumbed.

Then an announcement was made that all prisoners were to be transported from Grossrosen. In the past just the rumour of a camp being cleared was sufficient to provoke dread. This time we were not panicked, we took this news in our stride. On the contrary, I even felt a certain satisfaction when I heard about it. I had one dominant thought – "nowhere could be worse than here". I was strengthened by this notion. It kept alive the hope of a better future.

Preparations for the transport soon began. The first transports were assembled in the new camp. We anticipated that we would be given the order to begin marching very soon. Naturally we were curious about our ultimate destination. We knew that most of us could not survive a march lasting more than a few days. The mere mention of such possibilities terrified us. Until this time I had managed to avoid the dreaded condition of becoming a muselmann, which meant being unable to work and certain death. I was determined to work, no matter what the circumstances, because it meant I was free to move around and would receive a minimum of food to survive. In short, a better chance to stay alive and keep going until the end of the regime of terror. With this goal before me, I tried to remain with my friends from Fünfteichen. I knew from past experience that we could overcome many of the difficulties on the march if we could stay together. I was shocked to find these friends behaved very strangely towards me. They appeared alien and indifferent as they stood in front of me, as if I had demanded some impossible service from them. My initial disappointment finally gave way to resignation. The deathly and deadening environment of Grossrosen had even transformed both the appearance and mental condition of my friends. Everyone had to become an animal and take up the fight for life with sharpened senses and instincts. The defence of one's own life was the only rule. When compared to this, the suffering of our colleagues had no meaning. Ties of friendship were now severed so that they did not become an encumbrance that might otherwise have endangered one's own life. I knew what it meant to be alone. Those who had not yet been reduced to a state of total apathy found themselves in a new inner torment – yes, desperation. I had to lean against someone so that I would not become entirely dependent on the mercy of the Kapo. We all understood the ordeal that might lie before us. I realised that if I allowed myself to remain isolated and alone I was doomed. In my helplessness I turned to my old friend Bloch. He promised to allow me to join his group, but his offer was accompanied by a most unusual warning. He instructed me that I had to become totally self-reliant. He expressed concern that we might become separated during the transport. I was unsure how I should understand what he meant – either he had developed a pessimism I had never previously detected, or should I take his words of advice as a refusal? His behaviour conveyed a positive attitude. I was heartened that he was being honest with me and valued me as a member of his group. It was pointless to expect comforting words, and it was absurd to seek solace in our situation. I remained convinced that Bloch would help me whenever he could. His inner spark and the optimism with which he confronted difficult situations had been extinguished during the three weeks we had spent in Grossrosen. At long last came the evening Appell and with it the command to take a blanket to continue the march. I looked out for my friend Bloch, but in vain. My agitation slowly mounted as I went from column to column, searching for other friends, always without success. Finally I noticed that some of the inmates I remembered from Fünfteichen had left my group in order to join others. Apparently, they had learnt that their group was destined for a better labour camp. I also sought shelter in this group because I nurtured the hope that perhaps I could avoid the dreaded march and go on a train instead. The group was already well established in columns of five, so it was not possible for me to join when I approached it. The Kapos guarding the column knew exactly how many men belonged to their group. So I was chased away and had to return to my place in front of our barrack. While we were still standing around helplessly waiting for the piece of bread that would be our ration for the march, we were constantly counted and scrutinised. I became very uneasy when there appeared no end to the count. Finally it became clear that they were searching for some people from our barracks. The Block Elders and some Kapos went back into the barracks and rummaged through everything, even searching latrines and cesspits, all in vain. Finally the ss intervened. Sniffer dogs were let loose, and shortly afterwards two inmates who had hidden themselves between wooden boards of the external wall of the barracks, were found. They were father and son. Hardly had they been removed from their hiding places when the Kapos began beating them from every side. The Block Elder hurried by, demanding to know precisely where the two had hidden, and how it was possible to find room in such a narrow space. The two inmates stood there trembling, their heads drooping, bloody and beaten. They were then ordered by the Block Elder to return to their hiding place. Passively, and like puppets, they moved towards the wooden wall. The Kapos rained blows on them until they were stopped by the ss man. "No more beating! They shall return to their hiding place!" A few moments of breathless quiet were interrupted only by the shuffling of both inmates. The ss man watched, stony-faced, pulled out his revolver and aimed at the younger one. At this moment the older man threw himself protectively in front of his son, and caught the bullet with his own body. Lying on the ground, he pleaded in garbled German and Polish that they shoot him instead of his son, and should show mercy on a young life. We stood transfixed. Many Poles among us, observing this deadly drama, made the sign of the cross. It seemed impossible that this overwhelming gesture of love of the father could fail to elicit pity. However, seconds later the ss man pushed the old man away with his boot and aimed the revolver at the head of his son. The old man straightened himself, knelt next to his crumpled son, made the sign of the cross, and prayed out loud. The ss man continued, carefully aiming at the head of the praying father. Two shots rang out, and the praying man was finally silenced, the father slumped over the corpse of his child.

We kept hearing reports about missing inmates, and large troops of ss men with sniffer dogs who were sent to track them down. They systematically combed through and very thoroughly searched the barracks: the interior and external walls, the latrines and the entire sewage system. Suddenly the dogs began barking and used their paws as they first began to scratch and then tried to push aside a manhole cover. Inmates were forced to uncover the opening. Then the ss shone a torch into the hole. They sniffed out their intended quarry after a brief search. They screamed in jubilation, "We've got them! We've caught some of the pigs!" The Kapos stepped forward and insisted that all those in hiding reveal themselves. At first they were indistinguishable figures, but as they emerged from darkness into the daylight I recognised among them the friends for whom I had been searching. For a moment, I felt as if I had been enveloped in darkness. My friends from Fünfteichen stood before me: Kolatacz, Schabse, Jakob Bloch and two others. It was only in that moment I was able to make sense of recent apparent changes in the demeanour of my friends upon whom I had always been able to rely. I remembered my friend Bloch's words, the veiled hints that from that moment I had to fight for myself, there was no one else on whom I could depend. They were words of parting and farewell, because either he could not or did not want to include me in the plan to go into hiding. Perhaps the hole was so small that the number of accomplices and accessories had to be strictly limited. I knew I could never discover his motives for excluding me from his secret plan. As soon as they emerged from their hole, which had become their trap, first they were beaten by the Kapos and then the ss set the hounds on them. These howling dogs leapt upon the victims and tore them limb from limb. Their doubled-up blood-soaked bodies lay together in a moaning, twitching heap.

Words cannot describe my emotions at this moment. Had my heart seized up, or was the cold stiffness I felt, my body's automatic defensive response in a moment of the greatest anguish? All I knew was one thing: we could not scream, nor could we defend ourselves as we witnessed the torture of our friends.

Clearly delighted with his success and with the satisfaction of a job well done, the Block Leader came towards the rotten ss Leader and announced his great discovery in the sewer-hole. "Get up!" he screamed at the tormented ones lying bleeding on the ground. They got up only with the greatest difficulty. For the last time I saw my friend Jakob Bloch in front of me. With tears in my I eyes I looked towards him, but he did not see me. Trembling and broken he stood there, he who for more than four years had managed to get through so bravely, and had shown so much endurance, confidence and will to live. Now he was shattered, crushed, broken. His face was deformed and covered with blood. The ss Leader led the five victims behind the barracks and they silently took their final steps. A few seconds later a salvo of pistol-shots announced my friends' end.

They had been among the first who were deported for forced labour in 1940. They had experienced and suffered in many camps, and been forced to work on the Eastern Front. Now, so near to the gate of freedom, they had fallen victim to the bullets of the ss in February 1945.

Those were my last hours in Grossrosen. I lost my best friends. Images of unforgettable horrors were etched forever into my soul. Broken, and filled with painful, insane, tortured thoughts, I slowly marched out of the camp gate. Without thinking, I took my place the column as we marched five abreast.

Chapter Six

Flossenbürg

Where were we being taken, and why were we dragged relentlessly from one camp to another?" That was the question that pre-occupied us. We could not get a clear idea of the current situation because the snippets of political news we heard was confusing, but we all understood that by the beginning of 1945 the German Army had suffered catastrophic losses and the war fronts were collapsing. The Red Army had penetrated deep into German-occupied territory, and the Allies in the West were flooding across the Rhineland. Day and night Allied planes bombed German-controlled areas.

By this time the masses of prisoners had been reduced to a few thousand emaciated figures, who were, for the most part, incapable of work. These wretched figures were gathered together as one would sweep up rubbish, and assembled for transport. We knew full well that most of them could not survive the stress of the journey, that most would perish, and their end would be dreadful. With horror we asked one another, "What would our fate be if we were compelled to march once more?" Most of us were so weak and our perception so dulled, that we had become indifferent to the endless suffering and death around us. They appeared unconcerned as they awaited their fate in a state of complete apathy. Their dulled resignation showed that their senses, their feelings and their souls were already dead, long before their bodies died.

For several days this described my own condition, but every now and again I was revived by a spark of hope. However, this feeling of connection with life returned less and less frequently, and ultimately I was unable to resist bouts of deep depression.

I was by myself and without friends when we were finally assembled into a marching column, but I was no longer affected by this. I had no feelings of mourning or remembrance. Not only was I a stranger among strangers, I was also estranged from my own being. I had no memories. I could no longer remember names or thoughts. It was as if I had no past. We received our marching ration – a piece of bread – on which our life literally depended. I ate half the bread immediately. On the march from Fünfteichen to Grossrosen I had learnt how difficult it was to be hungry for a few days, so I wanted to save the remaining half for the journey. Many of my comrades ate their bread ration immediately. They enviously scrutinised every hand movement of their more prudent companions who had saved part of their ration and furtively transferred morsels to their mouth as we marched.

It was already dark when we descended down the hill where Grossrosen Camp was located. The street we used was blocked by tank traps. There were machine-gun settings on both sides of these obstacles. At first we had no idea for whom these machine-guns were intended. Were they intended to prevent any attempt we might make to escape as we were marching, or were they directed against the Red Army? Where were the liberating armies? Were they already close by? Would we have been better off if we had declared ourselves unable to march and remained behind in the camp? Had our comrades who had remained behind at Fünfteichen been unexpectedly liberated?

After the first hundred metres I pulled out my bread and bit off a large piece, but I was determined to save the rest. I could not withstand the temptation for long. At short intervals as we marched along I shoved my reserves into my mouth, morsel by morsel. Soon nothing remained. I no longer had reason to fear that anyone would steal my bread, but this was an inadequate consolation. I began to hope that we would reach our destination the following evening, and that there would be food waiting there for us – I thought I could manage one day without bread.

From snippets of conversation I overheard, I concluded that we might be destined for either Dachau or Buchenwald. According to some reports, conditions in these camps were still tolerable. Some comrades were even of the opinion that compared to Grossrosen, these camps were more like sanatoriums. However, all this conjecture could not conceal the fact that none of us knew what future the ss had planned for us. What, for example, would have become of us if we had not stepped forward of our own free will to go on the march?

As I write this account, the riddle is solved. We now know that all those who stayed behind and declared themselves unfit for the march had chosen their downfall. They did not have the luck of those who remained behind at Fünfteichen, instead they were all herded together and shot. When the courtyard was filled with corpses the ss searched the whole of the Grossrosen Camp with sniffer dogs and discovered many inmates who in that final moment had hidden themselves. The dogs bit them and dragged them into the daylight before these terrified people could leave their hiding place, after which they were condemned to lynch law. They were shot down on the spot. The sick and weak had already been shot where they lay on their bunks.

This all happened at the end of February 1945, a time when even the dimmest must have known that the Nazi regime was doomed to defeat. The hope of liberation was no longer an illusion, it was a reality that could catch up with us at any time. Yet the murders continued with an inconceivable frenzy. In all the camps, in their hundreds and thousands, the helpless, and the defenceless died a myriad of deaths. I, like many others, did not believe they would let me live if I declared myself unfit to march. In order to secure the remotest chance to live I took on the dreaded ordeal – that is – I continued to march. My feelings were dulled as I remembered the failed assassination attempt of 20 July[1]. I hoped that a similar day would return and a successful attempt would be made, and so bring about our longed-for liberation. Full of despair, a confused sequence of thoughts of salvation passed through my mind: like parachutists falling from the sky to assault the Nazi fortress and bring about the end of these bloodthirsty men, there must be an exit from all this hopelessness, eventually all kinds of suffering must come to an end! I forced myself to try to take just one step at a time towards this end. Fortunately it was still cold, for many inmates would have broken down after just one kilometre if we had been in the summer heat.

After a few hours we reached the suburban railway station at Schweidnitz. Waiting there was a train that consisted of coal wagons. We were quickly assembled into groups of 150, and like animals we were herded into the empty wagons. As usual, this was accompanied by a hail of blows with pistol butts by the ss men on guard. The wagons were so crowded that it was difficult to remain standing; sitting or lying down was out of the question. The weakest amongst us staggered to the floor. There they lay on the feet of those who remained standing and with their last strength they in turn struggled to free themselves from this burden by continuously pushing the bodies lying on the floor. The Kapos stood, legs apart, at the open wagon-doors, claiming more space for themselves. The Germans among them, mostly professional criminals and convicts, felt themselves superior to the masses of other inmates because it was rumoured they could join the ss. In actual fact many of them had applied for ss uniforms because they were impatient to exchange their hated concentration camp garb. Whether true or not, these Germans felt themselves compelled to claim their privileges. They quickly monopolised a large part of each wagon for themselves, beating and trampling those around them. The coal wagons were without a roof. The fine coal dust covered the floor and sides. Very soon it clogged every pore of our skin and lay suffocatingly on our throats. Between each of the wagons was a small roofed hut that provided shelter for the ss; they stood with

---

1. On 20 July 1944, an attempt was made to assassinate Adolf Hitler inside his Wolf's Lair field headquarters near Rastenburg, East Prussia.

their guns at the ready. As night fell, the cold became piercing. Tiny snowflakes fell incessantly upon us from the dark sky. Inconsolably, we stared into the void above us. Finally, we huddled closely together to keep ourselves warm and to protect ourselves from the penetrating cold and wetness of the snow. Although we wore our blankets over our heads and shoulders, the dampness was like a second heavy blanket that covered our bodies. After waiting for hours on end, we breathed a sigh of relief when the train began to move. The Kapos tried to divide us up into two groups. In turns, one group had to stand huddled closely together, while the other had to sit according to the method we knew from Grossrosen: that meant each inmate had to sit with his legs spread wide apart so that another could sit in the space in between. We had to swap so that in turn we all had the chance to rest for a few hours. There were some who were so weak they could not stand, and if those at the front or back did not support them they fell to the floor. They were pushed and trampled for so long until they cowered like beaten dogs in the corner.

There were neither buckets nor toilets in the wagons, so some urinated where they stood. We were in open wagons, so no one cared. Soon after, some who suffered with diarrhoea or dysentery tried to excuse themselves, but the Kapo sought to persuade them to wait. He consoled them that the train would soon stop and then they could relieve themselves. However when the train eventually did stop it was pitch black and none of us were allowed to leave the wagons to go to the toilet. Faced with this predicament, the sick began to do their business in the wagons. They huddled together for mutual protection in a corner as they did their business. But then they could not escape from the crush in the corner because the healthy ones endeavoured to keep the sick and weak at a distance.

I stood against the side of the wagon where I had been pushed by the others. At first I could not move at all, and was able to shift about a little only after the train departed. I was part of the group that had to stand. I managed to retain my place against the side. This had the major disadvantage of being colder than a place in the middle of the wagon, but on the other hand I did not have to protect myself from all sides. This was extremely important for me because it was the first time I had experienced being transported without being shielded by my friends. So I pushed myself against the wooden side for protection.

The train set off again, the silence broken only by the puffing engine. We felt the monotonous soporific rhythm of the wheels with every last fibre of our bodies. Imperceptibly, we were lulled into a semi-sleep where we stood. Now and then we were startled from our sleep, only to relapse back into a relieving stupor. We could hear nothing except the noise of the wheels turning endlessly. I succumbed to the noise, and my thoughts. Then it was my group's turn to sit. I had been content to retain my place against the side and hoped I could keep it whilst I sat. I was not aware of how it happened, but I was shoved into the second row. The man behind me was generous enough to allow me to lean against him. Was it because he understood my weakness and still had sufficient human feeling that he was willing to allow me to do so, or did he feel obliged to support me because he was the one who had pushed me from my place against the wall? Either way I was grateful. It helped me at least to some extent to conserve what remained of my strength, because soon after we had to remain standing for several more hours. I was dreadfully afraid that if in a moment of weakness I should sink to the floor or pass out I would be roughly handled or beaten. Faithful to my usual practice, I did what was necessary to avoid being beaten. Enticing as they may have appeared, I refrained from picking up remnants of food from the floor. The man next to me leaning against the wall began to draw me into a conversation. He whispered to me that he was Polish and a practising Catholic. He had been in concentration camps for a year. He seemed to think about nothing except escape. He could not understand the reason why we were transported from camp to camp. According to him, the ss were only searching for a suitable place where they could calmly shoot us all. I told him there was absolutely nothing we could do. Even when I was fit in Fünfteichen there was nothing I could do to change my situation; now I was so much weaker and disheartened, the idea of resisting my destiny seemed absurd. He changed the topic of conversation and asked me various questions as he tried to discover whether or not he could trust me. Finally, he pointed to his friend who was standing next to him and told me that they had already decided to escape. He asked if I wanted to join them, but I declined because I was so weak. He countered by promising to do all he could to help and support me, and be my friend. On the other hand, they had to ask for my help because he and his friend only spoke Polish. They did not want to draw attention to themselves during the escape because they were foreigners, so they needed someone who spoke German. After some hesitation I declined their invitation. I was not willing to risk trying to escape, although if I had been among friends I trusted I would have been willing to do so. We had heard so much about deception and betrayal that from the beginning I had been extremely dubious about attempting to escape in a group consisting of different nationalities. These two Poles could have proved their comradeship, but still I did not feel I could trust them with my life. So I then spoke frankly to them. For me escape was out of the question. I simultaneously reassured them that they need have no fear that I would betray them. "I will not say a single word about any of this, I have not heard anything, I know nothing," I reassured them.

Later, when our group had to stand once more, I knew the moment had arrived when the two Poles would make their break for freedom. I took the blanket that I wore on my shoulders and pulled it over my head. Isolated from all that was happening around me, I agonised; had I chosen correctly, or had I made a cowardly choice when I shied away from seizing a chance that might have saved my life. In the end, would it have been better to risk being shot in order to escape this miserable transport? Many thoughts crossed my mind: questions and answers in endless succession. This pointless self-doubt would have continued for a long time, but a wild shooting noise ripped me from my thoughts. I pulled the blanket from my head just in time to make out the shadow of a human body as it glided out of the wagon into the darkness. The shooting stopped. Instinctively I ducked and stared intently at the sky. The darkness deepened as the train rumbled through the forest. We were on a bend. This was the moment the two Poles were waiting for. Gradually I was choked with fear. I began to tremble and thought about moving to another part of the wagon. I was frightened that I might be betrayed by someone who may have overheard our conversation. I would be mercilessly beaten because, according to regulations, all escape plans must be immediately reported. I tried to remain as inconspicuous as possible. As the train continued on its meandering route and kept changing direction, so I was able to keep changing my position. Once again I put my head under the protective blanket. The wheels rattled without stopping. The train continued without a break. We never found out what happened to the two escapees. The following day the Kapos and ss told us that the fleeing Poles were stood in front of a firing squad and shot. Some were adamant that the ss told us this solely in order to frighten us. In reality both Poles managed to make good their escape.

As it became light we saw different small towns and villages as we passed through them. Early that morning the train slowed and eventually stopped on a railway siding. Workers on their way to work approached our wagons and enquired curiously as to what type of transport we were. We asked them to bring us something to eat, bread, potatoes, whatever they could spare. Some comrades begged for water. I saw a rail worker hauling a bucket of water, but he was immediately intercepted by the ss who forbade him to continue. In order to deter the workers, the ss told them we were all serious criminals; anyone who approached us would be punished. However, when more trains stopped on the sidings, we continued to shout even more urgently for bread and potatoes. Finally, our individual cries merged into one that passengers on other trains could not ignore. In fact many workers threw us singles pieces of bread and small parcels that probably contained their daily rations. Within moments a wild fight in the wagon ensued. I briefly thought whether or not I should join in this struggle because I was so hungry, but my fear held me back from joining the battle for the bread and parcels that fell on the floor. Many were injured as they tried to steal bread from one another's mouths.

After some time, our train began to move again. We no longer saw large towns. We heard sirens and the dull sound of bombs exploding.

Our train seemed to keep switching tracks. Our Kapos fobbed us off with assurances that rang hollow: that by evening we would reach our new camp, and there we would receive food. When this short February day came to its end our wagons were still being shunted aimlessly backwards and forwards. So began the second night, and still our journey seemed to be without end. The number of those weak, with dysentery and dying grew. One corner of the wagon was already filled with corpses and excrement. We all just ignored this squalor. With an indifference that today seems inconceivable, we registered sickness and death. I witnessed how someone with eyes dulled and death etched on their face crawled to the corner of death and shortly after stopped breathing. Some of the dying had a little foam between their lips, others noiselessly sank into themselves and gave no further sign of life.

The battle for space in the wagon gradually eased. As more people died, so those of us who remained alive had more room in which to stretch out. When night fell I was able to resume my old place against the side of the wagon. The arguments decreased, and even the Kapos assumed a more relaxed manner. Everyone was hungry and thirsty, and we were all overwhelmed with exhaustion. It was as if we experienced this second night in the wagon through a fog. When it was our turn to sit I found under me the body of a man who showed no sign of life. It was impossible to drag him away. I cannot easily remember in detail what followed. I was not unduly perturbed as I remained seated on the corpse. It was a huge relief to me to have an opportunity to sit, and I soon fell sound asleep. I was disturbed only by the hard bones beneath me. More people died through the night. Slowly we pushed the deceased to a heap of corpses which grew higher and higher.

Finally we passed a large station that was barely lit. We could decipher the signs: it was Plauen Station in Vogtland. Shortly after, we heard the noise of wailing sirens, and this was quickly followed by the whistling sound of falling bombs. These "enemy" bombs fell very close to us. We were surrounded by explosion after explosion. These were accompanied by huge tongues of flames that erupted from the ground before us. We hoped that our transport would also be bombed so that our endless journey would come to an end. Maybe the confusion, smoke and fire would make it possible for us to safely make our escape. Even this hope was unfulfilled. For some time after, columns of fire and smoke enveloped burning houses. As the next day dawned the fires subsided to reveal the fact that our pitiless destiny remained unaltered.

We continued our journey that morning. Slowly our thirst grew more and more unbearable. Drop by drop, we licked the dew that had condensed on the blankets that covered our shoulders. I was also able to wet and cool my tongue by licking the droplets that had formed on the iron bars as I stood against the side of the wagon.

Still there was neither bread nor water. We continued for a few more hours until we stopped at a small station. From a distance we could read the station name: Flos. We found out from our Kapos soon after that this was our destination, Flossenbürg concentration camp. We were so worn out we had ceased to care. We watched with complete indifference as the wagon doors opened. A commando of ss and inmates from Flossenbürg concentration camp came to fetch us from the train. Stiffly, we staggered out of the wagons. Almost a third of our comrades who were either dead or dying remained in the wagons.

Then the counting began once more. Even now, we had to stand waiting in rows and columns while the inmates from Flossenbürg pulled the dead and dying from the wagon and piled them close to us so that the final total was correct. This number had to be spot on: no one could be overlooked, dead or alive, everyone had to be accounted for. We turned around to take a final look at the corpses piled high on the platform before we departed from the small station. This transport cost the lives of several hundred inmates. We marched to the camp. Indescribably tired and hungry, we mechanically acquiesced to being driven forward. We were lost in sad thought, what horrors did this camp have in store for each of us? Time and time again we were tormented by the same thought: "Will they let us live or will they destroy us and if so, in which way?"

We marched on hard-packed snow. The peace and quiet of Sunday lay gently over the little town as we marched through. Our march became more and more arduous because we had to go up an incline. We were wretched, despairing figures as we struggled to drag ourselves along the white-covered streets. Suddenly, the loud noise of church bells rang in our ears. Before us, lay the church proclaiming Sunday. Although we retained only a pitiful glimmer of life and hope, the chimes of the bells touched something barely alive in each of us. Did this signify anything? Had the priest rung the bells on this peaceful Sunday morning to call together the good citizens of this small town to protest against inhumanity and indignity in general, and this awful procession of corpses in particular? We really wanted to believe, to hope that the world was at last alerted from its indifference and had eyes to see this dreadful drama as it passed before them – the martyrdom, torture and death of helpless people. Could they not see, hear and feel that in the face of this unfathomable mass murder they could not and should not any longer remain silent?

Just then the gates of the church opened and a crowded mass of people burst out. The service must have just finished. The faithful slipped off the pavement into the road, the same street where we had encountered the church-goers. The ss quickly tried to force us on to the left side of the street with a few blows from their batons. They passed by very close to us, this God-fearing community in their best Sunday dress, men, women and children, all pious clutching their prayer books in gloved hands.

They lowered their eyes and looked away as they passed by. Was it fear or indignation, dread or contempt? We could only believe it was their contempt; that was all we had been accustomed to for so long. And the bells rang louder and louder, really near, really loud. They seemed to ring directly from the hearts of the pious, those children of God, who only seemed to know about "love your neighbour" and compassion from the pages of the Bible. They calmly surveyed our misery and with hardened hearts observed us like statisticians contemplating criminals.

As I think back to my childhood, I remember the Catholic houses of God with their unique rituals and recall how their mystical semi-darkness had a strange appeal for me. Then I believed that those who prayed in those houses of God must have a special inner ability to take on board the pain and suffering of other human beings. Following the example of their God, wasn't one of the basic principles of this church an unconditional obligation to "love your neighbour"? The numbing reality of this encounter destroyed whatever remained of this childish fantasy.

The barbed-wire fence of Flossenbürg concentration camp loomed before our eyes. Our legs were tired, without feeling, like sticks of wood, as we walked as quickly as we could. As we marched through the camp gate we were directed to the far corner of the Appellplatz. Once again we had to submit to being counted, and it seemed to take forever because some of us kept falling to the ground from exhaustion and causing chaos in the ranks. After we had been counted forwards and backwards, we were assigned to Quarantine Blocks 21, 22, 23 and 24. I was allocated to Block 22 and in no time it was full to overflowing. Three or four people were shoved together to occupy each plank that usually served as a place for one person to sleep. I shared a space with three other comrades. We had to sleep head to toe. At night our feet disturbed one another, but at least we had a place to lie down.

Soon we were called once more for Appell. This time we were not marched to the Appellplatz, we were stood in front of our block where we were counted, first by the Block Secretary, then by the Block Elder. After that we had to wait until the Camp Secretary and the ss Blockführer arrived. We had to wait for many hours until it was our turn because they had to count the inmates in all the blocks.

Only then did we find out that just a plain fence separated us from the main camp. There was a suspicion that we were infected with typhus so we were kept in quarantine. Most of the prisoners in Flossenbürg were German. The majority of them wore a small piece of green cloth on their left chest to signify that they were criminals. Frequently they were supported by Ukrainians who undertook many of the menial camp duties. Some of these boys had incredibly long whips with which to beat us.

We had to submit to a very time-consuming procedure to be allocated a new Flossenbürg concentration camp number. We had to march in single file past the Block Secretary who sat at a big desk.

Shortly before I reached the table, the man in front failed to say his camp number and name as loud as was required, a Ukrainian room orderly drew back his arm to strike across the face. The man had the presence of mind to duck, so I was hit a heavy blow in his stead. I fell to the ground. My spectacles were broken as they catapulted from my face and fell to the floor. I had managed to retain my spectacles intact through all the camps; their breakage was for me an irreplaceable loss. It was very difficult for me to stand up, my head hurt so much. Full of fear, I quickly called out my number, "It's not your turn yet," shouted the room orderly as he grabbed me tightly by the throat. Trembling, I waited until it was my turn. When I had passed the desk I sensed I was bleeding. Finally, in strict order of our new numbers, soup was distributed. My number was 72,678; this entitled me to a portion of this thin soup which I slurped greedily, although it contained very few pieces of carrot and potato. Our old Block Leaders and Kapos gave out the bread ration in the evening. We were relieved about this because we knew them already and they were not as unpredictable as the Flossenbürg Kapos, but we also knew they were certainly no better.

Inmates began bartering immediately after the distribution of the bread ration, many swapped half their ration of bread for a plate of soup. The soup kettle was not completely emptied. The room orderly and Kapos put what was left in the soup kettle aside. Every functionary got a few extra litres that they were able to barter for whatever they wished. Those dying of hunger and half-dead from thirst were all desperate to fill their empty stomachs. Some of them gave half or all their bread ration for a few plates of soup, and so made their condition even worse.

The Kapo Hellmann from Fünfteichen also lay in my block. He was a distant relative of mine, and was appointed assistant room orderly. I expected some concessions from him because he had been a frequent guest in my parents' home. In his new position, in certain circumstances, he would have had the opportunity to pass me a plate of soup when he had enough. For a while I hesitated, uncertain whether or not I should forgo my pride and ask. Finally, my hunger triumphed over my inhibitions, and when he passed the wooden plank on which I lay, I enthusiastically answered his enquiry about my condition. I asked him to give me an extra meal, I would be grateful for anything. He said I should stay awake so he could secretly bring me something to eat while everyone was asleep; the others must not know about it. Of course it was not a present, because the soup that the functionaries retained was intended for everyone, so what he would bring me was our entitlement anyway. But who then thought about categories of justice? Everyone tried to participate in every opportunity for any type of theft in the least dangerous way, to obtain a plate of soup from the functionary by legal or illegal means. Some inmates swapped their bread and margarine ration for a ladle of soup. Others debased themselves cleaning the shoes of the camp "elite", others "organised" small utensils in exchange for a bowl of soup from the functionaries. I hoped to obtain some of this stolen soup from Hellmann.

Evening came, and soon it was time for bed. At last came the shout, "Lights out!" With open eyes I lay still and waited. When would Hellmann bring me the bowl of soup? But he stayed away. I waited for ages, until finally I dozed off. I awoke with a start when I thought I heard footsteps. Finally, I had to reconcile myself to the fact that I had waited for nothing, and fell asleep as my tummy kept rumbling. After this, I did not speak to Hellmann any more.

When we were woken the next morning I made my way to the latrine and washroom, which were both in the same building; but the way was in blocked by sick and weak comrades. Some were dead, some lay dying. Corpses littered the washroom. Some were naked, their limbs contorted with spasms before they died. It was apparent that others had taken their clothes. Comrades afflicted with foot-sores removed bandages from corpses to bind their own wounds. Those who were half dead looked on the others with apathy. I observed that they were already detached from this life, no longer capable of feeling pain, no longer aware of what happened around them.

At the morning Appell we had to line up the corpses and sit the weak living ones in front of us so everyone could be accounted for. Only then did the counting begin. Some of us were then allocated to various work tasks in the camp. We were not given any of the usual jobs because we were still in quarantine; so we had to sweep and wash the barracks, clean the latrines and the washrooms, and remove the dead. We dreaded removing the dead because this was so difficult. It required two inmates to remove each corpse. Each one took hold of a leg of the corpse; so that the stiff corpse was dragged across the floor. With each tug the head would bump on the ground. Several times I was ordered to move corpses. On one occasion, the Kapo ordered ten or twelve of our group to remove corpses to the crematorium. Together with a comrade I had to drag a dead person across an icy path that lead up to the crematorium. The crematorium was very narrow and there was hardly space for two men next to each other. The uphill gradient drained our final strength. Suddenly a corpse-carrier in front of us slipped and did not get up immediately, despite his efforts to do so. As we could not pass him we had to wait until he regained his footing The Kapo watched impatiently, he wanted to finish this detestable job as soon as possible. To the Kapo, the fallen inmate did not appear to be at the end of his strength. His face had not yet caved in, and his body did not yet resemble a Muselmann. The Kapo began to beat the helpless man on the floor. With it he bellowed, "You lazy dog, you faker, you're trying it on! I'll show you!" However, the fallen inmate lay motionless on the ground and gave no sign he felt any pain. Finally the Kapo stopped beating our comrade and shoved him with his foot. "Get up now. We have to continue! Get up!" The face of the fallen one became paler and his eyes stared listlessly. We tried to support his back and pull him up by his arms, but he slumped down with a faint death rattle, and stopped breathing. So they now lay together, the cold stiff dead, and the warm corpse.

Until now, I had been in camps that were not equipped with crematoria. When we were in Fünfteichen there were also many inmates who died from weakness, or who were beaten to death; but we did not live in close proximity to the crematoria, and this gave us a feeling of relief when we compared our situation to that of those inmates living in Auschwitz and other such camps. The first time I had seen a crematorium was from a distance, in Grossrosen. Here in Flossenbürg, I had to bring the corpses to the crematoria, and there I stood next to the ovens where I saw the fire, and inhaled the sweet smoke of burning human flesh. We were filled with a mounting dread of death as we watched the burning corpses. Until now, our apparent indifference had enabled us to get on, and to suppress our fears; but we were overwhelmed with fear as we observed this spectacle. "Will I too also end like this?" I asked myself, "And when?" I was terribly emaciated and bore all the external marks of a Muselmann. How long could I live like this? I did not know the answer.

The smaller my chance of survival became, the stronger became my will to live, at any price. I suffered more and more dreadfully as I was repeatedly assigned to remove the corpses and witnessed the flames of the crematorium and the gruesome, towering column of smoke.

The crematorium lacked the capacity to cope with the continuing flood of corpses, and so they heaped the dead into a mountain in front of the building. They lay in stacked on top of one another, first one way, then the other. When there was no room left for more piles of corpses, a ditch was dug adjacent to the barbed wire at the edge of the camp. It measured about seven to eight metres in width, length and depth. We threw the corpses into this ditch, poured tar over them, and set them on fire. The rising smoke polluted the air throughout the area. Both crematoria burnt day and night.

We became very anxious as rumours circulated throughout the camp. We speculated whether all Jews were to be removed from the various blocks, separated from the other inmates and collected together, and sent away on "transports". We could just imagine what they had in store for us. We cited as evidence, in support of our theory, the fact that a few Jewish Kapos and assistant Kapos, who until now, as Jews, wore the yellow triangles, removed their identity signs and replaced them with badges that denoted other identities.

All those who could speak Polish tried to sever their connection with their own (i.e. Jewish) people and loose themselves among the mass of other Polish inmates. We believed that the "Camp Prominenz" were well-informed, so this action on their part only heightened our fears. When we saw how they tried to conceal their Jewish identity we feared the worst. I deliberated feverishly, but I could not bring myself to do as they had done. I had no opportunity to acquire a different coloured triangle in exchange for my own. I only had one portion of bread, and that was not sufficient. I was also afraid that I might be beaten to death if I was discovered wearing the wrong emblem. So I did nothing that might risk incurring the displeasure of our Kapos. I took no action, and abandoned myself to my destiny.

I was not seriously ill and had managed to remain alive. I still had one priceless treasure: my shoes. If they had noticed them, my comrades would certainly have envied me. So they were not immediately identifiable as leather shoes which would them stare the Camp Prominenz in the face, I deliberately kept them quite dirty. Only by keeping them dirty, could I hope to keep them longer. Having leather shoes in the camp was an unimaginable help.

One day the camp administration decided that we should be released from the quarantine barracks. Those who were ill were sent to the sick bay, and the remaining inmates were allocated to other barracks. Then we had to assemble for Appell, where we had to remain standing motionless for a long time. We could not return to the blocks we had formerly occupied, that much was clear. After a while, we were led to the bath-house; there we had to wait once again for those who were in front of us to finish. Finally we were admitted into a large room and immediately ordered, "Everyone undress – naked! Shoes on one side, clothes on the other!" Many of the guards in the bath-house were Ukrainian, and without any cause they began beating us all indiscriminately. We stood around waiting for a long time. A Ukrainian began looking through the pile of shoes, searching for a leather pair for himself. I was appalled at the prospect that I might lose my good shoes, when I saw him holding them in his hands. Without thinking, I rushed forward to explain that they were my shoes, and anyway they were too small and would not fit him. On several previous occasions I had been able to save my shoes from the grasp of the Kapos because they were so small. The Ukrainian did not want to hear this, lifted up his rubber truncheon and repeatedly beat me. "What!" he screamed, "do you want to steal a pair of shoes from the others?" I realised that the beating would continue if I persisted. I quickly disappeared into the crowd of naked bodies that was huddled closely together because of the freezing cold. Now I had lost my last treasure and from that moment was numbered among the mass that had to make do with shapeless, heavy, wooden clogs.

Then there was a life-and-death moment which made this painful incident pale into insignificance. We had to form a single file. Each of us in turn had to go into a small room. There, our bodies were examined, perhaps to determine our physical condition. I was one of a number of inmates who were separated from the rest and sent to an adjacent room. Those who had been chosen were relatively few in number; but this served only to heighten our feelings – we were tormented by helplessness and fear. After a while a Kapo from the sick bay appeared. He used a red pen to paint a cross on our foreheads. We did not know what this meant. Some of us thought that we would be sent to the sick bay. I concluded that it could only be to our advantage; but someone else vehemently contradicted me, asserting that we would receive a murderous injection when we arrived in the sick bay. None of us felt able to dispute this opinion. We were apathetic, and our situation seemed hopeless. We stood, still naked, around the room with red crosses on our foreheads. The door opened and in walked two inmates who I knew well, the Kaiser brothers who originated from my home town. Four years ago, I had been with one of them in Grünheide Camp. I had met the other brother, who was older, in Fünfteichen where he was a Kapo; and it seems that also by this time he had managed to secure himself a favourable position here. He worked as a boiler man. Originally he had been a tailor, and in the camp he would sew for the relatives of the camp administrators. I had shared a locker with the younger Kaiser when we had been in Grünheide, and I also used to write his love-letters for him. When we were working in Grünheide in 1941 our relatives were mostly still at home, and every two weeks we were allowed to write short letters to them. The younger Kaiser had fallen in love with a girl from Mährisch-Ostrau. Like many others, she had been driven from her home and forcibly resettled in our town. The young lady only understood German, Kaiser only spoke Polish and Yiddish. So I wrote his letters and put in them twenty years worth of my heartfelt feelings of love and homesickness.

Camp life was such that these friendships soon lost their meaning, and one could not expect gratitude to be unending. I was utterly astonished that Kaiser remembered me and still felt obligated to me. He came towards me, squeezed two pieces of bread into my hand, and warned me to eat them quickly. Unable to believe the luck which befell me, I then asked him the meaning of the cross painted on my forehead. His face took on a helpless, blank expression. Then, a compassionate glance gave him away. I then understood. When people were selected for special treatment their fate was sealed. At first, I remained in my group, thinking: what could I possibly do to break out of this deadly isolation.

At that time Flossenbürg Camp was heavily overcrowded because new transports of inmates arrived each day. The camp administrators no longer knew how to cope with the unending stream of humans who arrived from every direction. The frail and the sick were eliminated to reduce the total number of inmates, and to prevent an epidemic of infectious diseases.

The isolation room gradually filled with skeletal humans, so much so that it would not be immediately obvious if an inmate left. I mustered all my courage and crept to the door that led to the boiler room where Kaiser worked. As I stood mute before him with pleading eyes he quickly washed the red cross away with soap and washing powder. Then he shoved me through the corridor into another room in which another crowd of men were standing naked. Amongst this new transport were some inmates who still looked half-human. When I spoke to them I discovered they were from Plaschow Concentration Camp, near Krakow. I was taken to the bath-house, which was equipped with showers that actually worked and soon the water started to flow. In the corner stood a container of liquid soap, and we were able to take a handful of this cleansing fluid. After we had washed ourselves we were sent to another room to get dressed, and without further delay I was assigned to Block 3 with my new comrades. Here I encountered once again some of the inmates who had been in the quarantine block with me. We stood and waited in front of the block. Our bodies were stiffened by the cold, and we tried to keep moving. Suddenly, I found myself staring at a very familiar face. At that moment my Uncle Leon ran towards me. He had been evacuated from Kittelstreben Concentration Camp to Flossenbürg. For a few moments we carefully scrutinised one another, and realised that since Fünfteichen there had been a serious deterioration in our condition. He had also survived foot-marches and exhausting transports in goods trains, and had become dangerously emaciated. However, we were both delighted with the coincidence to have discovered one another among the crowded masses that filled the camp. A huge sense of relief welled up inside me as I realised that here was someone to whom I could turn with complete trust and confidence. Our group was assigned to its planks; once again four men to a single sleeping space. Even so, there was insufficient space for everyone on the planks, so the remainder had to sleep on the floor.

The room orderly in charge of the part of the barracks in which I slept was a Pole. He was an experienced camp inmate, a criminal. Sometimes his raw voice ascended to become an insane scream. We could never tell whether he had become hoarse because of his scream-ing or the schnapps bottle that was constantly at his side.

Although we were no longer in quarantine we were not assigned any regular work. Our main occupation consisted of waiting hour after hour in front of our barracks. This standing began very early every morning. We had to stand for hours in rank and file until Appell was finally over. We could only move after the seemingly end-less process of being counted was complete. That year, March was a cold month and winter seemed to drag on into spring.

We were liable to be severely punished if we were caught leav-ing our block, so we had plenty of time to reflect upon our gloomy situation. Often we forged plans in case we survived the war. Even when I was in Fünfteichen I frequently occupied myself with a plan to go to Breslau and there, as a representative of the police, to hold the Nazis to account for their crimes, always provided that I survived.

Food was a constant preoccupation for all of us; sumptuous meals were a constant fantasy. For hours on end we recounted to one another the food that was cooked, baked and roasted for the Holy Days of the Jewish festivals and Shabbat. I vividly recalled from my childhood the festival days which we as children spent with my grandparents. What huge quantities of good things we demolished then! We often spoke of fresh bread and baking, and tried to recapture the fragrant taste of the crust. However, ultimately, every conversation returned to the same old question: "What would you do if you held two kilos of bread in your hands? Would you cut it thick or thin?" This magnificent thought gave satisfaction to our tongues. We also spoke about the forbidden pleasures of pork. In the camp we had often eaten pork and horsemeat, so many were of the opinion that in the future they should not forgo these foods. The call for Appell or for work tore us from these dreams and fantasies.

We were no longer bothered by the fact that the camp was constantly enveloped by the smoke of burning corpses. Tears filled our eyes when the wind blew this smoke towards us, and the prospect of our possible end filled our consciousness.

Each evening we returned to our barracks, our senses dulled. All too often this was followed by short fights over places on the planks. In the course of each day some inmates died or were transported elsewhere, and those who slept on the floor fought for the few vacancies on the planks as they became available. Fights sometimes turned into brawls because those places close to the stove were so much warmer than those on the frozen floor.

On one occasion, four inmates on a neighbouring plank were quarrelling. One claimed his comrade had pushed his feet into his face. The accused protested against this accusation. A menacing atmosphere spread amongst us. We were all so short-tempered we could resort to animal behaviour at the slightest provocation, any seemingly trivial incident was sufficient to trigger a confrontation. The light should have been extinguished some time ago. The noise attracted the attention of the room orderly who immediately stormed to those who were quarrelling. He pulled one inmate off the plank and beat him until he fell to the floor. He grasped two adjacent planks to lift himself off the floor before letting go and falling with all his weight on the prostrate figure, squashing him. Thus the murdered comrade lay on floor next to my plank all night. The next morning we carried him out of the barrack.

Day and night, death stalked the barracks of Flossenbürg. There was no relief. Our fear and horror was such that we were in a state of constant tension. Each evening we fell onto our planks, broken by tiredness and exhaustion. The short night hours passed in no time. So not even night brought the relaxation we longed for.

In the early morning, as once again we trudged back and forth in front of the barracks in the freezing cold, a Kapo approached us. "Who wants to come with to carry food?" he called out. "The soup kettles must to be carried to a factory outside the camp." From the Kapo's assistant we discovered that a transport of women who had been evacuated from other camps had arrived at a factory a few kilometres away. Naturally, I immediately thought of my sisters, who had been at Auschwitz. This concentration camp had been evacuated, and I hoped to meet friends or relatives who would be able to tell me about the fate of my sisters. It was for this reason alone that I freely volunteered for this arduous task, even though I knew I was unlikely to receive any reward. A pleasant surprise awaited us when the "carriers" arrived at the kitchen. Instead of the usual promises which were only given after work, if at all, each one of us was given a plate of thick soup. It originated from the kettle which was destined for the women. We handled the kettles with the utmost care, not wishing to spill a single drop and so risk incurring the wrath of the Kapos. Finally we loaded the kettles onto carts and pushed them out through the camp gates. The meadows and hills around Flossenbürg lay quietly and peacefully before us. It was as if we were immersed in another world. I turned to look back towards the camp a few times. I wanted to see what it looked like from afar. What picture did those who lived freely in the vicinity have of it? Do they think human beings live there, or is our camp an isolated island whose sounds and wailing are swallowed up by the landscape, where humans are forcibly marooned to wait and become beasts of prey, where the strong beat the weak and subsequently burn them to destroy the traces of their murder? What are the thoughts and feelings that stir in the minds of those people who look upon our camp from a safe distance? What do they think when they see us pass by, wretched figures in concentration camp garb, pushing our carts, accompanied by armed ss soldiers? What is the purpose of this barbaric island in the thoughts and feelings of the outsiders? How much do they know and understand about life behind the watchtowers and barbed wire, where day and night on both sides of the enclosed camp unbroken columns of burnt human corpses ascend incessantly, leaving no trace? Do the people that we encounter en route suspect anything of the blood-curdling events happening close by? As we briefly glanced at them their silent faces betrayed nothing, neither that they recognised our fate, nor did they waste any thought or emotion upon it.

There were ss guards on either side of the factory gates. With a hand gesture they beckoned us to enter with the kettles of soup aboard our handcarts. We pushed them into the courtyard.

Two women in uniform wearing small hats together with a group of about twenty wretched figures shrouded in striped concentration camp rags, mere shadows of their former selves, approached us. The monotonous clattering of their wooden clogs was the only way we could tell they were not ghosts. However, the female guards were very much a part of our reality. One of them rhythmically slapped her skirt with her whip as she marched. Some of these shadowy creatures wore small scarves around their heads from which their unnaturally large and sad eyes stared vacantly. The scarves were the only way we could tell they these prisoners were women. We could see that the heads of those without scarves were shaved and bald like us. Clad in their miserable overalls we could hardly tell if they were male or female.

This was the first time we had been in close proximity to female concentration camp prisoners and women guards. We were not able to linger and study them more closely because we had to push our carts into a factory hall which had a glazed roof.

As the doors of the hall opened we stared bewildered at the sight that greeted us: a vast mass of twitching concentration camp rags, the entire floor covered with female bodies shrouded in threadbare rags, a sea of work-weary bodies from which their bare shaven heads bobbed up. Sunken faces stared at us, faces distinguished only by the pale tip of their noses and hollow eyes. We looked into their eyes and could not look away, their staring eyes held us spellbound

and transfixed. At first glance we could not tell if they were men
or women, young or old. Their sunken faces were lifeless, but their
fearful, wandering eyes tracked our every movement.

We unloaded the soup kettles in a corner and remained there
only briefly. Gradually we were able to distinguish individuals among
this shapeless mass of humans: yes they were women, herded together
and sitting on the floor. They were so closely packed together they
were forced to sit legs apart, one in front of another. Thus thousands
of women sat on the floor, breathing with difficulty in a cloud of an
indescribable stink which rose from their bodies and the excrement
in which they squatted. They could no longer stand up or attend to
their bodily functions; hundreds of them just sat there, dying. A pitiable heap of humans laid spread out before us, suffering and dying.
With our eyes we searched in vain for some sign of their femininity,
but we could detect no trace in their faces or bodies. Shaven bare,
they resembled faceless animals, bodies shrouded in rags. Through
the rags we could discern their dried-out breasts hanging out, their
rags insufficient to provide for female modesty. Horrified, we stared
at these sick bodies covered in excrement, and a growing feeling of
nausea welled up in us and became worse when our eyes moved to the
floor in the middle of the hall where there was a hollow. Here, those
who had been eliminated were heaped up together with the bodies
of unconscious women as they lay dying and mostly half-exposed,
their naked female body parts filthy and besmirched. At this moment
we were gripped by indescribable horror. We stood there, numbed,
unable to comprehend the scene that confronted us, unable to recognise in this heap of misery any of our relatives or friends. We did
not know which way to turn, which shout to answer. No human
norm intruded upon all this. Here, the life of each individual was
meaningless, only a herd of condemned, dying female skeletons lying
pressed against one another in urine and faeces, dead or alive. Which
of them still had a name, which of them could be recognised? Half
in shock by what we had just experienced, we left the hall. However,
we took the look of those thousand, wide open, hopeless, lifeless eyes.
I'll never forget those eyes, which were only directed to the death
which was so close to them.

We marched back to our camp. Clouds of smoke drifted skywards from behind the hill that concealed the town. We hurried back despite the fact we knew the source of the smoke was the crematorium. How long had we been in that hell? We no longer knew. Had it been minutes or hours? The horrific nature of our experience had extinguished our sense of time. We smelt, felt and saw nothing but dirt, decay, sickness and death. We had been forced to confront many atrocities in the camps, but the spectacle of the women's camp, thus far surpassed them all; it was unbearable and we were deeply disturbed. Our senses no longer seemed to function, it was as if they denied our experience and wanted to obliterate it.

When we returned to our Block we were all gripped by the news of the day, so very few made any enquiry about what we had witnessed. There was much discussion about the major defeats suffered by the German Army on the Eastern Front and on the Western border. It was said that the Russians were on the way to Berlin and the Western Allies were already on the banks of the River Main. All this news was partly based on smuggled fragments of newspapers and partly on the fantasies of inmates. Most disturbing was news of the break-up and evacuation of our camp. Some thought that Jewish inmates would be singled out and transported; and if so, when and where? If yes, when and where? The question "where?" gnawed at our consciousness; a hundred possible answers flashed through our minds. "Are we going to be killed? How, in which way?" For a long time we had to accustom ourselves to being objective and dispassionate when we contemplated these questions. It was all we could do to maintain an outward appearance of composure. Within, it was the same turmoil as before. We revisited the one question that filled us with bitterness and outrage: should we die now, now – when the torturers' end was so near? We wanted to survive, to see with our own eyes when it was our murderers' turn. We longed for the day when our roles would be reversed, when the bloodhounds would become inmates in striped uniform, on starvation rations lying on planks. It was our most ardent wish to see with our own eyes how they would exist in our filthy barracks and latrines, how they would stand and be hounded on the Appellplatz. This was the one day we wanted to experience! May the world go down thereafter! Just one such day and we could die in peace. No – this must not happen: that we should die like dogs on the eve of our redemption.

About this time some of the inmates from our Block suddenly disappeared. They had identified themselves as Poles and assumed false names and concentration camp numbers in the hope of avoiding the unknown fate of the transport of Jews that would soon be assembled. This means of escape was only possible for those inmates who had non-Jewish friends to protect them. The remaining inmates would have been aware of their absence, and they could easily denounce them! The Poles, Ukrainians and Russians soon noticed when anyone tried to conceal their Jewish identity; the distinguishing character-istic of circumcision marks us forever and can never be removed.

Naturally, some of these inmates had already been caught, and if they did not enjoy the protection of influential functionaries they were severely beaten. Despite this, I did not relinquish my desire to disappear. In anticipation, I learned with others the Christian prayer "Our Father", but I could not find trustworthy non-Jewish friends who would protect and support me. In fact it was relatively easy to obtain a small iron cross in exchange for a ration of bread and hang it on string around one's neck. However, without non-Jewish friends I could do nothing, so I had no choice but to carry on living as before, to be watchful, and to avoid the beaters who relentlessly searched for victims.

One day after our midday meal we had to assemble on the Appellplatz. Then came the instruction we had anticipated, "All Jews, one step forward". We had to assemble as a single group and regis-ter our concentration camp number according to our Blocks. It was clear that they had made important plans for us. Any thoughts of disappearance had to be abandoned.

In the evening during the soup distribution it was announced that all Reich-Germans in the office should identify themselves. We did not have to wait long to discover the reason. In accordance with a new decree, all Reich-Germans had to report to the ss and were perhaps even forced to join, we never ascertain whether it was really compulsory or not. Either way many of them enrolled, especially criminals.

One night, about one or two hours after the order "Lights out!" we were startled from our sleep by crashing noises followed by screaming voices "Lights on! Who has stolen the bread and rucksacks? The culprit must give himself up immediately!" Confused, we blinked in the sudden bright light. A rowdy and heavily drunken mob of German Kapos dressed in prison uniform and ss caps on their heads broke in to our barrack, singing boisterously. They bellowed that their comrades in the adjacent block had been plundered, and the thieves had come from our barrack. With kicks and blows they chased us from our planks and searched feverishly for the stolen goods. As they did so, they discovered a few inmates had forbidden objects. These were immediately seized and the unhappy owners were tormented with beatings. Unfortunately, they found two small pots of potatoes on the stove which some inmates had planned to cook during the night. When the Kapos discovered the potatoes they screamed, "You have swapped the stolen rucksacks for the potatoes. Who do they belong to?" Silence ensued. Then they seized some of our comrades from planks close to the stove and began to beat them indiscriminately. The victims protested their innocence, but for the drunken Kapos it was not a question of right or wrong. They carried on beating wildly; they wanted to torture for tortures sake. They grabbed those comrades who tried to flee and threw them on top of the stove which immediately fell over, scattering burning embers on the floor. The sight of flickering flames provoked a new atrocity. Our weakened comrades were seized by their arms and legs and thrown on to the burning coals. Their bodies were pressed down onto the fire in an attempt to put out the flames. Then those wearing ss caps departed, and we heard them for a long while afterwards. We remained behind with our maltreated comrades, and were overwhelmed by the sad certainty of the difficulties that would confront us if these new ss people were to be our guards on our next march.

Chapter Seven

Leonberg

I arrived in Leonberg in March 1945. It was snowing and raining when they unloaded us from the cattle trucks in Leonberg Railway Station. For the first time since I left the death camp of Flossenbürg, I dared to hope that I would live to see the day of my freedom. I marched on wobbly legs from the station in to the camp. It was night when we arrived in the camp, shrouded in our blankets. Our despair and our fears that we would be destroyed (for this is what often happened to transports of skilled workers) were allayed when we arrived. We asked if they had a crematorium. "No". We breathed a sigh of relief.

The Appellplatz was small. The camp consisted of walled houses rather than barracks. The rooms were filled with bunks made with planks, and we, the new arrivals, were herded in. We were desperate for a drink of water, but this was forbidden because dysentery and typhoid were rife in the camp. The camp administrators and ss wanted to ensure that this epidemic did not become widely known. They tried to keep the camp going so they could keep their posts and thus avoid being sent to the battlefront. I could not sleep because of my agonising thirst, so I lay awake on the plank listening to my neighbour dealing with an old inmate. The latter wanted to show him where there was water, simultaneously warning that if he were caught with water or even going for it, he would be so badly beaten he would no longer need it. The old inmate demanded a few cigarettes in exchange for precise details of the exact route to this hidden water supply. A few minutes passed, then my neighbour returned, satisfied. He told me that he had drunk his fill; he also brought back a bowlful. He was ready to give it away for one cigarette, or even a half. I had nothing to offer. Uncle Leon lay next to me, and he was suffering terribly from thirst. Finally, my neighbour took pity on us. He called me over and whispered in my ear, "I have risked a beating and have given away cigarettes. Although I still have a bit of water, I have to keep it for myself. I am afraid of being thirsty. If you want, I will explain where you have to go to get water. Take your eating gear with you so you can bring some back for your Uncle. You've got to risk it!" Then he outlined to me exactly the way to the steps, a few steps down, continue to the wall, there count so and so many steps, then feel for the tap with your hand. I crept back to my plank and told my Uncle. "No", he said, "it is too dangerous, you are already too weak, if you are caught you will be beaten, and you will not survive. That will be the end of you".

For a while I lay awake, wracked with indecision. I was preoccupied by the thought of water in the cellar. My Uncle fell asleep. Carefully, I slipped from my plank and in the darkness made my way like a sleepwalker to the water supply. My heart was beating wildly. "If I am caught, I will be mercilessly and murderously beaten. That would be the end of me." Occupied with these thoughts, I made my way in the darkness. Down unfamiliar steps, I came to the aforementioned wall; then searching with the palm of my hand I suddenly found the tap. I carefully turned it on. Water began to flow. I sealed my lips tightly around the tap. I drank without drawing breath for as long as I could. Then, carefully, I filled my metal bowl to the brim for my Uncle. Then, quickly, I drank and drank from the tap until suddenly I heard steps and noticed something moving towards me. Petrified, I stood motionless, and the steps went away. I could hear nothing except the beating of my heart. Quickly I crept back to the steps, carefully cradling my precious possession. With total concentration I counted my steps and searched for my place among the many planks. Soon I recognised my Uncle, who was looking out for me from his plank. With a feeling of triumph I handed over the metal bowl full of water. That was our first night in Leonberg.

After the morning Appell, most of the people on our transport including me were assigned to the night shift to assemble components for aeroplanes. Some of us thought they were V2 rocket parts. The workshop was in an enclosed tunnel. There was a shortage of food, but the regime was not as strict as we had feared. We had little reason to fear being beaten. There were several air raid alarms nearly every day. We drew encouragement with every flight over our camp.

Typhoid and dysentery were continuously on the increase. The sick and dying lay everywhere; in the so-called toilets, in the gangways, on the stairs. It was not long after a frail or sick person sat down before a death rattle passed over their lips.

It was a major task for the Camp Commando to remove the dying and the dead. For these weeks Leonberg was no longer a work camp but a death camp. Death dominated all thoughts in the camp.

My legs were so weak it was all I could do to stagger to the night shift, although I was hardly able to work. I was assigned to a group using electric hammers to fix rivets. As I was so weak I could not hold the hammer properly and therefore my rivets were uneven. Our foreman was a Pole from Krakow. He warned me to work properly and hammer them in neatly. By this time I had also become a Muselmann; but psychologically I was not yet completely broken. Despite numerous warnings I could not rivet properly, so the foreman punched me in the face. Although I did not feel any pain I could feel the anger welling up inside me. "Have you now become a Muselmann who is beaten, but does not react?" I asked myself. I was weak and hungry and could hardly breathe. I kept returning to the water fountain to drink and I felt a little better.

I mustered my thoughts together and decided to make conversation with the foreman. He was not one of the criminals from Grossrosen, but he had been active in the Underground Movement.

In contrast to the Poles who had been in Grossrosen, those who had been members of the Resistance Movement had retained their humanity. So I said to the foreman, "Look, I have already been in different camps for four years and have gone through a lot. While I still had my strength I was happy to work but now I am too weak to hold this electric riveting hammer properly in my hand. It didn't hurt when you slapped my face. But I think you understand and can see that the war will soon end. Warsaw is already liberated. Whatever will happen to us, we are all destined to share the same fate. This is why I believe it is a crime for any one of us to beat another unless we are forced to do so." Deep in thought, he looked at me for a while; then he said, "Boy, you are right. In this inferno we often don't know what we're doing." He gave me a job which I was able to do sitting down. I had to fix various different-size screws where they belonged.

So the days dragged by until mid-April 1945. One morning just after we had returned from the nightshift we had to wait for longer than usual on the Appellplatz. After being counted several times they gave us 200 grams of bread and then we were ordered to leave the camp. It was said that the camp was to be evacuated, but where did they want us to go? We had no idea. For many it was their final journey. We marched towards Stuttgart. Long before we reached the town I threw away the blanket that always kept me warm because I was too weak to carry it any more. Those of us who sat by the roadside were shot. A little later I also had to abandon the coat I had received from a dying man because I couldn't carry it any more – a beautiful warm coat that in earlier times was only worn by camp prisoners of the highest rank. I was on my last legs when we arrived in Stuttgart. We marched in the town past ruins. There was a stationary tram at an angle across the road. The chaos that surrounded us clearly showed that the killer regime was coming to its end. The look on the faces of people in the street was also different: gone were the contemptuous looks which we had experienced until now; instead partly thoughtful, partly sad and serious, sometimes even compassionate. We felt encouraged and strengthened by all this, and this gave us the strength to continue marching to a suburb of Stuttgart where it was intended to load us onto goods wagons.

Once we arrived at the station we heard the usual screams of the ss guards to which we had grown so accustomed, and shoved us into the wagons using their rifle butts. A hundred inmates were squeezed into each wagon. We had to sit on the floor with our legs apart. When the wagons were full some tried to stand up but were unable to remain upright for very long. They were so weak they were soon compelled to fight again for space on the floor. There was absolutely nothing for us to eat or drink. The doors were not completely shut; two ss guards were posted at the opening. Then everything in accordance with our past experience: no space and no bucket for us to attend to calls of nature; the sick and the weak, especially those suffering from dysentery, could not keep anything in and were pushed by those who had the strength into a corner of the wagon.

The atmosphere in the wagon became very stressful as it became apparent there was little chance or hope we would survive. Some of those with diarrhoea used their final strength to resist being pushed into the corner of corpses and excrement. They flailed around with their wooden clogs; their piteous cries were heart-rending. Foaming at the mouth and with eyes glazed and protruding, one of those already bearing the mark of death defended himself and shouted like an animal, "I don't want to die in the filth! You murderers! Let me go! I'd rather be shot, you murderers!" Then another began screaming in desperation, crying like a lunatic. We all were greatly agitated by the screaming of the sick. An ss guard stormed in through the wagon door to re-establish "order". Literally every bit of space on the floor was covered with people, but with callous disregard he stepped on them where they lay. He stepped on hands and human bodies; everyone tried to avoid being trampled on. An outbreak of panic became a very real danger. The ss man began to stagger nervously as he rained blows on us. Those inmates who had some strength tried to soothe those who were screaming and encouraged them to calm down; they also sought help and quiet from those comrades who retained a semblance of normality. Despite this, one inmate remained standing and continued crying and screaming. He had lost his mind. He wailed and raged so terribly that some comrades had to restrain his arms to stop him thrashing about with his clogs. Finally, the only way we could silence him was with a few blows. He fell over, white foam covering his lips – and then he too was pushed into the corner of the dead.

Some inmates tried to negotiate with the ss to be able to attend to nature out of the wagon. After that the ss permitted two inmates at a time to go out of the wagon into either open fields or nearby woods. This was a welcome relief.

On the second evening I got stomach cramps. Was I now to be struck down with dysentery?

My brain was whirring as if I was affected by a fever. I was desperate for the train to stop, otherwise I could not see how I could save myself from the pile of corpses heaped in the corner. We heard that the next morning when we were due to arrive at the camp we would receive bread and soup, so I drew on my final reserves of physical and mental resilience. My Uncle Leon was sitting next to me, and he laid his hand on my body to warm himself. He kept on and on at me to persevere, and simultaneously tried to push me towards the door so that I would be among the first to get off and attend to nature when the train stopped. I felt a little stronger thanks to the cool air close to the door opening, and so was better able to control my stomach pains. I tried with all my strength to control myself and waited until the train stopped once more. All my thoughts and will were focused on this moment. Then I insistently begged the ss man to let me out. Hesitantly, he gave me consent as we stopped in a dark forest. I was not allowed to go more than two metres from the wagon. The ss man shone his torch and pointed his cocked rifle at me the whole time. My bowels emptied like a waterfall; I felt as though I was about to lose all my innards too. Weakened, I returned to the wagon. Then I felt my strength ebbing away. I slumped. I was constantly preoccupied by just one thought that hammered dully in my brain: tomorrow I will arrive at the camp. Tomorrow we will get bread and perhaps a plate of warm soup. Finally, I fell into a deep, exhausted sleep. In my dream I stood at the open wagon door; my mother stood on the sidings below. She gave me her hand and said, "Get out of the wagon!" I tried hard to reach her outstretched hand but I was so weak I couldn't lift myself. With all my strength I struggled to grab the saving hand of my mother. I woke up and realised that as I slept a comrade had rolled onto me. I freed myself from this burden and recalled my dream: the open wagon door and my mother's outstretched and supportive hand. This wonderful apparition strengthened my belief that my mother was standing by me in my worst hour. My heart suddenly lifted, it was as if my spirit had been liberated. In that moment I was suddenly strongly convinced that I would also survive this transport.

The following morning we stopped at a small station, I read its name: Kaufering. We were not far from Landsberg. It was a great relief to get out of the wagons, but about a quarter of our comrades had not survived, and we abandoned their corpses in the wagon. Some inmates from the nearby camp arrived and removed the bodies. We then marched into Camp 1 (in the vicinity of Kaufering there were a number of camps distinguished only by their number). We stood on the Appellplatz from where we were taken in groups to be washed and deloused. Everyone got a bowl of warm soup and a piece of bread when we left the bathhouse. Even though the soup was thin it was sufficient to sustain the will to live. There was no room in the camp for us so for a while we just stood in front of one of the barracks. The camp personnel were reluctant to let us enter because they had heard there were some among us who were suffering from diarrhoea and typhoid, and so did not want to expose their camp to the risk of infection.

We departed at twilight and marched a few kilometres until we reached Camp VII. We were not taken to the barracks, instead we were taken to the Narren. This was a narrow ditch covered with wooden boards with loose straw strewn on either side. We stayed there overnight. The following morning we had to line up separate from the other camp inmates. The only work we did was inside the camp, otherwise we were not allowed out of the camp.

As new arrivals we received less bread than other prisoners because we had not yet been allocated to a work commando. The ration of bread was more meagre than ever; sixteen slices were cut from each loaf. Some were driven by hunger to pull up grass and cook it in tin bowls. Each day the rubbish was swept up into a big heap and burnt, and some of them tried to cook the grass using the heat from this fire, and then ate it. My Uncle advised me against trying to ease my hunger in this way for fear of catching diarrhoea, typhoid, or any other illness. The following day I was terribly plagued by hunger. I could no longer control myself and I secretly tried to collect grass. But I couldn't find anything because the other comrades had already pulled it all up.

So for a while we vegetated, but despite our weakness we kept our spirits up; we had heard that the Red Army was outside Berlin and the Americans had crossed the Main.

One day we were called to Appell at an unaccustomed time. Quickly we were assembled into a column five abreast, and I had no opportunity to ensure I was alongside my Uncle Leon. When our group numbered seventy-five the order, "March in Step, March!" was given, and before we knew it we had left the camp. I looked back towards my Uncle who had remained behind on the Appellplatz with many others. I would have willingly run back to bring him with me, but it was too late. I was driven forward by those around me. Once again uncertainty began to nag – "where to now?"

Chapter Eight

Mühldorf

I looked out for friends in the marching column and, incredibly, I recognized a few old friends from Markstadt. After a short march we arrived at a train station. Once again, for the umpteenth time, we were loaded into wagons. It was the middle of April 1945. The air was soft and mild, and gratefully we soaked up the sun's reviving rays.

Now, suddenly, the Kapos and the ss treated us surprisingly decently. Despite the difficulty we had in understanding each other, they no longer found it beneath their dignity to engage in conversation with us as we made our way. We took advantage of this new approach to find what was happening on the battlefront, and what the ss intended to do with us in case of a (German) capitulation. However, the ss, now consisted of a strange assortment of nationalities and included many Volksdeutsche (ethnic Germans) from Ukraine, Poland, Romania, etc. They suddenly showed a lively interest in prisoners who originated from their native countries. Some ss people cultivated prisoners by helping them to get bread and potatoes.

A man from the part of West Ukraine that belonged to Poland walked next to me with whom I could communicate easily with in

Polish. He asked me what region of Poland I originated from, and what was my family name. He told me that at home he was also friendly with Jewish families, and that he found them to be refined and cultured people. Then he assured me that he sincerely regretted the disgrace and suffering inflicted on the Jews. His words were a stark contrast to his hat and uniform, which bore the death's-head symbol.

Another ss man approached as we talked. As I fearfully fell silent, my conversational partner said to me in Polish, "He doesn't understand what we are saying; he is a German, a son-of-a-bitch." These comments seemed strangely at odds with my previous experiences of ethnic Germans. In all the years of my camp life, I knew that the ethnic Germans in the ranks of the ss often sought to distinguish themselves by exceeding the brutality of the ss. In the new circumstances created by the tightening grip of Allied forces surrounding Nazi Germany, they would have loved nothing more than to shed their Nazi skin. As everything collapsed around them it seemed opportune for them to befriend us in order to secure their own future.

When we had been loaded into wagons, a friend confided in me that "his" sentry had regretted the gruesome extermination of Jews. He claimed that he had always distanced himself from these crimes, at least in his own mind. My friend took him at his word, and begged him to turn a blind eye if an opportunity for him to escape would arise. The ss man assured him that he too had often thought about making his escape, but the surrounding area was so densely populated that it would be almost impossible to remain undiscovered. Still, the two agreed to meet in the new camp to continue planning their escape.

The Spring brought new hope. The beautiful season and other changes in our life enabled us to contemplate the future with new-found courage. This transport was so different from all previous ones. We were no longer herded like cattle into the wagons; instead we were able to climb in slowly and without undue haste. On the march we no longer heard the nerve-wracking clicking of guns which had been the invariable accompaniment to all earlier transports. This time, those who were weak were helped along, not murdered on the spot.

The pace was no longer dictated by the rapid march of the Kapos and ss; instead it was regulated by the faltering steps of the weakest.

Our train passed through small towns and villages which apparently bore no scars inflicted by the war. We felt a benefit both from inhaling the clean air outside the camp, and the view from the train of a world which had not suffocated by violence and blood from which we had been excluded for so long. The uncomprehending indifference with which the people of this world stared at us, the unchanging rhythm of their lives stood in stark contrast to our suffering, and pained us deeply.

The train stopped at Mühldorf Station in the evening. The ss opened the doors of the wagons and shouted, "Get out!" Astonished, we observed that close to the train there were columns of prisoners repairing wrecked railway tracks. Large craters along the tracks were evidence that the station had been recently bombed. Then a passenger train rolled by on an adjacent track. As it passed by so slowly we could clearly observe the passengers. In the main, they were well-dressed and seemingly well-nourished people. Many young women among them stared at us blankly without feeling.

Some of us spoke with those inmates repairing the tracks. They were inmates from a camp for Jewish prisoners. However, when the ss realised we were calling to one another, they stopped all further contact. Then we were assembled into a marching column five abreast, counted and then marched away. Bad as our physical condition was, we did not give up because of our growing conviction that our circumstances were about to improve. For the first time we had not lost anyone during the march, and that filled us with great happiness. Until then, during these marches so many inmates had died that their corpses made mountains at the stations when we arrived; disheartening views for all of us as we had to continue with fears we did not dare to admit to: that very soon we too would belong to those who were treated like rubbish and buried in no man's land.

It was not long before our dulled sense of fear of the unknown came to an end when we reached the camp. There was not the same regime of terror in Mühldorf, unlike that which I had experienced in Grossrosen, Flossenbürg and Fünfteichen. From the outside, my new camp resembled Grünheide, the first camp I was in. However, the barracks were surrounded by barbed wire, but there were no high watchtowers, nor were there the twofold electrified wire fences. Individual guards outside the fence kept watch. Here the atmosphere was less strict than the sadistic concentration camp regime we had come to fear. To our astonishment, camp inmates wore their own civilian suits with yellow stars stitched to the front and back. Compared to us most of them were well-nourished.

They led us in groups to the wash-barracks where we were able to wash ourselves thoroughly with soft soap. I was shocked when I saw my pelvis and thigh bones from which almost all my muscle-flesh had disappeared. I was overwhelmed with disgust for my own body. It was as if I was looking at a stranger that I wanted to have nothing to do with. I was in a state of mental turmoil; it was as if in my own mind I was confronted by two people who provoked a feeling of hostility: one suffering because of their interminable gruesome experiences, and the other who was reluctant to believe the evidence of his own eyes and condemned what he saw. For a long time, I was deeply troubled by these feelings and thoughts. I very clearly remember these thoughts and feelings to this very day, but I cannot completely comprehend them after so many years.

We were assigned to barracks that were already occupied. We did not receive a warm welcome from the current inmates because our arrival left less space for those already in residence; moreover, they were shocked by our appearance.

Most of the camp inmates spoke Hungarian; the majority of the camp hierarchy and officials were Hungarian. The Camp Elder was a Hungarian familiarly known as "Bacsi", which means Uncle; this was very strange to our ears. Until this time I had managed to pick up a few phrases of the prevailing camp language in Czech, Ukrainian, Russian, Flemish and Dutch, but I found it unexpectedly difficult to understand words in Hungarian.

There was a nasty surprise in store for us when we began searching for a place to sleep. There were no vacant planks for us, so we had to share; when our Hungarian roommates returned from work they protested vehemently. It became a confrontation, and we were barely able to make ourselves understood in response to their Hungarian abuse. The outcome was that the old lags preferred to keep to themselves rather than share with any of us. So I was able to share a plank with a friend from Markstadt. Some of us had to content ourselves by lying on the floor.

The old prisoners had the best of everything, but that was nothing new. As new arrivals we were last in line when food was distributed, first in line for the most difficult, dirtiest work, first in line for extra duties, and had to make do with the least favourable spaces in which to sleep. However, there were other reasons why we were openly discriminated against which only made sense if one understood the enormous gulf that separated us from Hungarians Jews. It was a gulf that arose both from the fact that we came from different countries, but also from our very different experiences.

Polish Jews had been deported and many of them murdered long before Hungarian Jews were deported to the concentration camps in Spring 1944. Those who remained alive languished in the few remaining ghettos and concentration camps. For three years Eastern and Western European Jews endured inhumanities under German occupation until their "Judenrein" campaign (literally, to make Europe empty of Jews) was implemented and they were finally murdered in what was called the Endlösung (Final Solution). However, during these three years the Hungarian Jews lived as free people. It was only in Spring 1944 that Eichmann's campaign led to the destruction of over half a million Hungarian Jews in Auschwitz.

On the first night after my arrival I left my barrack as usual to search for friends and acquaintances. I was delighted when I encountered my old school friend Passermann. Although he looked well-nourished and cared-for, I hardly recognised him at first. It was so long since I had seen anyone wearing civilian clothes in such good condition. When I saw him approaching me, I was so overwhelmed with joy that I wanted to hug him. I was dumbfounded when he merely put his hand out and took an unmistakeable backwards step. My condition was such that it was inadvisable to touch me. Most of us Muselmänner were full of lice and so physically weak that we did not care about basic personal hygiene. The worst of it was that we were no longer aware of our pitiable condition. At first I was deeply hurt by my friend's behaviour; after a moment I understood why he found me so repulsive. He had endured Auschwitz, and his instinct for survival had taken precedence over the stirrings of friendship. He immediately gave me a piece of bread, an object that was worth more than all the treasures in the world. Not only that, he promised to provide me with bread the next day. This happy news filled me with incredible joy. Before we separated he told me about two other people from our home town who were also there.

One night when I lay in the barrack, I suddenly heard a muffled voice call out my name several times. Surprised, I went to the door and saw a man about twice my age standing there. He asked me to confirm who I was. He held out a plate of soup which he clearly intended to give away. For a few seconds I tried desperately hard to recognise him and to remember his name; the warm soup was the incentive for my effort. Although his face was familiar to me, with the best will in the world I could not remember his name. My pitiable appearance made it difficult for him to recognise me. When I told him my father's first name he told me that he had studied with my father and that his name was Stützky. Only then did I recognise him, and I was able to tell him about his family, their house near the cement factory and about others too. I could see he was gripped with pity for me. He quickly gave me the plate of soup, and then content, I lay down on my plank to sleep. How I thanked destiny that had led these helpful people to me.

In general, we all felt somewhat relaxed by the milder atmosphere that pervaded the camp. The prospect of the imminent end of the war lifted our mood. It could only be to our advantage to await events in a small camp like Mühldorf.

On another morning at the Appell they organised the work commandos. The inmates ran about aimlessly; the Kapos, still with their clubs, tried to organise the number required for their labour groups. Some inmates even tried to change from one labour group to another in the hope that they would be given lighter work. The Kapos retrieved these runaways with screams and beatings, so it took some time before the marching column began to move. One could hardly imagine our amazement at these events. In earlier camps, inmates hardly ever dared to attempt to change their labour group; it was often the end for anyone caught doing so. The confusion in this camp was an agreeable relief for those of us who were disciplined long-standing inmates.

At first, because we were new arrivals, we had to stand apart from other prisoners. Each Kapo chose whoever they thought would be useful; I was assigned to the building commando. A third person from my home town who had already been in this commando for some time was Chaim Goldstein. He recognised my pathetic condition; he encouraged me and gave me hope. Immediately he begged his work colleagues to give me a job that I could manage with my limited strength.

So I began my first working day in this camp with confidence. I worked in a column that had to carry bricks. Most inmates had to carry three bricks, but because of Goldstein's earlier input I had to carry only two. I soon realised that the foreman took no notice of me so occasionally I was able to avoid this work. I soon resorted to a long-established camp "trick" and asked for permission to visit the latrine. No one expected me to return quickly because I was the weakest member of our group. Until lunchtime I was able to relax lying on wide planks, and the warm April sun also helped to lighten our mood. Goldstein, who worked a few hundred metres away from me at the building site, brought me some potatoes boiled in their skins – I ate them with great relish. That afternoon I was able to carry bricks with a strength I had not felt for some time. In the evening when I returned to camp my father's former pupil Stützky looked me up after supper and brought me a bowl of soup. Only then did he take the time to talk to me and tell me about his experiences and ask in which camps I had been stationed. Stützky had survived the death camp at Auschwitz. He was surprised I had withstood four years of camp life. I told him about Hermann, who had almost treated me like a son, and who had trained me as an electrician – the time spent with him had ensured my survival. Stützky then told me he supervised youths who had to sort potatoes in a large store. Straw was also stored in the loft of these storehouses, so it was strictly forbidden to make a fire in any of these rooms. It was impossible to cook potatoes in secret, let alone smuggle any into the camp. Since he was the supervisor, he knew he would be held responsible for any theft, so he had to be vigilant with his workers. However, he had discovered that in other camps it had proved possible to cook potatoes using an electric current. Could I, as an electrician, manage this trick? I thought about it. Perhaps I could try it with coils, would a zinc bucket and wire be suitable for this experiment? Before I could do so, Stützky had to persuade the Kapo of the working column that I could join his group.

The following morning the work assignment was no stricter than it had been the day before. I pushed into the front row to make myself conspicuous because I did not want to have to carry bricks any more. Feverishly, I searched for Stützky, but I could not attract his attention because he was preoccupied counting his work group. Without hesitating, I called his name out loudly, and finally he gave me a wink. He lined me up in a group of about thirty young people, some of whom were not even sixteen years of age. With a profound sense of relief I joined them. My fellow inmates envied my new-found privileged status as a member of the camp "elite". We worked inside the building where we were not exposed to the wind and rain. Occasionally, youths were able to take advantage of their working circumstances to cook potatoes or exchange them for other food.

When we started work I quickly acquired a zinc bucket and a few metres of electric wire. Then I had to prove my worth. I disconnected the fuse and connected the flex to the circuit. Then I connected an old insulator to the end of the wire and attached the other end to the bucket, level with the surface of the water. I laid the potatoes carefully around the insulator, and then filled with suspense we watched and waited for the outcome of this experiment. In fact steam slowly began to rise from the bucket and the fuse coped with the additional load. Finally the potatoes were cooked; the experiment was a success. Stützky was even more pleased than I was. At lunchtime the potatoes, with their beautiful aroma, were carefully spread out, counted, and fairly distributed. As a reward for my efforts

I received a double ration. This episode brightened the gloom of my camp experiences to date.

One evening after Appell, I met up with some acquaintances from Fünfteichen, including Schlamek Metz (who fell in the Israeli War of Independence in 1948) and Rosmarin. They went to a corner and began to cook a sugar beet. I wanted to help them by making wood shavings, but I pushed the blunt blade of the knife deep into the flesh of the ball of my thumb, leaving behind a long scar. Whilst the sugar beet slowly cooked over the fire until it was soft we discussed that day's rumours about the liquidation of the camp. Since the camp was not closely guarded we toyed with all kinds of ideas about plans for our escape. Our camp was joined by a women's camp; we were astonished that "elite" inmates from our camp could go in and out. From this we could hardly fail to conclude that security was unusually lax. Our thoughts of escape began to take shape. The fear of another transport inspired the boldness of our plans. A quick escape might finally end the interminable, debilitating waiting. Schlamek Metz was an enthusiastic supporter of our plans but at the same time he said that under all circumstances he must take his father with him as he had taken him everywhere and looked after him until now. So we began to examine our planned escape in more detail. The best prospect of success appeared to be from the side of the camp directly into the forest. If necessary we could either cut through or dig a hole underneath the wire fence. We decided that when it next rained during the night we would steal silently past the guards, slip through the fence, and make our way into the forest. We were all too weak to attempt anything heroic; but time pressed on, and we did not have very long to think about it.

We were able to "recuperate" for two weeks. Then one day we were ordered at Appell not to go to work but instead march to the station where a goods wagon awaited us. So it was not liberty that greeted us, nor our longed-for escape, but instead, once again, the hated and feared transport. We were no longer together among a circle of helpful friends; the secret cooking of potatoes had abruptly ended. Wistfully, I thought back about recent weeks. I dreamt about the tight mesh of the wire fence that I had stared at for hours on end, which in my thoughts I had already broken through. All that was now in the past; the present was transport – transport to where? There were many answers to that dreadful question: one version went like this: we would be taken to a big holding camp where Jews from all the camps in the surrounding area were being accumulated. Another whispered rumour that inspired fear and dread: we would be deported to a camp in Tyrol where all the Jews would be murdered. We did not voice our fears because we craved the comfort of hopeful illusions. There was one fantasy that we often spoke about: that we would be cared for by the International Red Cross and taken under its auspices to Switzerland. We embellished this dream with many tantalising details and endlessly speculated how it might happen.

We later found out that an order was issued from Himmler's headquarters for us to be transported without delay to Tyrol where the ss planned to build a mountain fortress. In Himmler's headquarters there were various opinions about what should be done with us; some were of the opinion that we should be murdered with other Jews in the Tyrol, others thought we should be detained so we could be ransomed to the Americans.

At Mühldorf Station we were loaded onto wagons. After being shunted about for a long time our transport slowly got under way. The train kept stopping because it was repeatedly attacked by low-flying Allied aircraft, so our journey was more stop than go. Only at night could the train travel without interruption. The train could not travel quickly because it was forced to make so many detours. In parts the rails were ripped apart in bomb craters; apparently there were insufficient workers to repair the damage. When, on the second day of our transport, we had to wait for a long time at a small station we found out that we were not far from Munich. The station was called "Poing". Our train stopped on a siding at the edge of the forest. The ss took advantage of the break to rest and warm themselves in the April sun. We tried to find out from them what they intended to do with us at this station. We did not learn very much from them, but we did discover that we were not far from the concentration camp at Dachau, so we concluded that was where they intended to take us.

Suddenly we became aware that the ss guards who were guarding our wagons had disappeared. We looked out of the wagon and saw the guards gathered around the camp leader, who gave a short speech. After a few minutes the guards returned, opened the wagon doors wide, and told us we were free. Was this reality? Was this the moment we had yearned for, for years? Had they really let us get away alive? Some of us joyously hugged one another, and even effusively shook the hands of the guards. We were overcome with joy because we had escaped death. While this scene unfolded, the ss and some from our ranks went to plunder the food wagon attached to the train. We had not had anything to eat for twenty-four hours, and we were ravenous.

I was so overcome with my new-found freedom that I myself forgot my hunger, and silently observed the scene with indifference: how old camp inmates came together, how women and girls from the wagons joined them. They had emerged from other wagons attached to our train; they had all originated from a camp adjacent to our own.

Then I saw how some people carried whole loaves of bread under their arms, how others carried large packs of margarine. When I asked where they had got their booty from, they pointed to the wagon at the front of the train. Quickly I also ran there, but the food wagon was already engulfed by a dense crowd. Even so, people pushed and shoved as they tried to get into the wagon. Some of the Block Elders and Kapos called for the ss to help to push people back, but the mass of starving people seized the wagon and plundered it. Everything that could be moved was carried away, and soon not a single piece of bread or cheese remained. Those of us who failed to get any of this treasure circled the wagon in the gloom like hungry hyenas, staring into the darkness. Some of us scraped margarine off the floor after it had been trampled on in the stampede.

Gradually people rearranged themselves into groups sorted by the town or country from which they had originated. The group from our home town consisted of Stützky, Passermann, Goldstein, Rontschkele and myself. Rontschkele and I had only recently arrived in the camp. The five of us began to discuss what we should do next and to whom we might turn for help, spurred on by the fact that some groups had already left the station. Some of the ss men and women who had guarded the Women's Camp began to mingle with these groups. In the confusion of these radical changes the boundaries between the former torturers and their victims was erased. We exchanged clothes with the ss; we sat together and ate with them at the edge of the forest. One of our group thought we should find out the whereabouts of our home town; actually he wanted to walk all the way home. I advised him against this because our home was so far, far away, and the war had not yet ended. After some discussion, we decided that first we would go to a farmer and eat until we were full up, then we would to listen to the radio to find out what was happening at the Front, and only then would we calmly make our way to the next town. We went in search of a railway station. When we had walked a few hundred metres we entered a yard that was already filled with a number of inmates who had already eaten all the available food. We continued and found a farmer who allowed us to stay; the whole of the rest of the village was already occupied by inmates from our camp, so we were lucky to find this accommodation. A Polish woman who worked for the farmer had shown us the way, and it was thanks to her that we were able to stay there.

When we asked for bread we were told that there was none left, but the farmer's wife promised to cook soup and potatoes for us. We rested and asked the farmer to switch on the radio, but it did not work. We were facing him and waiting for our soup when without any warning we heard wild shooting outside. Shocked by the clatter of pistol and machine gun fire, we recoiled from the benches. After a few moments, the Polish woman worker looked outside to see what had happened. Shortly after she returned, she wrung her hands, and made the sign of the cross. She told us that the ss had chased the former inmates, and all those who did not stand still were shot with pistols and machine guns. We begged the farmer to hide us in the cellar or barn, but his former friendliness evaporated and we read his rejection in his facial expression. Stony-faced, he said he could not hide us and told us to leave immediately. We had no time to think before the ss burst into the farmyard and aimed their cocked machine guns and bayonets directly at us. From their uniform we could tell that these were not our usual guards, but an ss army unit stationed in the forest. When they discovered that a transport of concentration camp inmates had been liberated in their vicinity, they chased us and took us all prisoner. (Later, I found out that news of our liberation had been announced on the radio by "Action – Free Bavaria". When the American forces reached the suburbs of Munich a group of Germans had seized the initiative and for a brief time occupied the radio station, calling on German soldiers to lay down their arms. This group was overpowered by local ss units.)

Most of our former guards had disappeared into the distance when we had been freed, but this ss Army unit did not need their help. They carried out their duties thoroughly and quickly. With guns at the ready they hounded us and quickly scooped us up into groups, and then chased us back into the wagons. The road from the village of Poing to the station was littered with our dead and injured comrades who had been chased. Some were laying on the ground in pools of blood, groaning and writhing and pleading for help, but there was nothing we could do for them, each of us had to run for our lives. Those who could not move quickly enough were stabbed or shot. I felt the prick of a bayonet, but I did not turn my head. With all that remained of my strength, I ran for my life. Stützky, who was just a metre behind me, was speared by a bayonet. He let out a short scream, fell down and remained motionless on the ground. The murderous hounding continued, our running punctuated by the whistle of flying bullets and the cut and thrust of bayonets. We arrived at the station, panting for breath. More guards at the station gestured with the butts of their rifles to encourage us into the depths of the wagons. With a final effort I climbed into the wagon. A few hours ago I was still united with four friends from home; we had all believed that the gates of freedom had opened for each of us. Now, with bitterness and grief, I realised that only two of my friends had survived this bloodbath. I myself had heard Stützky's death cry. Goldstein was also missing, but I did not know what fate had befallen him. Passermann told me that Goldstein had been beaten up as we ran towards the wagons; when he struggled to stand up and rejoin his comrades he was cut down by a volley of machine gun fire.

The wagons were locked from the outside. Cowering and frightened, we lay on the floor. Some inmates had wounds inflicted by bayonets and bullets, and we did our best to bind up their injuries with improvised bandages, but we did not have enough rags; it was bitterly cold, so none of us was willing to sacrifice our rags. The injured groaned and whimpered when anyone touched them. I still could not grasp what had happened in the last few hours. One hour ago I had believed I was a free human being, now I was locked in this train, lonelier than ever, two of my dear friends who had endured so much suffering and even withstood the hell of Auschwitz were now dead. With their death their entire family line was extinguished.

Outside, the drone of approaching aeroplanes drowned out the noise of the firing of the ss guards whose presence put us all in jeopardy. As the noise became ever louder we could clearly see through gaps in the wagons the low-flying Allied planes and the panic-stricken ss rushing headlong into the forest. Slowly, and at low level, the planes flew over our train. Salvoes of flak from anti-aircraft batteries close to the station rose to engage with the planes. Shortly after, dense swarms of aeroplanes clouded the sky, flying towards us in a tight formation, firing their machine guns at the station and the trains. The bullets drummed on the sides of the wagons, and occasionally even penetrated the wooden walls. We knew this because we heard the sudden screams of people being injured in the wagons. We three comrades huddled down and even closer together until the gunfire stopped. When I looked up I saw that one of the three of us lay motionless – he was the youngest of us and called Händchen. We shook him in the hope that he might have fainted or been injured, but Händchen showed no sign of life. On the back of his felt coat we noticed a small burnt hole. Like statues, we remained motionless, staring at our dead friend. Was the whole world really conspiring against us, determined to dispatch us to our death, no matter how? A few hours ago we had been five comrades (from my home town), five people, the sole survivors of large families. In just a few moments three of us had been murdered. We were inconsolable after these terrible events. Silently we looked first at one another, then at the corpse who lay next to us as if asleep.

A sudden cloudburst drummed on the roof of the wagon and was a welcome distraction. Paradoxically, we felt more secure inside the wagon as the storm raged outside. What had they planned for us? We were like cowed animals, almost glad to sense the narrowness of our cage, fearful that otherwise we might be shot like creatures in the wild. Our resistance had been broken long ago. We were relieved that the train was once again in motion and carried us away from the scene of this bloody episode. Quietly we lay there, listening to the monotonous rhythm of the wagon. When morning dawned we talked to people in other wagons. We asked where the train had stopped, and where the train was going. Apparently we were in the sidings at Munich Station, but we later discovered this was not true. We were increasingly tormented by hunger. Next to me in the corner of the wagon lay an inmate who had hidden some food under his clothes. He would like to have eaten it, but was openly afraid that others, seeing him take out his reserves, would either steal them or beg him to share them. So he went to outermost corner of the wagon where I lay, to be undisturbed. Apparently, he was not afraid of me as I appeared too emaciated and weak. When he began to eat at leisure I could not help but follow his every movement with greedy eyes. He must have been moved by my hungry look because he gave me a piece of the cheese that he had stolen from the food wagon. He had an entire piece of cheese that he consumed bit by bit. Other comrades gave me some raw potatoes. I held them for a long time in my hand. Should I eat then raw, as many others did? I had not eaten for two days and my hunger was so great that eventually it outweighed my fear of becoming ill so I cut potatoes into thin slices and sucked them. I let the precious few crumbs of cheese melt on my tongue and spat out the sucked-out pieces of potato, persuading myself that I had eaten them. So I partly calmed my rumbling stomach.

Our wagons were shunted back and forth, and the motion caused the injured among us to groan with pain. But we could do nothing for them.

Night fell. We were tormented more by thirst than by hunger. After the massacre of Poing we were so terrified that we acquiesced to whatever happened to us without complaint. Artillery and gunfire rumbled on all around us through the night, and each new attack awoke new hope in us. We were on tenterhooks because of the noise of the fighting; it was music to our ears, and time passed quickly. The unbroken noise of weapons firing heralded the imminent end, the delivery for which we could hardly bear to wait. Whenever the firing abated we fell into a shallow slumber, only to be startled awake yet again. Dawn had hardly begun to break when we were woken up, not by noise, but by silence. The morning of 30 April 1945 dawned, becoming always lighter, but still a dreadful silence all around. We peered through the gaps in the sides of the wagon to find out what this silence meant, but there was nothing of note we could see. Suddenly there was a babble of voices. The wagon-doors were torn open by figures in unfamiliar uniforms appeared before us. Hesitantly, we left the wagons. We looked carefully in every direction, but could see no trace of the old guards. Our comrades crowded around a few tanks parked next to our train. We were all crowded around, anxious to examine these strange vehicles. We were all extremely curious; were they friend or foe? Then we recognised the insignias on the tanks; they were American vehicles. Slowly I pushed myself forward until I was close enough to be able to touch this grey giant by stretching out my hand. On top of the tank sat two soldiers who, full of pity, threw various foods to us, and started to speak to us in English. We stumbled joyously about, touching the gun barrel and lying down on the tracks. We would have gladly embraced the soldiers and thanked them for the great fortune that we were once again allowed to be free people, now face to face with American soldiers. However, our appearance made ordinary people recoil and try to avoid coming into close contact with us.

We stopped hugging one another. Our bodies and souls were beaten and crushed, utterly drained and exhausted. The heavy snow fell remorselessly, and we shivered terribly in our pathetic rags. We stood helplessly close to the Tutzinger Station, and an icy wind swept across the Stamberger Lake. Everything we touched was freezing: the barrel of the guns we embraced, the clear frosty night, even those people we met on the morning of our freedom. Now we were free, but what remained of our past? Our homes had been destroyed, our families annihilated. We were solitary islands in a freezing, foreign world. These first days were strange; our minds were numb, as if we had been intoxicated by our freedom. We could go wherever we wanted, could do whatever we wanted, but we always encountered dismissive, uncomprehending faces. The world could not or did not want to understand our pain. Had these people been so hardened by their own suffering that the tragedies of others was an unbearable burden, a burden they were unwilling to bear, regardless of the circumstances?

Gradually the first stirrings of our happiness turned to deep disappointment. No warm nest awaited us; no helping, healing, consoling hand was laid upon us to cure our wounds. Our injuries were still fresh and they bled and hurt at every touch. Slowly our hopes melted away, the hopes that had sustained us for so many years in the concentration camps, and changed to resignation and bitterness. It was all too clear that the free world did not understand us; they justified their coldness with well-worn phrases, either "we too have been through a lot", or with the superficial excuse "we did not know or had not heard about the gruesome atrocities you have suffered". Nor could the material compensation of later years heal these wounds. We still carry the burden of our bloody past in our heart and wrestle to find the strength to cope with it.

On 30 April 1945 our freedom was restored to us, but still today, twenty-one years later, as these memories are recorded, the mental shock of the concentration camps remains, the camps still hold me prisoner.

So I wish to close my report with the words of the ex-concentration camp inmate Professor Viktor Frankl. They are words that resound in his book, *A Psychologist Experiences the Concentration Camp*:

> There is no luck on earth that could ever make up for what we suffered. It was nothing to do with luck. What sustained us through our suffering, sacrifice and was not luck. Nevertheless, on misfortune – one can barely focus. Many of those who were liberated found they could not escape the anguish of their experiences even in their new found freedom.

For every liberated person there will come a day when, looking back on the totality of the experience of the concentration camp, will have a strange feeling: he will not understand how he was able to withstand the demands of life in the camps.

Photos

The author's father, Usher Bornstein

The author aged circa 15

The author aged circa 30

Renee (nee Koenig) and Ernst wedding December 1964

The Bornstein family in 1976

The Author working in a medical laboratory as a medical student

The Author with a memorial he established in Bavaria. It states: "To the honour of the Dead and to warn the living"

May 1969, the Author giving the inauguration speech at the Dachau Memorial for Concentration Camp Victims, which he created

The Author with Franz Josef Strauss (6 September 1915 – 3 October 1988) who the chairman of the Christian Social Union from 1961 to 1988, long-time prime minister of the state of Bavaria (1978–1988). The Author frequently corresponded with Herr Strauss on issues such as the resurgence of Neo Nazism. On the Author's death, Herr Strauss wrote a warm personal letter of condolence to his widow Mrs Bornstein.

Addenda

Appendix A

National Religious Groups in Zawiercie and Their Institutions*

YIZKOR

It is with a holy fear that every one of us remembers the Kedoshim[1], who during their lifetime kept alive the flame of Judaism, with the feeling of national self-awareness that one is a Jew. This was the spiritual burning bush which burnt inside them like a fire, until their pure souls left them.

---

* Appendix A and B were written by the author in the Yiddish language and were contributions to the "*Sefer Hazichron of Zawiercie*" which were books written after the Holocaust as memorials to Jewish communities destroyed in the Holocaust. They were usually compiled by survivors from those communities and contain descriptions and histories of the community, biographies of prominent people and lists of people who perished.

1. The term "*kedoshim*" is sometimes also to refer to the six million Jews murdered during the Holocaust, because these people fulfilled the commandment of bringing honour, respect, and glory to God.

We, children and brothers of the Kedoshim, do not simply want to recite "yizkor[2]" and "kaddish[3]" for our deceased loved ones; we also say "yizkor" in the ears of future generations: see and remember what became of the entire Polish Jewish population. Remember too, that all the achievements in Israel, the strength and Jewish national pride, which uplifts you and purifies you, today, tomorrow and the day after, is all thanks to the initiative and dare of those who died (for the sanctification of God's name – *a Kiddush Hashem*).

AN EXAMPLE OF THE PHYSICAL DESTRUCTION

Let us illustrate the degree of the physical destruction of our nation, by describing just one house, in one town in Poland, the large apartment building and dirty yard on 21 Aptetchne Street, in the town of Zawiercie. It was in that house that I spent my youth.

Only a few individuals remained alive from the many inhabitants of that building. Entire families, like Mendel Osokov's family, were wiped out, and no memory remained of them. Both Osokov brothers, Moshe and Elazar, who were members of the "Hashomer Hadati" movement, are no longer with us. Osokov's two daughters, Chana and Frumtche, are no longer with us. No memory remains of the families: Naftoli Weill, Dovid Weill, Mendel Zandberg, Hillel Katsike, Getsel Lefkowitz and from Family Birnfreind. From the large families of Leibel Kvat, Mordechai Kravietz and Dovid Tcherkowsky, there remained only a single daughter from each family.

The heart constricts when one remembers all that. Who am I, that I should be worthy of saying "Yizkor" for all those above mentioned families who are still so fresh in my memory? I feel small and lowly compared to these who have given up their pure souls amidst the most terrible tortures; people with whom I used to play during my childhood and with whom I spent time during the Jewish holidays

---

2. A special Yizkor "Remberance" prayer for Holocaust victims is recited at various times during the year.
3. A special Memorial Prayer for Holocaust victims is recited at various times during the year.

like for example when we celebrated the holiday of Succot[4] together in the succot[5] that were set up in the yard?

The words of kaddish stay stuck in our throat, when we say them for our father and mother, relatives, close friends and acquaintances. Our spiritual leaders, rabbis, teachers, our fellow pupils and comrades in the youth movements, in my case as a student in the Mizrachi *cheder* "Torah Vodaas" and an activist in the "Shomer Hadati" movement, which during a certain period was a strong movement in Zawiercie.

Yiskadal V'yiskadash

THE "TORAH VODAAS" SCHOOL

Everything that had an influence on my spiritual development later on in life, stems mainly, from the time when I started going in the above mentioned modern cheder (more correctly, school). The school "Torah Vodaas" was situated on the Marszalkowska Street, in Hendel Hammer's house. It was there that the headquarters of the Mizrachi and Zeirei Mizrachi were located.

The classrooms there were large ones, and had large windows. Hanging on the walls in the largest room, were portraits of Herzl, of Rabbi Mohilever and Rabbi Kook, as well as of our national poet Bialik.

On another wall hung a large picture of the beloved bochur[6] from Zawiercie who had recently passed away at a young age, Moshe Dovid Shklozsh. He was the son of a shoemaker, a simple, honest, kind hearted, dear Jew, who honoured the Rabbis. His young widow (I think she was called Malle), who was also a daughter from a well-to-do shoemaker and a fine Jewess, was well liked in town, thanks to her refined ways and kind heartedness, her delicate manners, and her lovely smile. This made her husband, who already as a boy was well liked in town, even more popular. Their wedding was held in the presence of a large crowd. Rabbi Moshe Dovid Shklazh was a popular boy in the

---

4. Festival of Tabernacles.
5. A temporary structure with a roof of branches in which Jews eat and, if possible, sleep during the festival of Succot *Also* called a "tabernacle".
6. Young, learned student.

"Migdal Oz" Yeshiva – a scholar, who was later very involved with the Zeirei Mizrachi movement. He used his youthful vigour especially for helping to organise the "Torah Vodaas" school. His funeral was one of the most imposing in Zawierce at the time.

His friends (Yisroel Hermann, Yehoshua Grinberg, my father, may God avenge his blood, Osher Yechiel Bornstein) used to organise remembrance ceremonies in the "Torah Vodaas" school in Shklazh's memory. At one of those ceremonies I sang a song which Moshe Dovid Shklazh had written in Ivrit.

The school was somewhat of a revolution in the life of religious Jews in Zawiercie, just as the Mizrachi movement was at that time in Zawiercie.

I feel fortunate that I spent my youth in the atmosphere of the above mentioned school, where we learnt not only Talmud, but also Tanach, Ivrit, Jewish and general history in the spirit of modern Jewish thinking. There, we celebrated the national holidays including the fifteenth of Shevat, the anniversary of Theodore Herzl's death, Lag B'Omer, and the Proclamation of the Balfour Declaration. Ivrit was much developed there. In those days this was something new in our town, because I do not think that a Tarbut[7] School was already established there at that time.

Studies of nationalistic nature were greatly encouraged. Stories in the Talmud and the Midrash which were in line with nationalistic ideology, such as the story of Bar Kochba and his uprising, were taught to us children in much detail.

I spent my time in the classrooms of "Torah Vodaas" not only during school hours. I would go there also on Shabbat and on certain evenings, when Zeirei Mizrachi held their meetings. My father would often take me along to the debates and speeches. Despite the fact that I was still a child – and I would often fall asleep during the debates and discussions – a lot of it nevertheless remained engraved in my memory.

---

7. The Tarbut movement was a network of secular, Hebrew-language schools in parts of the former Jewish Pale of Settlement, specifically in Poland, Romania and Lithuania. Its existence was primarily between World War I and II.

Y. D. Erlichman and Leibush Yehuda Erlich of Tel Aviv – who invested much effort and resources in the "Torah Vodaas" school, in order to raise the youth in the spirit of national-religious Judaism and pioneering – are, to the best of my knowledge, the only survivors from amongst the leading members of Mizrachi and Zeirei Mizrachi. The name of Shabbtai Chazan who used to be the leader of the school was often mentioned with much praise and as a model of pioneering because he made *aliya*[8] and settled in Israel and worked there in agriculture.

Unfortunately, many of the activists in "Mizrachi" and "Zeirei Mizrachi" had planned to make *aliya*, but due to family commitments they did not manage to actualise their plans (this was also the case with my father). My father's friend Yehoshua Grinberg returned from Israel. Sadly, he did not survive the war. I also did not hear from his son Avraham, one of the best in the "Torah Vodaas" school, after the great catastrophe. My father, my mother, my youngest brother Leib and my younger sister Naomi died in Auschwitz.

As mentioned earlier, Shabbtai Spivak was principal of the "Torah Vodaas" school. The teachers were Mordechai-Mottel Schechter, Dovid Werdyger (later Reb Shabbtai's son-in-law, today of Magdiel, Israel). I think that Koppel Mintz was also a teacher there. Secular studies were taught by Leibel Wigdorzohn and Shlomo Spivak during a certain period of time.

"HASHOMER HADATI"

From the "Torah Vodaas" school we continued into the "Shomer Hadati". That Mizrachi youth movement was industriously organised by Zvi Rubinstein. He trained us to become group leaders and encouraged us to publish a wall newspaper. Shortly before World War ii, the "Shomer Hadati" was considered the largest youth group in town. The leadership of this group consisted mainly of the younger contingency like for example: Manek Rosenberg (who died unfortunately), later also Shalom Granek, Zoshye Vigodska, Yechezkel Schachter (today in Sweden) and myself. Granek died in combat in Israel.

---

8. Aliyah is the immigration of Jews to the Land of Israel.

At the Mizrachi headquarters there was also a large library which contained almost the entire *haskala* literature in Ivrit; Yiddish literature and many general literary classics.

For a short while I was the assistant librarian, together with Zvi Rubinstein. As assistant librarian I often used to take books to the town rabbi, Rabbi Shlomo Elimelech Rabinowitz. The truth is, as a child I felt antipathy towards Rabbi Shlomo Elimelech, due to the well-known controversy about the rabbinate. As a child I aligned myself with the supporters of the Koziglever Rov out of a feeling of fairness. When my father took me on the eve of Rosh Hashanah to Rabbi Shlomo Elimelech, the town rabbi, I grudgingly and in a not very friendly manner, stretched out my hand to him to wish him "a good year". I could not forget the controversy, as well as the injustice done to the children of the Koziglover Rov, who walked around in threadbare clothes and about whom people in town said that they were literally starving. As a child I could not easily forgive the Kaminsker (i.e. Rabbi Shlomo Elimelech) this injustice and this was the cause of my childish antipathy.

However, later when I used to bring to Rabbi Shlomo Elimelech books from the Mizrachi library – my attitude to him changed completely because from the short conversations that I had with him I discovered his refined nature and kindness. In 1945 I met him again in a camp, just before his death. More about this later.

THE GREAT DESTRUCTION
In 1939, shortly before the outbreak of the war, the Jewish-nationalist youth from all denominations were well organised in Zawiercie. Generally, nationalistic fervour was strong amongst all national-religious Jews in Zawiercie. Tens of national-religious pioneers travelled to Israel.

Nevertheless the overwhelming majority remained attached to their town – mostly because of family commitments. The mind was oriented towards remaining in the town. We continued believing in the "civilized world" and it did not occur to anyone that on the 1 September 1939 German airplanes would start bombing Zawiercie (already at 6 o'clock in the morning).

Appendix B

Fellow Residents in the Ghetto and Camps

Surely many others will write about the odysseys of the Jews of Zawiercie after the first bombing of the city, as well as about the escape of almost all Zawiercie residents to Piltz. Therefore I will not elaborate on that account. All I will add is that amongst the refugees in Piltz there were also Jews from Bedzin, Sosnowiec and from other Cantons in Zaglembie.

Before the refugees had managed to figure out what their next step would be (on Monday morning), the German tanks and troops were already standing in the town square in Piltz. The German beasts immediately shot dead a few Poles and Jews. Polish hooligans took advantage of the disorder and started robbing Jewish businesses, with the pretext that Jews were hiding merchandise for selling on the black market. My grandmother's store too, was plundered. The hooligans continued their plundering until a German officer passed by and forbade them to continue.

I personally remember the bloody Wednesday (March 1941) because that was when I was sent off to a work camp. According to what I heard later, there was a second bloody Wednesday in 1942.

On the first bloody Wednesday the first big raid took place, when the Nazis pulled out hundreds of Jews from their beds. Accompanied by beatings and shootings, these Jews were packed into the hall of Berent's factory. The Nazis pulled out the beards and payot[1] of many Jews. There were many dead.

I too was pulled out of bed by the Nazis. I barely got dressed and – beating and pushing me with their riffles – they shoved me down the stairs. I still managed to behold my mother's crying eyes, which accompanied me into the deep, dark night.

I never saw my mother again.

On that night the Nazi murderers rounded up many victims like me.

I was sent off by the Nazi beasts to a camp in Germany. There we built the motorway. Afterwards I was sent from one camp to another and I witnessed the suffering and death of many Zawiercie Jews.

In 1943, after many wanderings, I arrived in the camp of Markstadt (30 km from Breslau-Wratislav). There were many Zawiercie Jews there. The conditions for many of them were very harsh and inhumane. Also there, one of the most beloved young men of Zawiercie, Lipa Shpeizer, passed away. Avrohom Habermann and Tchebiner, the eldest of the Tchebiner brothers (a brother-in-law of Yoske Yoskowics) also died in the Markstadt camp. Tchebiner was taken away on a transport, to destruction.

In Markstadt I also met my uncle, Leib Libermentch, who arrived there in 1942. His wife and a one year old child were sent by the Nazis to Auschwitz. He was murdered by the ss a few hours before the liberation by the Americans (April 1945). He lies in a mass grave in Eggenfelden (Bayern, Germany).

---

1. "Payot" is the Hebrew word for sidelocks or sidecurls. *Payot* are worn by some men and boys in the Orthodox Jewish community based on an interpretation of the Biblical injunction against shaving the "corners" of one's head.

At the camp I was assigned to work together with a German socialist, a Nazi opponent. Thanks to him I was able to keep up correspondence with my parents, who were still living in the Zawiercie Ghetto. Thanks to him, I was also able to help fellow Zawiercie residents, such as Hersh Hochberger and Mordechai Shlechter. Sadly, both of them perished during the last weeks of the war, in the year 1945.

In 1943 I received a letter from my parents, through the above mentioned German, that they were already sitting on their bags waiting for the train to Auschwitz.

Tens of Zawiercie residents in the camp had family members in the Zawiercie ghetto. We all knew that now the fate of our loved ones was sealed. We felt even more resigned that our turn would come next. Our premonition about the lot of our loved ones sadly turned into reality and took on dreadful forms; like the death of the Kedoshim in the house on 21 Hoshe Street about which I found out much later. In that house a bunch of elderly Jews hid out in a cellar during a raid, knowing full well that during such a time they would be the first victims. These Jews decided to remain locked up in that cellar and to die there of hunger and thirst. Amongst those Jews were Reb Henich Bentzlovics and my grandfather Reb Mottel Bornstein.

Two weeks later, the cleaning-up commando of Jews who still remained in the T.E.Z. factory, removed these Kedoshim from the cellar and brought them to Jewish burial. My father's brother, Yisroel Yitzchok (also a brother of Yessochor Bornstein of Tel Aviv) who later was killed from an ss bullet in the Buna camp on Rosh Hashanah 1944, was also a member of this commando. He was very active in the "Zeirei Mizrachi" and very beloved amongst his friends.

At the end of 1943, a new department was formed near the camp where I was incarcerated with the name "the Fünfteichen camp". Many Zawiercie residents ended up there. I took advantage of the kindness and gentleness of my colleague and protector, the humane German, Wilhelm Hermann. He took me to the workplace where the Zawiercie residents worked – under the pretext that we must carry out some work there. That way I was able to meet up with many acquaintances – amongst them: Yisroel Hermann and my uncles Yoske Meisels and Hillel Zimmerman. We were strictly forbidden from talking to each other, but we ignored this. Under great danger Yisroel Hermann nevertheless spoke to me. He told me about the ghetto and about Auschwitz. As he started telling me about my father's last will, may his death be avenged, (with whom he was in the death camp Auschwitz) – an S.S. man suddenly arrived and pulled me away from him and started hitting me because I was conversing with an inmate. A couple of days later Hermann died from a terrible beating. After the above incident with the S.S. man I had not had the chance to speak with him or see him. My uncles too died a few weeks later from beatings. Before their death I used to help them regularly procuring tobacco (through which they tried getting hold of bread). But the supervisors – Polish Katset members – would always confiscate the tobacco from them and on top of that hit them badly too. Hillel Zimmerman died first from these terrible tortures and later Yoske Meisels succumbed as well. The dead bodies of the Kedoshim were taken by the Nazis to the head-camp Grossrosen, were they were burnt in a crematorium.

At the end of 1943, the Nazis also transferred our camp to Fünfteichen. In January 1945, when the Red Army marched in the direction of Breslau, the Nazis led our camp on foot to the main camp in Grossrosen.

It was a march of a few days on foot – a death march – because those who could not walk it, were instantly shot dead.

While I describe this march, I would like to mention the heroism of a young teen, Yaakov Bloch, a son of the butcher from Myszków. This boy used to carry sick people in his arms when they did not have the strength to walk. By doing so he saved them from sure death. He also used to oppose a group of Polish and Ukrainian inmates when they acted abusively. One night, while we were lying down, they pulled out a few Jews – mostly weak people – and strangled them in order to take away from them their piece of bread. We, the Zawiercie residents who used to keep together, noticed this terrible crime, but we were starving from hunger and thirst and we did not have the strength to move.

Again we witnessed how the Ukrainians and Poles pulled out a Jew with the intention to murder him. Suddenly Bloch got up. He removed his boots from his feet and started hitting them right and left – so much that a few of them fell down – dead. Then they started fighting amongst themselves and robbing their own fallen and dead friends. From then on they did not dare to attack the Jews anymore.

This dear boy Yaakov Bloch, who always helped and tried assisting his Jewish brethren to survive this terrible time, was shot dead by the ss in Grossrosen, when he tried to escape in March 1945.

After a few days of bloody wanderings we arrived in the main camp of Grossrosen. There we found many thousands of inmates from Auschwitz. There wasn't any place to lie down, not even on the floor.

Here, in Grossrosen, I found the Zawiercie Rabbi, Rav Shlomo Elimelech. Despite the fact that he was physically completely broken, he was filled with optimism and faith that the end of Nazis is coming near. He recounted to me how the Zawiercie residents in Auschwitz had helped him. Zawiercie girls used to smuggle flour to him. They even managed to bake him challot for Rosh Hashanah.

He would greatly praise Regina Rosenzweig (now in Haifa) and Dora Pultorak, who supported him with food under the most difficult circumstances.

Many people acted to the Rabbi like his Chassidim. They honoured him greatly and tried to help him as much as possible. Jews were jealous of me when they saw me walking alone with the Rabbi and conversing for a long time.

When we had to leave Grossrosen on another death-march, the Rabbi – who was unable to walk – remained behind. The ss shot him dead.

Another person – who was very beloved in Zawiercie as a person – Yitzchok Kartush, was also shot to death during that march.

After weeks of marching and wandering on the roads, on which thousands of inmates lost their lives, I started to feel that my strength was leaving my battered skeleton. Nevertheless I continued walking. In the middle of April, I arrived at a camp, in which there were several Zawiercie residents.

I knew that the Red Army was positioned not far from Berlin and that the Allied forces had already beaten the Nazi military. However, I too was totally crushed. I was just skin and bones. I felt like my soul was lying on my lips and that my days were numbered. I was terribly tortured by the thought: It was clear to me that the Nazis were being conquered, but, but – will I survive and be a free man again?

Yes, I knew that the end of the Nazis was a question of days, but – would I survive these few days?

The Nazis transferred me to the camp in Mühldorf, which was a branch of the Dachau camp.

I was only there a few hours when I heard someone calling my name: "Bornstein, Bornstein!"

Who could be calling me here? I thought to myself. Who knows about me?

I did not have to investigate for too long. It was Stützky, who used to live in Ogrozensky and later in Zawiercie. (There he was my father's pupil in Zeirei Mizrachi). Stützky brought me a plate of camp soup with a few potatoes. My hopes of surviving the misery became more realistic.

After this nice reception he brought me potatoes every day. Other Zawiercie residents in the camp also supported me with food. Those were: Osher Passerman, the Tzimbler brothers (today of New York) and Moshe Chaim Goldstein.

At the end of April the Nazis wanted to transfer us to the Tyrol Mountains, in order to destroy us there. They packed us into boxcars and transported us to the direction of Munich.

While we were in transit, the Americans mounted an offensive and captured the train tracks.

We were free.

We left the boxcars. We, the Zawiercie residents – Stützky, the Tzimbler brothers, Moshe Chaim Goldstein, Osher Passerman and a son of the baker from "Small-Zawiercie" whom we called "Rontschkele" – kept together. We went over to a farmer and procured some food. Outside the American and German soldiers were engaged in battle. After a short while the ss entered the farm and drove us out of the house.

When we came outside we saw another group of ss murderers taking a group of Jews and killing them. The ss men, who had taken charge of us, drove us back into the train wagons. On the way to the wagons, they shot the boy who was always ready to help, Moshe Chaim Goldstein, the good hearted Stützky and the young boy Rontschkele. They were buried in a mass grave together with other Kedoshim from the mass murder. The grave is situated 20 km from Munich, in a forest near the train station Poing.

In the morning we were liberated by the Americans. For a long time we remained standing by the mass grave where our Zawiercie brothers lay, who, even in extreme hunger, had shared their last potato with another.

Sadly, they did not survive "the last minute before twelve": they died twenty four hours before the actual liberation, when they could have become free men.

Standing by the mass grave, we swore that we would take revenge from the Nazis and carry a "Yizkor plaque" in our heart – for the future generations of our people – in which is engraved these two burning words: "Al Tishkach – Don't Forget!"

Derelict Mass Graves: A Bitter Revisitation to Leonberg*

Shame and Accusation 1963

The following article does not make easy reading. Its language is harsh. It is brutally forthright. We are not afraid to publish the article virtually unabridged – even though we may be criticised for doing so.

Having been invited, as a visiting doctor, to attend a number of most interesting operations carried out by the chief physician of a well-known hospital in Stuttgart, I took my leave of the colleagues who had welcomed me so hospitably and helpfully in the early afternoon.

---

*   Appendix C was published in the *Neue Juedische Nachrichten, New Jewish News* of Munich.

My second time in Stuttgart! After an absence of more than 18 years, I was driving through its streets on a one-day visit, my car filled with suitcases, my wallet filled with money – a well-fed citizen of this land of economic miracles. I was on my way to the International Convention of Dentists in Cologne. I couldn't help thinking about the time when we were staggering through these streets, some of our number sitting down at the roadside in utter exhaustion, waiting for the shot to the head that would spare them the pain of further marches. No, it was not a proud feeling to be one of the few who survived the bloodbath, to have gone on to university and gained two doctorates. I felt sad and despondent.

How indifferent everyone is towards the events of those days. We, the concentration camp inmates would never have expected such an attitude. Who wants to hear about our experiences nowadays? Not even our own brothers are sufficiently sympathetic to the horrors we suffered through several years in the shadow of death.

Yes, this is what I want to tell you, my comrades who lost their lives here in Stuttgart. I am coming back to you and, in my thoughts I want to join you, all you many hundreds of victims, carried off by hunger and dysentery, hastily and namelessly buried in mass graves – your dreams buried with you. A father's dream of seeing his children once more; or that of a child: to meet her mother and siblings one more time. All this lies buried under a bit of soil in Leonberg.

First of all, I went to the Jewish Community in Stuttgart. Busy secretaries in fine offices were working away on modern typewriters. Notices concerning a variety of compensation problems hung on the walls. I went inside and asked for directions to the mass graves of Leonberg. "What, Leonberg?" came the reply. "Never heard of it. A concentration camp, or a grave of brothers for the victims of the concentration camp – here? Never heard of it." One person arrives, saying that he has heard of a forced labour camp for foreigners in Leonberg, but "as the Jewish Community we have no interest in this." The office manager of the Community begins to question me, as to whether I am fully Jewish or a half-Jew, and what was I doing in Leonberg anyway? I was appalled by their questions. "Yes, there were some non-Jews in Leonberg, but the majority of the inmates were Jewish." All we need to do is go through the "Incomplete Lists" stored at the registry office in Leonberg, and soon we will know who the victims were. The Lists also include the names of Jews from Germany, Holland, Poland, Russia, Czechoslovakia, Hungary and so on. After I had described, in a few brief words, the life and death of hundreds of Jews and non-Jews during the final weeks of the war, the head of the Community Office telephoned the mayor's office in Leonberg. He was told that there were two mass graves containing former inmates of concentration camps in Leonberg, and that some of the bodies had been exhumed. The mayor's office was staying open late today, and the registry officer in charge of the administration of mass graves would await me if I could arrive soon.

Feeling resentful and mortified, I left the Community Office. I was ashamed for my brothers who sit in their offices, busily administering church taxes and refunds, but oblivious of their brothers hastily buried in mass graves a mere 15 minutes away, without any memorial or mark of respect.

And yet, just recently a polemic concerning the erection of a monument for the mass graves in Leonberg had been published in the south German press. But it would appear our community officials do not read such publications. With deep bitterness, I glanced back at the Community Office building, which also displays the sign for a Regional Association and a Regional Rabbi.

The Jewish rite ordains that once a year a prayer be said for each deceased relative. For the dead who have no relatives, the community or the community Rabbi is to fulfil this task.

You, my perished concentration camp comrades, are of no interest to the Regional Association, nor to the community and not to the community Rabbi either! I find it hard to reproach the others, seeing members of my own faith act in such a neglectful manner.

The registry officer in Leonberg was emphatically welcoming. He declared that he perceived his office not merely as a duty, but was concerned about the concentration camp mass graves at a human level. He asked me to join him in his car and took me to the municipal cemetery, which has a mass grave containing the bodies of former concentration camp inmates, some of them previously exhumed. In a space of a few square metres, the nameless victims lie in immediate proximity to other graves. However, the concentration camp grave is overgrown by coarse grass. Slightly embarrassed, the officer stated that there ought to be a board somewhere indicating that this is a concentration camp grave. We searched for it, without success. The neighbouring graves are well cared for, marked by stone borders and headstones and planted with flowers. The grave of my brothers does not even have markers for its borders. No sign, no board, no flowers, just coarse grass to cover it. I stood in a corner, quietly and said the prayer for the dead: "May you find peace beneath the divine wings. The soil, however, cannot cover this bloodshed by innocents. Honour be to your memory."

From the cemetery, the officer took me to the large mass grave on top of a hill. We drove past beautiful, newly-built villas, until we arrived at the resting place. It consists of a section of unkempt field, overgrown by weeds. It is neither fenced in nor marked. Ahead of us we see a woman, walking her dog in this field.

The registry officer explained, apologetically, that a monument ought to have been erected here by the corporation of Leonberg, but the project had been delayed by certain disagreements. I asked why no flowers had been planted here and was told that, according to the town planning architect, the climate on this hill was unsuitable. My dear concentration camp comrades, you lie underneath this soil, trodden by dog-walkers. All around, the newly-built villas are surrounded by flourishing gardens. Only where you are, no flowers will grow: so says the architect. A wooden cross stands here, in the name of charity. But no sign speaks of those who lie under this soil. You are surrounded by "charitable" Christian villa owners, but no one will plant a flower for you, will mark your resting place with a tombstone. You are a nuisance, obstructing the view of the landscape that harmoniously extends all the way into the town and is observed to great advantage from here. What a wonderful panorama this hillside reveals, but at its top, right in the middle, there is a large mass grave soaked in the blood of innocents. It is an unwelcome sight. It disturbs the peace of its privileged surroundings, so blessed by the economic miracle. You have been forgotten, even by your brothers who reside in Stuttgart in their hundreds. They pray in the synagogue, observe the feast days, enjoy the community dances, and process compensation claims. But the elementary reverence due to the tormented victims has been neglected by our brothers, while the others do not wish to be reminded of these events at all.

Having wiped the tears from my eyes, I was approached by the official who, in an embarrassingly apologetic tone, expressed his hope that by next year there might be a well-kept cemetery in this place, and two years from now the long overdue memorial would be ready at last.

I then asked the registry officer to take me to the spot where the camp used to be. We approached by car. The area was all but unrecognisable. There are houses everywhere; the new streets and gardens are in impeccable condition. However, I immediately recognised the buildings that used to house the concentration camp. Old people were looking out of the windows. It is now a housing scheme for senior citizens. The windows are curtained and adorned by flower pots. I would have liked to peep behind those curtains, for I cannot possibly imagine how such immense human suffering and pain can be glossed over by middle-class finery. The residents looked on in astonishment, as I took photos of the smooth, featureless walls, the yard, the former mustering ground where the inmates had to line up twice a day, no matter whether they could stand up or were slumped on the ground, close to death. The yard is now planted with simple flower beds. Through tiny cellar windows I gazed into the rooms where eighteen years ago I had risked my life to steal drinks of water so I would not die of thirst. They now house middle-class laundry rooms. I walked along the walls to the entrance of the estate, hoping to find at least a plaque indicating that innocent people had been imprisoned and faced death here. "Honour their memory!" But their memory has been wiped out – without a trace. Merely a few files, languishing unnoticed on registry office shelves, list their names – in bureaucratic terms – in "incomplete registers".

The kindly registry officer later took me to the old town hall, which houses the registry office. He gave me the registers listing the names of buried concentration camp victims. Searching for acquaintances, I looked at the entries with obviously Jewish forenames. I tried to think, but I could not bear to stay any longer in this calm, bureaucratic environment. My eyes were stinging with sorrow and anger. The names on the pages took shape, living corpses. In their tens and their hundreds they crowded all around me, with their drained faces and sunken eyes. They were staring at me, questioningly. Hastily, I opened my eyes and took my leave of the registry officer – but the gaunt faces went with me, staying with me for a long time as I went on my way.

Neglected Brothers' Graves*

The first of May, a public holiday for the German people, is a feast day for me, too. On this day, I regained my much longed-for freedom, after four years of ignominy in a number of concentration camps. The American army arrived as we awaited our fate, shut into cattle wagons in Tutzing station on Lake Starnberg. In accordance with an order given by super-beast Himmler, we were to be taken to Tirol, there to be murdered in a ravine. On 1 May 1945, when the American army smashed open our wagons, hundreds of us had already died and hundreds more were so mortally ill that they could not be restored to life, even by liberation. Thus, freedom began with a large funeral, which lasted more than a week.

That was twenty years ago. Now I am back in this place that held so much sorrow and so much hope for me in those days. I have

---

* Appendix D was a pamphlet published by the author to coincide with the annual commemoration held at the former Dachau Concentration Camp in May 1965.

come to visit the grave of my brothers, those who did not live to enjoy the new-found freedom. On a lonely, but neat path I climb up to the graveyard. A well-tended cemetery with many flower-bedecked graves lies before me.

I am looking for the graves of my brothers, but I cannot find them on this site. My comrades are at rest a few steps further along, separated from these graves by a thin mesh-wire fence. But all I can find here is a desolate and neglected space.

I see hundreds of individual graves and one large mass grave, but no flower, no token of loving remembrance adorns this space. The large mass grave where many, many victims were laid to rest has on its bare stone only a two-line inscription indicating that here lie the peaceless and homeless. The words say nothing about their fate, about their suffering. They do not tell that these victims used to live peacefully in their homes and became peaceless and homeless only through the barbarism inflicted on them by the Nazis. The stones are overgrown by unkempt shrubbery. Broken gravestones piled up in a heap, mark the sad resting place of my brothers in suffering. No flower, no well-tended tree, no passable, neat path anywhere. What a contrast to the general cemetery on my right, where the graves display evidence of loving, caring hands, and where colourful flowers flourish and grow! Our cemetery is desolate, neglected and destroyed.

Thus I stand by the broken stones and remember my friends, who for years had to live through the torment of the concentration camps, only to lose their lives here, just as liberation was at hand. Could any of them have imagined that Jewish communities live just thirty kilometres from the destroyed cemetery where they were laid to rest – Jewish organisations and hundreds of Jewish people who do not care for these graves at all? Jewish presidents will visit some site or other, every now and then, but nobody comes to visit you, my brothers – you, who lie at rest here, in devastated graves.

Disappointed by the world and disappointed by our own brothers, I now light a candle in this lonely place, the candle for your soul, and I quietly say: *Yisgadal v'yiskadash sh'mei rabbah* (Exalted and hallowed be thy name).

Anti-Human

The Times Literary Supplement, April 25 1968

The place names—Grünheide, Mühldorf, Fünfteiehen, Gross Rosen—which provide this book's chapter headings read like a stage-coach itinerary through Germany's arcadian backwaters. Alas, the author of *Die lange Nacht* was no Lake District poet honing his sensibility on the emanations of forest-girt romanticism; to him the German equivalents of Green Heath, Mill Village, Five Pools and Great Roses were stages along a personal Calvary of slave labour which, miraculously, just—and only just—stopped short of extermination.

"Extermination through work" was that variation of the Nazi genocide programme which, in contrast to the gas chambers, offered Jews an infinitesimal chance of survival in exchange for draining them of the last ounce of physical and psychic energy before disposing of their husks. Ernst Israel Bornstein had been eighteen when his world collapsed; youthful adaptability, self-possession and, above all, luck combined to preserve his husk in seven work camps which might have been modelled on the sequence of Dante's circles of hell.

The basic theme of stories like Bornstein's is by now so sickeningly familiar that publication of this book might seem a labour of supererogation—until one considers the amnesia syndrome of the collective psyche. (Recently while former guards of Sobibor death camp were actually on trial at Hagen in Westphalia a local poll established that only one in ten townspeople had heard of Sobibor, some interviewees thought it the name of a new detergent.)

Die lange Nacht is however far more than an aid to memory; not the least of its additional merits are the pointers it provides towards the adumbration of a sociology of concentration camps. It touches on the symbiosis between hunters and hunted which turned *Judenälteste* into lethally grotesque simulacra of S.S. camp commandants, and delineates the archetypal camp pyramid broadening down from the tiny *Lagerprominenz* apex through narrow middle strata, to the vast base of moribund *Muselmannen*.

The law governing camp life was the biblical adage, "To him who hath shall be given", formulated with the pitiless logic of social Darwinism. Thus it was a conditioned reflex of the semi-autonomous *Lagerprominenz* to assign easier duties to fit inmates and back-breaking labour to shuffling skeletons.

In the last analysis, however, neither sociology nor psychology is adequate to the task of explaining the inexplicable. Despite Professor Adorno's "there can be no poems after Auschwitz", the poet can probably come closer to illuminating the darkness of the long night than anyone else.

Though Mr. Bornstein is no German-speaking Primo Levi, many passages of his book mark him as a poet—none less so than the description of a Day of Atonement service held secretly in a boarded-up but at the back of the *Arbeitslager*. Having accidentally happened upon this conventicle of chanting and—*incredibile dictu*—voluntarily fasting wraiths, he had first reacted with pitying incredulity to their supplication of an inescapably dead Godhead. Then after only agreeing to be "tenth man" (ten worshippers is the quorum required for the recitation of Jewish prayers) with utmost reluctance, he soon found himself involuntarily swept along by a cataract of prayer and tears having its source at the very core of his being.

If—as Beckett told us in *Godot*—the amount of laughter and tears in the world at any moment is perfectly equipoised huge cachinnations should rend the air away from where this book is being read.

ANTI-HUMAN

ERNST ISRAEL BORNSTEIN : *Die lange Nacht.* Ein Bericht aus sieben Lagern. Foreword by Max Mikorey. 246pp. Frankfurt : Europäische Verlagsanstalt. DM28.

The place names—Grünheide, Mühldorf, Fünfteichen, Gross Rosen—which provide this book's chapter headings read like a stage-coach itinerary through Germany's arcadian backwaters. Alas, the author of *Die lange Nacht* was no Lake District poet honing his sensibility on the emanations of forest-girt romanticism ; to him the German equivalents of Green Heath, Mill Village, Five Pools and Great Roses were stages along a personal Calvary of slave labour which, miraculously, just—and only just—stopped short of extermination.

"Extermination through work" was that variation of the Nazi genocide programme which, in contrast to the gas chambers, offered Jews an infinitesimal chance of survival in exchange for draining them of the last ounce of physical and psychic energy before disposing of their husks. Ernst Israel Bornstein had been eighteen when his world collapsed ; youthful adaptability, self-possession and, above all, luck combined to preserve his husk in seven work camps which might have been modelled on the sequence of Dante's circles of hell.

The basic theme of stories like Bornstein's is by now so sickeningly familiar that publication of this book might seem a labour of supererogation — until one considers the amnesia syndrome of the collective psyche. (Recently while former guards of Sobibor death camp were actually on trial at Hagen in Westphalia a local poll established that only one in ten townspeople had heard of Sobibor—some interviewees thought it the name of a new detergent.)

Die lange Nacht is however far more than an aid to memory ; not the least of its additional merits are the pointers it provides towards the adumbration of a sociology of concentration camps. It touches on the symbiosis between hunters and hunted which turned *Judenälteste* into lethally grotesque simulacra of S.S. camp commandants, and delineates the archetypal camp pyramid broadening down from the tiny *Lagerprominenz* apex through narrow middle strata, to the vast base of moribund *Muselmannen.*

The law governing camp life was the biblical adage, "To him who hath shall be given", formulated with the pitiless logic of social Darwinism. Thus it was a conditioned reflex of the semi-autonomous *Lagerprominenz* to assign easier duties to fit inmates and back-breaking labour to shuffling skeletons.

In the last analysis, however, neither sociology nor psychology is adequate to the task of explaining the inexplicable. Despite Professor Adorno's "there can be no poems after Auschwitz", the poet can probably come closer to illuminating the darkness of the long night than anyone else.

Though Mr. Bornstein is no German-speaking Primo Levi, many passages of his book mark him as a poet—none less so than the description of a Day of Atonement service held secretly in a boarded-up hut at the back of the *Arbeitslager.* Having accidentally happened upon this conventicle of chanting and—*incredibile dictu*—voluntarily fasting wraiths, he had first reacted with pitying incredulity to their supplication of an inescapably dead Godhead. Then after only agreeing to be "tenth man" (ten worshippers is the quorum required for the recitation of Jewish prayers) with utmost reluctance, he soon found himself involuntarily swept along by a cataract of prayer and tears having its source at the very core of his being.

If—as Beckett told us in *Godot*—the amount of laughter and tears in the world at any moment is perfectly equipoised huge cachinnations should rend the air away from where this book is being read.

Seven Camps

Allgemeine Düsseldorf, 1 March 1968

A few weeks ago, I stood inside the impressively simple memorial of Yad Vashem, high above Jerusalem (the museum underneath is not so solemn and dignified), reading, on the dark stone floor of the memorial, the names of some of the most dreadful concentration and extermination camps from the National Socialist period of atrocities. Naturally, the members of my party, Jews and non-Jews, were similarly depressed and upset: Almost without exception, they were of the same generation as the victims or their contemporaries. And yet, I could not help wondering what younger people and the next generation – Germans as well as Israelis – might feel in this quietly-distinguished place of remembrance. Twenty two years have passed since the incinerators stopped smoking, since the raiding parties and Kapos finally stopped their mass-murdering, and the gates opened for those emaciated figures who, in tiny groups, had managed to survive the years of crazed persecution and destruction – gates, through which they had no longer hoped to march towards the light of freedom.

The Europäische Verlagsanstalt in Frankfurt, well established as one of the responsible and most progressive publishing houses for contemporary and intellectual history in Western Germany, has added to its merits in publishing *"Die Lange Nacht"* by Dr. Ernst Israel Bornstein.

"Yet another concentration camp book!" might be the response of some readers who imagine that, following the Nuremberg trials, the publication of Kogon's "The ss State" and the court proceedings of recent years, they know everything there is to know about the persecution of Jews inside the concentration camps and elsewhere. Even well-intentioned people (who were neither Nazis nor are present-day sympathizers with the Nazis or their successors) will sometimes opine that enough is enough, and that a line should be drawn under the past; that forgiveness and forgetting are required and appropriate: This is, on occasions, even the opinion expressed by victims of concentration camps and persecution who, for entirely different reasons, can no longer bear to read about and re-live the unimaginable measure of cold-blooded barbarity inflicted on countless innocents – largely, but not exclusively Jews – between 1939 and 1945. However, no objective reader can dispute that a report of the kind compiled by Dr. Bornstein fulfils an important political and educational, psychological and ethical/moral purpose. In more ways than one, *"Die Lange Nacht"* surpasses a number of similar works: This comparison is not based on literary grounds (for who would wish to apply literary standards to this topic – although it must be said that the writing is amazingly vivacious and eminently readable), but on the author's objectivity, which gives his book its particular impact. He does not rant, and neither does he hide his feelings. One of six survivors out of a family numbering seventy two, he is wary of collective judgements and points to the decency of some of the guards, but nothing is sugar-coated or concealed. He has very obviously not given in to the temptation of over or understatement. In his deeply thoughtful preface, Professor Dr. Max Mikorey pays homage to Dr. Bornstein's reports which, beginning in the Ghetto of Pilica (the author relates remarkable things about the Jewish Councils) then informs us about the stations of torment of Grünheide, Markstadt, Fünfteichen, Grossrosen, Flossenbürg, Leonberg and Mühldorf.

Professor Mikorey ranks Dr. Bornstein's book on a par with Dostoevsky and Anselm von Feuerbach.

May many thinking Germans of all ages read this book, which is in equal measure harrowing and thought-provoking. It deserves many readers.

Dr. Hans Lamm

The Path of Inhumanity

Aufbau [Development], 24 May 1968

E rnst Israel Bornstein's work is not for those who do not wish to upset themselves. Among all the reports from the camps, this is one of the most harrowing and the most significant.

Now resident in Munich, the author who became a physician and dentist after the end of the war, devoting a large part of his working life to associations of the victims of persecution and the Jewish Community, has published a document of his own fate. He dedicates his book to his parents and siblings who were gassed in Auschwitz. He recounts, and that is all. He tells a story of repetitions and escalations: the days repeat themselves, endless, grey, and dreadful. The escalations increase in suffering, despair and, ultimately, in the hope – kept alive almost beyond belief – that an end to the horrors might come. His hopes may have been helped by a few strokes of fate and the fortitude of youth; nevertheless, the fact that Bornstein and others were able to survive appears as inconceivable as the facts themselves.

His is the entirely personal report of a human being on his forced march into inhumanity. A depiction of beings and of an "order" defying any classification for the magnitude of the terror they inflict. The descent takes him further and further down the ladder, from camp to camp, one year of persecution being followed by another, one hard crust of bread by the next – as long as such crusts were still available. Without being drawn into any discussion of political problems, the author provides many answers to questions that are asked again and again: How could this happen – why did people tolerate this – what caused these wounds that refuse to heal to this day?

It is irrelevant whether or not this book is a literary work of art. It stands like a memorial for millions who were transported into everlasting silence and for the truth, the forgetting of which would be the greatest sin humankind could commit. Each one of us will have to decide whether they wish to avert their eyes as they pass this memorial or whether they are prepared to pause awhile in awestruck silence and absorb its message.

Hilde Marx

Speech by the Author

Thirty Years Later – 1975

Address by the Chairman of the Regional Association for Jewish Victims of Persecution of the NS Regime, Dr. Ernst Bornstein on the occasion of the ceremony commemorating the 30th anniversary of the liberation of the concentration camp in Dachau.

Thirty years have passed, since the gates of prisons and concentration camps, previously guarded by SS, opened up into freedom. Much has been written and spoken about the twelve years of tyranny under Nazi rule, which brought genocide to Europe.

My esteemed preceding speakers have, in moving words, given expression to the pain and suffering inflicted on our brothers and sisters. However, I must take issue with the sentiment of my preceding speakers that a Jewish minister in the Federal Republic signifies a safe homeland for Jews in Germany. Walter Rathenau was not able to prevent the ascent of the NSDAP. Only the state of Israel is our assurance that Auschwitz and Dachau will never recur. The blood of the fighters in the Warsaw Ghetto with the *"Ani-Ma'amin"*[1] by the crematorium have convinced us and Israel that only "Medinat Yisrael"[2] warrants a safe future for us.

We can never be determined enough in our work against the spirit of the time, its tendency fades out and cover the trails of blood from so many murders. For it requires superhuman fortitude to express what we, what our fellow victims have suffered in Auschwitz, Treblinka, Majdanek, Buchenwald and here in Dachau.

Following his visits to the liberated concentration camps and conversations with former inmates in 1945, Leiwik, one of the last great Jewish poets, wrote: "The pen cannot describe nor can the mind express that which occurred under the concept of – Final Solution to the Jewish Question. All we have is mute and deep silence."

One ought to have the strength to go to the various mustering grounds of former concentration camps on the day of remembrance and stand there, expressing one's pain in a mute scream of protest. For it is only in deep silence that we can hear the cries of pain that fell on the deaf ears of the world.

Who has the strength to express the pain those Jewish children suffered as they were pushed into the gas chambers and crematoria?

When we were liberated thirty years ago, we swore that we would never forget. This holy remembrance has nothing to do with feelings of revenge or similar emotions. It is the expression of the voices of our brothers and sisters, of the many victims who, in their Yizkor[3] voice, their lament to us, our children and those around us.

Eli Wiesel, who as a young man was a concentration camp prisoner himself, says: "I defy a cheap liberalism that, in the name of political and religious considerations, requires us to forgive and forget. Murder is, in essence, the denial of the human. Murder is final, not an intermediate stage. Whosoever kills a human being, kills God. It is therefore not sufficient to battle against murder and

---

1. *Ani Ma'amin* means "I Believe". It is the prosaic rendition of Maimonides' thirteen-point version of the Jewish principles of faith.
2. *Medinat Yisrael* is Hebrew for the State of Israel.
3. *Yizkor* means remembrance and is the Jewish memorial prayer.

killers; we have to sever any connection with them by placing them beyond the wall of hatred."

For this reason we demand in our Yizkor, in our inability to forget and determination not to forget, that there must never be a law allowing a statute of limitation for Nazi crimes. The negligible sentences handed to Nazi mass murderers, too, are a mockery of justice and a slight on the memory of those who perished as victims of the Nazi regime.

So I will finish with the words of the unforgettable Kaddish-sayer who by himself visited the various grave sites of concentration camp victims week after week to say Kaddish; the man who through his tireless exhortations and demands and on his own initiative and expense was instrumental in the creation of the first Jewish memorial, erected in Dachau in 1964 by the Association of Jewish Persecutees.

Never released from the duty of eternal remembrance, Isidor Rosenberg the Kaddish-Kadosh, God rest his soul, told us ten years ago in Dachau, by the memorial in the forest cemetery: "Do not forget the torment your parents and relatives had to suffer. Just as at each Passover, the symbol of our liberation from Egyptian bondage, we declaim the words: Each one of us is duty-bound to put them-selves in this place, as if their own body had felt the pain of slavery as well as the liberation; so we shall pass on to our children and our children's children all that we have seen and experienced."

These words shall also be devoted to his memory, as we now say our prayer *El Malei Rachamim.*[4]

---

4. *El Malei Rachamim* means "God full of compassion". It is a Jewish prayer for the departed that is recited at funeral services and on visiting the graves of relatives.

Author's Obituary

On the Death of Dr. Med. Ernst Israel Bornstein

Neue Juedische Nachrichten [New Jewish
News of Munich], 18 August 1978

The Jewish community of Munich was shocked and deeply grieved to hear of the sudden and completely unexpected death of Dr. Med. Ernst Israel Bornstein, who was taken from us at the age of 56. Even now it appears inconceivable to us all that this scintillating, dynamic figure, involved in so many different fields of activity and, just a few days ago, engaged in stimulating conversation, discussing plans for the future, is no longer with us.

Dr. Ernst Bornstein, at whose bier we stand in deep shock, was born in Zawiercie. His character was formed by the unique ambience of his parental home, a synthesis of deep-rooted religiousness, expansive Jewish erudition, human warmth and heartfelt community spirit.

His urge towards intellectual pursuits, which had inspired him to publish articles in the Jewish press at a very young age, caused him to study medicine after his release from the hellish detention in concentration camps. He conducted his studies initially in Regensburg and later in Munich, where he earned his doctorate.

Inherited from his father, his devotion to "*Askanut*" spurred him into action in [initiating memorials in] the concentration camps of Buchenwald and Bergen Belsen, inspiring him to come to the aid of people even more unfortunate than himself, and to participate in the founding of the Association for Jewish Victims of Persecution, whose leader he remained until the day he died. It was Dr. Bornstein who took the lead in arranging commemorative events in Dachau and other Bavarian places of Jewish martyrdom, in the tender care of less well-off fellow sufferers and in the publication of the Bulletin for the Association. Over the past thirty years, there has been no commemorative event without a moving speech by Dr. Bornstein.

His sense of duty towards society inspired him to take an active part in the rebuilding of the Jewish community in Munich, where his main concern was the advocacy for the needs of young people. He was involved in a number of organisations who could always count on his assistance, despite his gruelling workload as a physician.

This deep bond with Jewish tradition and his Hasidic ancestry found expression in his regular attendance of the Synagogue in Georgenstrasse where he had his regular seat, in the choice of his spouse, descended from an equally deeply religious Strasbourg family, with whom he was to spend fourteen happy years, and in the traditional Jewish upbringing he gave his three charming, talented children.

In Dr. Ernst Bornstein we have lost a highly gifted, high-minded, sensitive, kind-hearted and upright human being who, having come through the dreadful Nazi-era unbroken in spirit, though physically damaged, devoted his life's work to his traumatised people and the common good.

At this sad time all our sympathy goes to his loving wife, his beloved three children and also his only surviving sister, who mourn him at his bier. In all their sadness, may they find some solace in the certainty that Dr. Bornstein's memory will forever live in our loving and grateful hearts and in the hearts of the many friends he made all over the world.

On the Death of Dr. Med. Ernst Israel Bornstein

The Talmud says: "The righteous do not need monuments, for it is their deeds that uphold their memory".

May his gentle soul be forever bound into the tome of the ever-living.

Rabbi Abraham Hochwald

Rabbi Abraham Hochwald conducted Dr. Bornstein's funeral in Strasbourg in August 1978. Rabbi Hochwald was born on 9 June 1923 in Trieste, the son of Polish World War I refugees. In 1939, his family again fled to Jerusalem, where he later studied at the Yeshiva Chevron. In Germany, he served first in the 1960s and 70s in Munich, together Rabbi Yitzhak Grünewald. Thereafter he was Rabbi in Lower Saxony. Later he served for many years as Rabbi in Dusseldorf and Aachen. On his retirement he settled in Antwerp and died on the 6 July 2006 at the age of 83.

About the Author

D r. Ernst Israel Bornstein was born in Zawiercie, a city in the Silesian province of southern Poland (60 km from Auschwitz) on the 26 November 1922. He was the oldest of four children. He was educated in Jewish schools and won a national essay prize at the age of fifteen. He was incarcerated in seven concentration camps, enduring the infamous "death march" until finally being liberated by American soldiers near Lake Starnberg in Bavaria on 30 April 1945. Thereafter, he lived in Munich, Germany, studied at the University of Munich graduating as a Dentist (Dr. Med Dent) in 1952 and as a Doctor of Medicine (Dr. Med) in 1958. He practiced as an oral surgeon. He married Renée (née Koenig) on the 20 December 1964 and they had three children, Noemie (Lopian) born August 1966, Muriel (Davis) born July 1967, and Asher Alain born May 1971. Dr. Bornstein died on the 14 August 1978 aged 55.

Dr. Bornstein was the founder of the Association of Ex-Concentration Camp Inmates in Munich, whose chairman he remained until he died, was a member of the executive committee of the Jewish Community in Munich and chairman of the Consortium of Associations of Persecutees in Bavaria. He originally wrote this book, *"Die Lange Nacht"* (*The Long Night*) shortly after the War, setting out his Holocaust experiences, whilst his memories were fresh and his feelings raw. This book was originally published in Germany, in 1967.

The Toby Press publishes fine writing
on subjects of Israel and Jewish interest.
For more information, visit www.tobypress.com